OUR RIGHT TO DRUGS

BOOKS BY THOMAS SZASZ

Pain and Pleasure

The Myth of Mental Illness

Law, Liberty, and Psychiatry

Psychiatric Justice

The Ethics of Psychoanalysis

The Manufacture of Madness

Ideology and Insanity

The Age of Madness (Ed.)

The Second Sin

Ceremonial Chemistry

Heresies

Karl Kraus and the Soul Doctors

Schizophrenia

Psychiatric Slavery

The Theology of Medicine

The Myth of Psychotherapy

Sex by Prescription

The Therapeutic State

Insanity

The Untamed Tongue

OUR RIGHT TO DRUGS

The Case for a Free Market

THOMAS SZASZ

PRAEGER

New York
Westport, Connecticut
London

Library of Congress Cataloging-in-Publication Data

Szasz, Thomas Stephen, 1920–
    Our right to drugs : the case for a free market / Thomas Szasz.
      p. cm.
    Includes bibliographical references and index.
    ISBN 0–275–94216–3 (alk. paper)
    1. Pharmaceutical policy—United States.   2. Narcotics, Control
of—Moral and ethical aspects.   3. Narcotics, Control of—United
States.   4. Drug legalization—United States.   I. Title.
RA401.A3S93   1992
362.29—dc20   91–30378

British Library Cataloguing in Publication Data is available.

Library of Congress Catalog Card Number: 91–30378
ISBN: 0–275–94216–3

First published in 1992

Praeger Publishers, One Madison Avenue, New York, NY 10010
An imprint of Greenwood Publishing Group, Inc.

Printed in the United States of America

The paper used in this book complies with the
Permanent Paper Standard issued by the National
Information Standards Organization (Z39.48–1984).

10 9 8 7 6 5 4 3 2 1

You have rights antecedent to all earthly governments, rights that cannot be repealed or restrained
by human law; rights derived from the Great Leg-
islator of the Universe.

—John Adams

Contents

Preface

When the history of human error comes to be written, it will be difficult to find examples of equal power; and the future will be amazed that such competent men, such eminent specialists, could in their own chosen field remain so blind, so stupid.

—Ferdinand von Hebra (1816–1880)[1]

In this book, I use many ordinary terms and phrases—such as *addict*, *drug abuse*, and *drug abuse treatment*—whose conventional meanings I reject. To avoid defacing the text, I have refrained from putting such prejudging expressions between quotations marks each and every time they appear. Instead, I should like to state unequivocally that everything I say in this book is premised on my contention that in today's American society there are two kinds of diseases and two kinds of treatments. The first kind of disease, exemplified by AIDS, is discovered by doctors; the second kind, exemplified by drug abuse, is mandated by legislators and decreed by judges. Similarly, the first kind of treatment, exemplified by the surgical removal of a gall bladder, is advised by doctors and authorized by competent patients; the second kind, exemplified by participation in a court-ordered drug treatment program, is imposed by judges on defendants accused or convicted of violating drug laws. I repudiate the scientific validity of placing rule-breaking behavior in the same category as bodily disease—and accepting both, on equal footing, as diseases. And I reject the moral legitimacy of equating a convicted defendant's coerced submission to a court-imposed intervention with a free adult's voluntary participation in a medical intervention—and accepting both, on equal footing, as treatments.[2]

Finally, for the sake of brevity and convenience, I use the terms *psychiatrist*, *mental patient*, and *mental hospital* to refer to mental health professionals, mental health clients, and mental health institutions of all kinds.

Acknowledgments

Among the many persons who have helped me with this book, I want to thank especially my daughter Suzy and my brother George for their unflagging devotion and advice; Charles S. Howard, for important suggestions for amplifying my argument; Roger Yanow, for conscientious reading of drafts; Peter Uva, librarian at the SUNY Health Science Center at Syracuse, for boundless patience in humoring my requests for references; and Elizabeth Alden, my secretary, for meticulous attention to details in preparing the manuscript.

Introduction

I never write on any subject unless I believe the opinion of
those who have the ear of the public to be mistaken, and this
involves as a necessary consequence that every book I write
runs counter to the men who are in possession of the field.
                                        —Samuel Butler[1]

For good or ill, this has been true as well of the books I have written,
this one included. In the present case, it is because the contemporary
debate on drugs, drug abuse, and drug legalization is a monument to
our collective ignorance and eagerness to forget.

From the founding of the American Colonies until the Civil War,
marijuana was an important cash crop, yielding the raw materials
needed for the production of canvas, clothing, and rope. The colonists,
including George Washington, grew marijuana.[2] Of course that is not
what they called it. They called it "hemp," just as they called their Negro
slaves "three-fifths Persons."[3] Although few people realize that the Constitution so stamps some of the people who built our country, at least
those who do realize it understand how such fictitiously fractional persons became real, full-fledged human beings. But how many people
know that hemp, coca, and the opium poppy are ordinary plants, understand how they became transformed into dreaded "dangerous
drugs," and realize that in losing our rights to them we have surrendered
some of our most basic rights to property?

This book, then, is about rights, responsibilities, the law, and the Constitution—not as abstractions in philosophical treatises or legal briefs, but as the practical realities of our daily lives. Specifically, it is about our laws and lawlessness concerning the substances we choose to call "drugs."

Casting a ballot is an important act, emblematic of our role as citizens. But eating and drinking are much more important acts. If given a choice between the freedom to choose what to ingest and what politician to vote for, few if any would pick the latter. Indeed, why would anyone be so foolish as to sell his natural birthright to consume what he chooses in return for the mess of pottage of being allowed to register his preference for a political candidate? Yet this is precisely the bargain we the American people have made with our government: more useless voting rights in exchange for fewer critical personal rights. The result is that we consider the fiction of self-government a blessed political right, and the reality of self-medication an accursed medical malady.

In 1890, less than half of adult Americans had the right to vote. Since then, one class of previously ineligible persons after another has been granted the franchise. Not only blacks and women, as they deserved, but also others with questionable claims to that privilege—for example, persons unable to speak or read English (or read and write any language). During this period, every one of us—regardless of age, education, or competence—has been deprived of his right to substances the government decides to call "dangerous drugs." Yet, ironically, most Americans labor under the mistaken belief that they now enjoy many rights previously available only to a few (partially true only for blacks and women), and remain utterly unaware of the rights they have lost. Moreover, having become used to living in a society that wages a relentless War on Drugs, we have also lost the vocabulary in which to properly articulate and analyze the disastrous social consequences of our own political-economic behavior vis-à-vis drugs. Mesmerized by the mortal dangers of fictitious new diseases such as "chemical dependency" and "substance abuse," we have become diverted from the political perils of our totalitarian-therapeutic efforts at collective self-protection. Long ago, Frederic Bastiat (1801–1850), a French political-economic thinker and pioneer free marketeer, warned against the dangers of precisely such folly. "Protection," he wrote, "concentrates at a single point the good that it does, while the harm that it inflicts is diffused over a wide area. The good is apparent to the outer eye; the harm reveals itself only to the inner eye of the mind."[4]

Precisely wherein lies our drug problem? I submit it lies mainly in the fact that most of the drugs we want are ones we cannot legally make, sell, or buy. Why can we not do these things? Because the drugs we want are literally illegal, their possession constituting a criminal offense (for example, heroin and marijuana); or because they are medically illegal, requiring a physician's prescription (for example, steroids and Valium). In short, we have tried to solve our drug problem by prohibiting the "problem" drugs; by imprisoning the persons who make, sell, or use such drugs; by defining the use of such drugs as diseases; and by coercing drug users to undergo treatment (coercion being necessary because drug users want drugs, not treatment). None of these measures has worked. Some suspect that these measures have aggravated the problem. I am sure of it. They have had to—because our concept of the nature of the problem is mistaken, our methods of responding to it are coercive, and the language in which we speak about it is misleading. I submit that making, selling, and using drugs are actions, not diseases. Authorities can go far in maintaining the illusion that (ab)using a drug is a disease, but an illusion it remains.

Moreover, the complex set of personal behaviors and social transactions we call "the drug problem" does not, in the literal sense, constitute a problem susceptible to a solution. Arithmetical problems have solutions. Social problems do not. (The solution of an arithmetical problem does not, ipso facto, create another arithmetical problem, but the solution of every social problem inexorably creates a new set of social problems.) It is a grievous mistake to conceptualize certain drugs as a "dangerous enemy" we must *attack* and *eliminate*, instead of *accepting* them as potentially helpful as well as harmful substances, and learning to *cope* with them competently.

Why do we want drugs? Basically, for the same reasons we want other goods. We want drugs to relieve our pains, cure our diseases, enhance our endurance, change our moods, put us to sleep, or simply make us feel better—just as we want bicycles and cars, trucks and tractors, ladders and chain saws, skis and hang gliders, to make our lives more productive and more pleasant. Each year, tens of thousands of people are injured and killed as a result of accidents associated with the use of such artifacts. Why do we not speak of "ski abuse" or a "chain saw problem"? Because we expect people who use such equipment to familiarize themselves with their use, and avoid injuring themselves or others. If they hurt themselves, we assume they did so accidentally and we try to heal their injuries. If they hurt others negligently, we punish them by both civil and criminal sanctions. These, in brief, are the means by which we try to *adapt* to—rather than *solve*—the problems presented by potentially dangerous devices in our environment. However, after generations of living under medical tutelage that provides us with protection (albeit illusory) against dangerous drugs, we have failed to cultivate the self-reliance and self-discipline we must possess as competent adults surrounded by the fruits of our pharmacological-technological age. Indeed, as I shall show throughout this book, our medical-statist policies with respect to drugs closely resemble the Soviets' economic-statist policies with respect to consumer goods. After a protracted war on self-medication, we are thus mired in a mess that is its direct result—just as after a protracted war on private property, the people in the Soviet Union are mired in a mess that is its direct result.

My thesis is that what we call "the drug problem" is a complex set of interrelated phenomena that are the products of personal temptation, choice, and responsibility, combined with a set of laws and social policies generated by our reluctance to face this fact in a forthright manner. If that is false, then nearly everything in this book is false. But if it is true, then nearly everything the American government, American law, American medicine, the American media, and the majority of the American people now think and do about drugs is a colossal and costly mistake, injurious to innocent Americans and foreigners, and self-destructive to the nation itself. For if the desire to read *Ulysses* cannot be cured with an anti-*Ulysses* pill, then neither can the desire to use alcohol, heroin, or any other drug or food be cured by counterdrugs (for example, Antabuse versus alcohol, methadone versus heroin) or so-called drug treatment programs (which are coercions masquerading as cures).

Unlike most criticisms of the War on Drugs, which are based on pharmacological, prudential, or therapeutic arguments, mine is based on political-philosophical considerations. I shall argue the following:

1. The right to chew or smoke a plant that grows wild in nature, such as hemp (marijuana), is anterior to and more basic than the right to vote.

2. A limited government, such as that of the United States, lacks the political legitimacy to deprive competent adults of the right to use whatever substances they choose.

3. The constraints on the power of the federal government, as laid down in the Constitution, have been eroded by a monopolistic medical profession administering a system of prescription laws that have, in effect, removed most of the drugs people want from the free market.

4. Hence it is futile to debate whether the War on Drugs should be escalated

or de-escalated, without first coming to grips with the popular, medical, and political mind-set concerning the trade in drugs generated by nearly a century of drug prohibitions.

I am familiar with recent essays arguing the impracticality of drug legalization.[5] I share that view. The idea of selling cocaine as we do cucumbers while preserving our prescription laws restricting the sale of penicillin is obviously absurd. But this proves only that unless we are willing to come to grips with the profoundly paternalistic implications and perilous anti-market consequences of prescription laws, which I discuss in this book (especially Chapter 7), we are doomed to impotence vis-à-vis our so-called drug problem. "The collectivist," warned A. V. Dicey in 1914, the year the first law protecting us from dangerous drugs was enacted, "never holds a stronger position than when he advocates the enforcement of the best ascertained laws of health."[6]

The result of our protracted drug-protectionist policy is that we now find it impossible to re-legalize drugs—we lack both the popular will for it and the requisite legal-political infrastructure to support it. We long ago decided that it is morally wrong to treat drugs (especially foreign, plant-derived drugs) as a commodity. If we are satisfied with that state of affairs and its consequences, so be it. But I believe we ought to consider the possibility that a free market in drugs is not only imaginable in principle, but, given the necessary personal motivation of a people, is just as practical and beneficial as is a free market in other goods. Accordingly, I support a free market in drugs not because I think it is—at this moment, in the United States—a practical policy, but because I believe it is right and because I believe that—in the long run, in the United States—the right policy may also be the practical policy.

OUR RIGHT TO DRUGS

1

Drugs as Property: The Right We Rejected

> In its larger and juster meaning, it [property] embraces every-
> thing to which a man may attach a value . . . [and includes
> that] which individuals have in their opinions, their religion,
> their passions, and their faculties.
>
> —James Madison[1]

Surely, it would be wrongheaded to contend that drugs do not belong
on Madison's foregoing list. In principle, every object in the universe
can be treated as property. Two questions thus arise: Whose property
is X? And should owning X, qua private property, be legal? X may stand
for the shirt on my back or the sidewalk in front of my house, the money
I earn as a gardener or the marijuana I grow in my garden. That drugs,
like diamonds or dogs, are a form of property no one can deny. Accordingly, we must now ask why the private ownership of drugs should
not be just as legal as the private ownership of diamonds or dogs.

THE RIGHT TO PROPERTY

In the English-speaking world, especially since the seventeenth century, the word *freedom* has meant the inalienable right to life, liberty,
and property, the first two elements resting squarely on the last.
"Though the Earth, and all inferior Creatures be common to all men,"

wrote John Locke in 1690, "yet every man has a *Property* in his own *Person*. This no Body has any Right to but himself. The *Labour* of his Body and the *Work* of his Hands, we may say, are properly his."[2] More than any other single principle, this idea informed and animated the Framers of the Constitution. "If the United States mean to obtain and deserve the full praise due to wise and just governments," wrote James Madison in 1792, "they will equally respect the rights of property and the property in rights."[3]

The quintessential feature of capitalism as a political-economic system is the security of private property and the free market, that is, the right of every competent adult to trade in goods and services. As Milton Friedman pithily put it, " 'Free markets,' properly understood, are an implication of private property."[4] To ensure such a free social order, the state is obligated to protect people from force and fraud and, to the maximum extent possible, abstain from participating in the production and distribution of goods and services. Of course, no such perfect capitalist order has ever existed or, perhaps, could exist. Still, it is a beacon that lights the way toward respect for persons and social cooperation based on the mutual, noncoercive satisfaction of needs.

The extraordinarily heavy emphasis on the right to property in our Anglo-American tradition does not mean that property is more important than life or liberty, or—as the enemies of individual liberty like to put it—that property is more important than people. It means only that property is "the convention" that best protects life and liberty; that "when life and liberty are at stake, they are already in jeopardy"; and hence that the right to property constitutes "a kind of 'early warning system' to invasions of life and liberty."[5] We ought to heed our loss of the right to drugs as precisely such a warning. Moreover, inasmuch as this alarm was first sounded nearly a century ago, the warning can hardly be said to be early. On the contrary, the sirens have sounded for so long that we no longer hear them: On no other front have the American people been subjected to so relentless a state pressure against their constitutional rights than on the issue of the right to drugs; and on no other front have the American people yielded their rights to encroachments by the federal government so readily, willingly, and indeed eagerly as on this one. I want to show that—because both our bodies and drugs are types of property—producing, trading in, and using drugs are property rights, and drug prohibitions constitute a deprivation of basic constitutional rights.[6]

Negroes and Narcotics: What Counts as Property?

My argument that drug prohibitions constitute a deprivation of the constitutional right to property hinges on our accepting drugs as a form of property. Depending on one's values, that may or may not be an obvious proposition. In any case, if the issue of what counts as property affects emotionally charged customs and vested economic interests, then nothing is obvious, and everything is subject to the fiction-making powers of lawmakers—as the precedent of slavery, which holds an important lesson for our problem with drugs, illustrates.

In his classic 1792 essay on "Property," Madison flatly asserted that "government is instituted to protect property of every sort."[7] The legality of slavery rested, of course, on the definition of the Negro as property, a definition that could not be challenged within the slave system. When the judicial system of the United States finally *allowed* it to be challenged, in the celebrated *Dred Scott* case, the formal articulation of the controversy signaled the beginning of the end for slavery.

Dred Scott was an illiterate Negro slave who had been purchased in Missouri, in 1833, by a U.S. Army surgeon named John Emerson. Emerson subsequently traveled with Scott to Illinois, a free state, and then, after a sojourn in Louisiana, took him back to Missouri, a slave state. In 1846, with the help of an anti-slavery lawyer, Scott sued Emerson's brother-in-law John Sandford, who became Scott's owner on Emerson's death, for his freedom (as well as for the freedom of his family, having in the meanwhile married and become the father of a child). The ground for Scott's suit was that his residence in a free state made him a free man. The lower court upheld his claim, but the Missouri Supreme Court ruled against him; the case was subsequently heard by the U.S. Supreme Court. Thus did *Scott v. Sandford* (1857) become one of the most famous and notorious decisions ever rendered by that high court.

The gist of the Court's decision, written by Chief Justice Roger Taney, was that because Scott was property when he was bought and was property when he brought his suit, he had no legal standing to sue; while Sandford, his owner, had a constitutional right to his property— that is, to Dred Scott. I cite a few illustrative lines from Judge Taney's opinion:

> They [Negroes of the African race] are not included, and were
> not intended to be included, under the word "citizens" in the

> Constitution. . . . He [Scott] was bought and sold, and treated as
> an ordinary article of merchandise and traffic. . . . This opinion
> was at that time fixed and universal in the civilized portion of
> the white race. . . . No one of that race [black Africans] had ever
> migrated to the United States voluntarily; all of them had been
> brought here as articles of merchandise. . . . No word can be
> found in the Constitution which gives Congress a greater power
> over slave property, or which entitles property of that kind to
> less protection than property of any other description. The only
> power conferred is the power coupled with the duty of guarding
> and protecting the owner of his rights.[8]

Volumes upon volumes have been written on this case, to which I
can probably add nothing. Note, however, that Taney specifically cited
the fact that the Negroes were bought and sold like property as proof
that they were property. What I find remarkable in bringing together
the *Dred Scott* case and the Harrison Narcotic Act is that in 1857, American whites had a constitutional right to own American blacks, because
Negro slaves constituted property; and that a mere half-century later,
in 1914, Americans no longer had a right to own opiates, because Congress declared them to be "narcotics," which could not be bought and
sold as "articles of merchandise." From the fiction that Negroes were
property and the laws built on it that empowered whites literally to
enslave blacks, the nation moved to the fiction that certain drugs (metaphorically) enslaved people and to the legislation built on it that outlawed the slave-holding drugs. (For further discussion of this theme,
see Chapter 6.) *Sic transit infamia mundi*. How terrifyingly right Edmund
Burke was when he observed,

> We do not draw the moral lessons we might from history. . . .
> History consists, for the greater part, of the miseries brought
> upon the world by pride, ambition, avarice, revenge, lust, se-
> dition, hypocrisy, ungoverned zeal, and all the train of disor-
> derly appetites which shake the public. . . . These vices are the
> *causes* of those storms. Religion, morals, laws, prerogatives, priv-
> ileges, liberties, rights of men, are the *pretexts*. The pretexts are
> always found in some specious appearance of a real good.[9]

The Body as Property

The phrase *right to life, liberty, and the pursuit of happiness*, once a vi-
brantly defiant proclamation, has become meaningless cant, a kind of

semantic mummy—the carefully preserved corpse of what only yester-day was a courageous Man. As the preamble to the Declaration of In-dependence and the Founding Fathers' other writings on political philosophy imply, they saw Man as a being endowed by his Creator with inalienable rights, among them the right to life, liberty, and prop-erty. To exercise such rights, Man must be a self-disciplined adult pos-sessing a right anterior to those they enumerated—a right so elementary it never occurred to the Framers that it needed to be named, much less that its protection needed to be specifically safeguarded. They viewed self-ownership thus because, as did Locke, they assumed it precedes all political rights and because, as exemplars of the Protestant Enlighten-ment, they had a clear view of the distinction between God and state, self and society. Indeed, albeit only in passing, Thomas Jefferson alluded to the crucial importance of bodily self-ownership as a political issue. He mocked would-be statist meddlers into our diets and drugs by re-minding his readers that "in France the emetic was once forbidden as a medicine, the potato as an article of food. . . . Was the government to prescribe to us our medicine and diet, our bodies would be in such keeping as our souls are now."[10] But is this not precisely what our government is doing now? Is it not what we expect and demand of it? Foolishly, we embrace the state's "prescrib[ing] to us our medicine and diet" as fulfilling its enlightened duty, guaranteeing us our "right" to health—instead of rejecting it as a crass deprivation of our right to our bodies and to the drugs we want.

It is clear that the Founders took for granted that Jesus' admonition about the soul applied to the body as well, and could be paraphrased thus: What does it profit a man if he gains all the rights politicians are eager to give him, but loses control over the care and feeding of his own body? Mark Twain's following remarks—provoked by the American medical profession's earliest attempts to monopolize the practice of heal-ing—still reflect that point of view:

> The State . . . stands between me and my body, and tells me what kind of a doctor I must employ. When my soul is sick, unlimited spiritual liberty is given me by the State. Now then, it doesn't seem logical that the State shall depart from this great policy . . . and take the other position in the matter of smaller consequences —the health of the body. . . . Whose property is my body? Prob-ably mine. . . . If I experiment with it, who must be answerable? I, not the State. If I choose injudiciously, does the State die? Oh, no.[11]

I contend that, strange as it may sound, we have lost our most important right: the right to our bodies.[12]

How We Lost the Right to Our Bodies

How can a person lose the right to his body? By being deprived of the freedom to care for it and to control it as he sees fit. From the time the Pilgrims first landed until 1914, the American people had the freedom as well as the obligation, the right as well as the duty, to care for and control their bodies, manifested by legally unrestricted access to the medical care and the medicines of their choice. During all those years, the government did not control the market in drugs or the peoples' use of drugs.

To follow the critique of the War on Drugs presented in this book, it is crucial that we keep in mind this question: How can a person lose the right to his body? And that we not waver from answering thus: A person can lose the right to his body the same way he can lose the right to his life, liberty, or property—namely, by someone's depriving him of it. When a private person takes away an individual's life, liberty, or property, we call the former a criminal, and the latter a victim. When an agent of the state does such a thing, and does it rightfully, according to law, we regard him as a law enforcement officer carrying out his duties, and regard the person deprived of his rights as a criminal receiving his just punishment. However, when agents of the therapeutic state deprive us of our right to our bodies, we view ourselves neither as victims nor as criminals, but as patients. There is, of course, a third way we can lose our right to property, namely, by taxation.

When a criminal deprives us of property (to enrich himself), we call it "theft." When the criminal justice system deprives us of property (to punish us), we call it a "fine." And when the state deprives us of property (to support itself, ostensibly to serve us), we call it a "tax." Taxation and drug prohibition are both coercive state interventions, and both are justified largely on paternalistic grounds. In the case of taxation, the state lets us buy those things it considers we can manage by ourselves (for example, food and lottery tickets), while it extracts that proportion of our income it deems "socially just," ostensibly to provide us with those things it considers we cannot provide for ourselves (such as health care and postal service). Similarly, in the case of drug controls, the state lets us buy those drugs it considers safe for us to use (over-the-counter drugs), and it removes those drugs it considers unsafe for us to use (prescription drugs and illicit drugs). Then, in the process of taxing us and depriving us of drugs, the state also expropriates sufficient funds to provide politicians and other government parasites with a comfortable living. Surely, it is not an accident of history that only one year separates the enactment of the Sixteenth Amendment, creating the legal authority for the federal income tax (1913), and the passage of the Harrison Narcotic Act (1914), creating the legal authority for the first federal drug prohibition. In short, when the state deprives us of our right to drugs and justifies it as drug controls, we ought to regard ourselves not as patients receiving state protection from illness, but as victims robbed of access to drugs—just as when the state deprives us of our right to property and justifies it as taxing personal income, most of us regard ourselves not as beneficiaries receiving state services for our needs, but as victims robbed of some of our income. Indeed, the deep sense that our property rights are inalienable—that they are not gifts of the government—accounts for the ineradicable streak in the American spirit that continues to regard taxation as legalized robbery.

At this point I want to note briefly that I recognize a need for limiting the free market in drugs, just as I recognize a need for limiting the free market in many other goods. The legitimate place for that limit, however, is where free access to a particular product presents a "clear and present danger" to the safety and security of *others*. On such grounds, the state controls the market in explosives, and on such grounds it may legitimately control the market in plutonium or radioactive chemicals used in medicine. But this is not the basis for our current drug controls.

Since the beginning of this century, through a combination of medical licensure and direct drug-control legislation, the American government has assumed progressively more authority over the drug trade and our drug use. The ostensible aim of these restrictions was to protect people from incompetent doctors and unsafe drugs. The actual result was loss of personal freedom, without the gain of the promised benefits. It is important to keep in mind that our elaborate machinery of drug controls rests largely on prescription drug laws, which, in turn, rest on a medical profession *licensed by the state*. While in *Capitalism and Freedom*, Milton Friedman does not mention drug controls, he addresses the even more sacrosanct subject of medical licensure, and gives it its libertarian due. "The conclusions I shall reach," he writes, "are that liberal principles do not justify licensure even in medicine and that in practice the results of state licensure in medicine have been undesirable."[13] Regardless of their lofty motives, drug controls encourage people to expect politicians and physicians to protect them from themselves—specifically, to protect them from their own inclinations to use or misuse certain drugs. The result is state control of the drug market and an interminable War on Drugs—symptoms of our having, in effect, repealed the Constitution and the Bill of Rights.

The Breached Castle

Consider the following imaginary scenario. Don, a retired widower in his sixties, lives alone in a suburban home. He has many friends, enjoys good health, is economically secure, and has no dependents. His hobby is gardening in the greenhouse attached to his home. A genius at making things grow, Don's home overflows with exotic plants and fresh flowers, and his tomatoes are legendary. Let us imagine further that Don, an adventurous and enterprising person, acquires some marijuana, coca, and poppy seeds, plants them in his greenhouse, nurtures the seedlings into mature plants, harvests them, and produces some marijuana, coca leaves, and raw opium. Much given to privacy, Don does not even let a cleaning person in his home, though he could well afford it. Hence, there is no way for anyone, legally, to know about his miniature drug farm. Finally, let us assume that on an occasional Saturday evening, Don, alone at home, smokes a little marijuana or chews some coca leaves or mixes some opium powder into his midnight tea.

What has Don done, and how does American law—criminal *and* mental health law—regard him and his behavior? Ownership of land and buildings is a basic property right. Privacy, especially since *Griswold v. Connecticut* and *Roe v. Wade*, is also a basic right.[14] Thus, Don has simply exercised some of his property and privacy rights: his right to his land, his home, and the fruits of his labor in his own home. He has deprived no one of life, liberty, or property. Conventional wisdom and medical disinformation to the contrary notwithstanding, Don has not harmed himself either. Nevertheless, American criminal law now regards him as guilty of criminal possession and use of controlled and illegal substances, while American mental health law regards him as a psychiatric patient suffering from chemical dependency, substance abuse, personality disorder, and other psychopathological aberrations as yet undiscovered. Moreover, stigmatizing Don as a mentally sick person, criminalizing his behavior as that of an evil-minded lawbreaker, dispossessing him of his home and imposing an astronomical fine on him, and incarcerating him as a dangerous offender—all this is now considered to be perfectly legal and constitutional. At this point, the reader might wonder how legal scholars and justices of the Supreme Court reconcile such seemingly excessive—and hence "cruel and unusual"—punishment with the Constitution.

Justifying Therapeutic Slavery

How can the government of the United States—crafted and considered to possess the most prudently limited powers of any government in the world—prohibit a competent adult from growing or ingesting an ordinary plant, such as coca leaf or hemp? And how can it impose such staggeringly disproportionate punishment—compared, for example, to the punishment imposed on many persons convicted of murder—on an individual who inhales the products of such a plant?[15] The answer is that where there is a political will, supported by popular opinion and powerful factional interest, there is a legal way, paved with the legal fictions necessary to do the job. At the end of the eighteenth century, operating in the context of the old practice of slavery plus the new principle of apportioning congressional seats by population, the manufacturers of legal fictions fabricated the ingenious and ignominious concept of three-fifths persons. Since 1914, the politicians' desire to control the use of certain common plants and their biologically active ingredients, together with the public's fascination with and fear of certain glamorized and scapegoated substances, has led to the fabrication of analogous legal fictions to justify the prohibition of the production, even for private use, of plants or substances deemed dangerous by the government.

The trick to enacting and enforcing crassly hypocritical prohibitions, with the conniving of the victimized population, lies in not saying what you mean and avoiding direct legal rule making. Thus, the Founders did not declare, in so many words, "To justify slavery, in the slave states blacks shall be counted as property; and to apportion more congressional seats to the slave states than they would have on the basis of their white population only, black slaves shall be counted as three-fifths persons." Similarly, our lawmakers do not say, "We shall impose draconian criminal penalties on anyone within the borders of the United States who ingests marijuana he has grown on his own land for his own personal use only." What, then, do they say? Why do legal scholars consider such a prohibition to be constitutional?

The answer to these questions is briefly this. Under the police power,

the states can prohibit a wide range of activities regarded as endangering
the public welfare, for example, gambling, obscenity, and drugs, notably
alcohol. However, Congress has no police power over the nation as a
whole. That is why making the sale of alcohol a federal offense required
a constitutional amendment. However, there is another route to federal
drug prohibition, namely, through the Constitution's Commerce Clause
(Article I, section 8, clause 3), which empowers Congress to close the
doors of interstate commerce to any unwanted product. Thus, the key
subterfuge undergirding the alleged constitutionality of our federal anti-
drug laws is that their purpose is to protect commerce, not to punish
persons for crimes. But where is the commerce in producing a plant for
one's own use only? Or in picking a plant found growing in the wild
and ingesting it?

Of course, the constitutionality of the drug laws, beginning with the
1906 Food and Drugs Act, was challenged in the courts. Not surprisingly,
it was consistently upheld by the Supreme Court, as for example in the
1913 *McDermott* case, where the Court declared,

> [Congress] has the right not only to pass laws which shall reg-
> ulate legitimate commerce among the States and with foreign
> nations, but has the full power to keep the channels of such
> commerce free from the transportation of illicit or harmful ar-
> ticles, to make such as are *injurious to the public health* outlaws
> of such commerce.[16]

In his scholarly review of the constitutionality of drug laws, Thomas
Christopher concludes that "there has been no serious discussion by
that body [the Supreme Court] of the over-all constitutional question [of
drug regulation]. *It would seem that that issue is too well settled.*"[17] Here
we come to the nub of the matter. Under the pretext of the Commerce
Clause plus the prevailing medical legerdemain about dangerous drugs,
the Supreme Court has, in effect, become the mouthpiece of the Food
and Drug Administration and of organized American medicine. Christopher puts it more elegantly. The Court, he writes, "has always shown
great respect for the Food and Drug Administration, and for its admin-
istrative findings and rulings. . . . [d]oubtless [this] is owing to the fact
that health matters are involved."[18]

The Commerce Clause as a decoy for the paternalistic-prohibitory
purposes of drug laws is a contemporary example of the use of a powerful legal fiction in the service of a popular cause. But the therapeutic
state thus engendered is no fiction. The *Wickard* case exemplifies the

implausible ends to which the means of Congress's right to regulate commerce may be put in order to justify depriving Americans of their right to manage their own self-regarding, drug-using behavior.

In 1940, pursuant to the Agricultural Adjustment Act of 1938, an Ohio farmer named Roscoe C. Filburn was allotted 11.1 acres for his 1941 wheat crop. He sowed 23 acres. Seeking exemption from the regulations, Filburn filed a civil suit against Secretary of Agriculture Claude Wickard, asking the court to enjoin him from enforcing the act against him. The lower court ruled in Filburn's favor. But in *Wickard v. Filburn* the Supreme Court reversed the decision, holding that the act could be applied to Filburn. What was Filburn's violation? Committing "farm marketing excess." What was Filburn's defense? That he used his crop "to feed part to poultry and livestock on the farm . . . some in making flour for home consumption . . . and keep the rest for the following seeding."[19] The Supreme Court ruled against Filburn, declaring:

> The Act includes a definition of "market" and its derivatives so that as related to wheat in addition to its conventional meaning it also means to dispose of "by feeding (in any form) to poultry or livestock which, or the products of which, are sold, bartered, or exchanged. . . . Hence, marketing quotas . . . also [embrace] what may be consumed on the premises. Penalties do not depend upon whether any part of the wheat . . . is sold or intended to be sold.[20]

Note the Court's redefinition of the word *market* so as to include supplying one's own needs, and its candid admission that such redefinitions may legitimately be manufactured ad hoc—in this case, "as related to wheat." The result of using the Commerce Clause as a pretext for drug prohibition is that, de facto as well as de jure, the American government is empowered to deprive us, as it sees fit, of our ancient freedom to grow—on our own soil, for our own consumption—any crop of its choosing.

Rights: Opportunities vs. Risks

The normal reader, defensive of the rationale of current drug prohibitions, might be inclined to dismiss my hypothetical scenario about "Don" as irrelevant to real life, and might want to change the subject to real problems such as intravenous drug use, AIDS, crack babies, and other assorted horrors. My rejoinder is two-pronged. First, let us re-

member the adage that hard cases make bad law. Hence there is merit
in considering the easiest case first. If such a case suggests that a particular law violates an important political principle, it ought to make us
think twice about casually overriding the violation in the name of some
temporarily fashionable social cause. Second, let us keep in mind that
the essence of freedom is choice, and that choice implies the option to
make the wrong choice, that is, to "abuse" freedom and suffer the
consequences. Thereby hangs a long tale, with a hopeless quest and
many enthusiastic questers as its leitmotif. Like medieval searchers for
the Holy Grail, these modern seekers look for the correct answer to an
absurd question, namely: How can we reduce or eliminate the risks and
undesirable consequences of liberty, while retaining its rewards and
benefits? The fact that we cannot do this has not stopped people, especially "democratic socialists" and other optimistic statists from trying.
Indeed, the history of modern welfare states is, in part, the history of
that self-defeating effort.

Rights entail opportunities as well as risks. This is why some people
see the right to property as giving us prosperity and liberty, and others
see it as giving us booms and busts; why some see the right to property
in land and houses as giving us builders, real estate agents, and landlords
who provide us with homes, while others see it as giving us unscru-
pulous moneylenders and greedy slumlords to exploit people's home-
lessness. Similarly, we can see the right to drugs as giving us control
over our medical and physiological destiny, or as giving us drug abusers
and crack babies.

Both images are real. Both are true. And the *choice* is ours. For example,
we choose to view the owners and managers of American supermarkets
as providing us with the best and most bountiful food and drink in the
whole world, not as malefactors determined to make life difficult for
troubled anorectics and bulimics. We do not blame the obesity of fat
persons on the people who sell them food, but we do blame the drug
habits of addicts on the people who sell them drugs. Obviously, the
supplier of every good or service is, ipso facto, a potential seducer as
well; the only question is whether he is a successful or unsuccessful
seducer. The successful seducer becomes a flourishing businessman or
entrepreneur; the unsuccessful one goes broke or quits the market. This,
in a nutshell, is the free market—the one and only secure foundation
of individual liberty. If we try to redefine liberty in such a way that it
is not liberty unless its results are individually and collectively
"healthy"—which, in the case of drugs, means providing us with ef-

fective and affordable treatments for disease *and* protecting us from the abuse of drugs by both patients and doctors—we fool only those foolish enough to believe in miracles. Sometimes, that category includes the majority. We then speak, usually in retrospect, of a crowd madness.[21]

THE RIGHT TO DRUGS AS A RIGHT TO PROPERTY

Obviously, viewing the right to drugs as a species of property right presupposes a capitalist conception of the relationship between the individual and the state, incompatible with a socialist conception of that relationship. We are familiar with the fact that capitalism is premised on the right to property. As for socialism, *Webster's* defines it as "a system or condition of society or group living in which there is no private property."[22] Q.E.D.: Drug censorship, like book censorship, is an attack on capitalism and freedom. Psychiatrists either ignore this cardinal connection between the chemicals we call "drugs" and politics, preferring to treat drug use as if it were purely an issue of mental health or psychopathology, or—if they recognize it—treat the relationship with their customary hostility to liberty and property. To illustrate this point, I shall juxtapose the views on liberty and property of two of the most important thinkers of our age: Ludwig von Mises and Sigmund Freud. Although both men lived in Vienna at about the same time and addressed some of the same momentous issues, I have never seen their differing judgments compared and brought to bear on our current views concerning drug controls.

Ludwig von Mises vs. Sigmund Freud

In 1922, Ludwig von Mises—the most unappreciated genius of our century—published a book entitled *Socialism*, establishing his reputation, at least among the cognoscenti. His closing sentences in that work read thus: "Whether Society is good or bad may be a matter of individual judgment; but whoever prefers life to death, happiness to suffering, well-being to misery, must accept . . . without limitation or reserve, private ownership of the means of production."[23]

Seven years later, Sigmund Freud—the most successful charlatan of our century—published *Civilization and Its Discontents*, adding more lustre to his already considerable fame especially among the scientistically minded enemies of capitalism and freedom. "I have no concern," declared Freud, "with any economic criticism of the communist system;

I cannot inquire into whether the abolition of private property is expeditious or advantageous."[24] Freud's anti-capitalist remarks were not isolated comments, tossed off at the spur of the moment. Years before, he greeted the Bolsheviks' declaration of war on private property and religious freedom with a mixture of naiveté and optimism. "At a time when the great nations announce that they expect salvation only from the maintenance of Christian piety," he wrote in 1917, "the revolution in Russia—in spite of all its disagreeable details—seems none the less like the message of a better future."[25] In public, Freud chided the United States for not sharing his disdain for religion; in private, he conducted his business in U.S. dollars only.

Unfortunately, modern liberals continue to focus on *human* rights rather than on *property* rights. Why? Because it makes them appear socially concerned—"caring" and "compassionate." By splitting off property rights from human rights, liberals have succeeded in giving the former a bad name, undermining the moral legitimacy of all other rights in the process. But property rights are not only just as valid as human rights; they are anterior to, and necessary for, human rights.

Liberty as Choice

Private property is indispensable as an economic base and precondition for forming a government *fit for freedom*. I use this unfamiliar expression to emphasize that no government is, or can be, *committed to freedom*. Only people can be. Government, by its very nature, has a vested interest in enlarging its freedom of action, thereby necessarily reducing the freedom of individuals. At the same time, the right to private property—as a political-economic concept—is not a sufficient foundation for a government serving the needs and meriting the loyalty of free and responsible persons. It may be worth remembering here that Adam Smith, generally regarded as the father of free-market capitalism, was not an economist (there was no such thing in the eighteenth century). He was a professor of moral philosophy. As such, his brand of economics made no attempt to be value-free. Today, professional economists and observers of the economic scene err in their efforts to make the study of these human affairs into a value-free social "science."

What, then, is the moral merit of the free market? What is good about it, besides its being an efficient mechanism for producing and delivering goods and services? The answer is that the free market is good because it encourages social cooperation (production and trade) and discourages force and fraud (exploitation of the many by a few with the power to coerce), and because it is a legal-moral order that places the value of the person as an individual above that of his value as a member of the community. It is implicit in the idea of the free market that persons who want to enjoy its benefits must assume responsibility, and be held responsible, for their actions; that they look to the principle of caveat emptor—not the paternalistic state—for protection from the risks inherent in the exercise of freedom; and that among the risks with which they must live are those associated with drugs and medical treatments. In short, the fundamental precepts of moral philosophy and political economics cannot be separated: They are symbiotic, the one dependent on the other. "It is . . . illegitimate," Mises warned, "to regard the 'economic' as a definite sphere of human action which can be sharply delimited from other spheres of action. . . . The economic principle applies to all human action."[26]

If we are willing to use our political-economic vocabulary precisely and take its terms seriously, we must conclude that just as the Constitution guarantees us the right to worship whatever gods we choose and read whatever books we choose, so it also guarantees us the right to use whatever drugs we choose. Mises's observation about the characteristic conflict of the twentieth century—which, with welfare-statism in mind, he offered at its beginning—remains true toward its end and applies with special force to the drug problem:

> In the sixteenth and seventeenth centuries religion was the main issue in European political controversies. In the eighteenth and nineteenth centuries in Europe as well as in America the paramount question was representative government versus royal absolutism. Today it is the market economy versus socialism.[27]

Mises never ceased emphasizing that our bloody century is characterized by a struggle between two diametrically opposite types of economic systems: command economies *controlled* by the state, exemplified by socialism (communism), versus free-market economies *regulated* by the supply and demand of individual producers and consumers, exemplified by capitalism (classical liberalism). States based on command economies are inherently despotic—a few superiors issuing orders, and many subordinates obeying them. States based on market economies are inherently democratic—individuals deciding what to produce, sell, and buy and at what prices, producers and consumers alike being free to engage or refrain from engaging in market transactions.

The American Drug Market Today

To clearly understand what has happened to the market in drugs in the United States during the past century, it is necessary, first, to distinguish between consumer goods, which are depleted in use, such as food and clothing, and capital goods, which are used to produce goods, such as machines and tools. This distinction immediately alerts us to the fact that the term *consumer good* has a distinctly individualistic (non-paternalistic) connotation: It implies that an individual, qua consumer, has an interest in a particular product. After all, not everything a person might be able to consume is—at all times, for all individuals—a consumer good. To qualify, there must be consumers who want it. And the only way we can be certain that a customer really wants a good or service is if he is willing to pay for it. This is what economists call a "demand" for a good. And this is the meaning of the adage "People pay for what they value, and value what they pay for."

Obviously, the presence or absence of demand is an economic and cultural—not a scientific or medical—issue. For example, in the United States today, there is a demand for marijuana, but there is no demand for the powdered horn of the rhinoceros (except perhaps in San Francisco). To be sure, the concept of demand (like the concept of illness) is a man-made category: In each case, the contours of the concept may be redrawn to suit the strategies of the definers; and both "conditions" may be imposed on individuals against their will. Courts now routinely order persons who use illegal drugs to attend drug treatment programs, from which mental health experts and economists conclude that there is a huge demand for drug treatment services in our society. (This creation, by court orders, of drug abusers and a demand for drug treatment services is similar to the creation, by court orders, of mental illnesses and a demand for mental health services. The pathetic and now discredited principles of statist—that is, Soviet—economics thus continue to flourish in our own drug-control and mental-health systems.)

Let us suspend our customary concerns with the drug user's motivations, society's judgments of drug use, and the pharmacological effects of particular drugs. And let us focus instead on the various ways an American who wants to use drugs now actually gains access to them. We can then categorize drugs according to their availability or mode of distribution, as follows:

1. No special government controls limiting sales: for example, coffee, aspirin, laxatives. Produced by private entrepreneurs; distributed through the free

market. Product called "food," "beverage," or "over-the-counter drug"; seller, "merchant"; buyer, "customer."

2. Government controls limiting sales:

   a. To adults: for example, alcohol and tobacco. Produced by private entre-preneurs; distributed through the free or state-licensed market. Product called "beer," "wine," "cigarette"; seller, "merchant"; buyer, "customer."

   b. To patients: for example, digitalis, penicillin, steroids, Valium. Produced by government-regulated pharmaceutical manufacturers; distributed through state-controlled physicians' prescriptions and pharmacies. Product called "prescription drug"; seller, "pharmacist"; buyer, "patient."

   c. To addicts: for example, methadone. Produced by government-regulated pharmaceutical manufacturers; distributed through special federally approved dispensers. No legal sellers or buyers. Product called "drug (abuse) treatment"; distributor, "drug (treatment) program"; recipient, "(certified) addict."

3. Government controls prohibiting sales to everyone: for example, heroin, crack. Produced illegally by private entrepreneurs; distributed illegally through the black market. Product called "dangerous drug" or "illegal drug"; seller, "pusher" or "trafficker"; buyer, "addict" or "drug abuser."

As such a market-oriented perspective on drug distribution shows, we have nothing even remotely resembling a free market in drugs in the United States. Nevertheless, most people mistakenly think of pre-scription drugs, and even of specifically restricted drugs such as meth-adone, as "legal."

Although it is a truism, it is perhaps necessary to repeat that the uncorrupted concept of liberty implies no particular result, only the proverbial level playing field where all can play—and win or lose—by the same rules. Despite all the rhetoric to the contrary, no one is, or can be, killed by an illegal drug. If a person dies as a result of using a drug, it is because he *chose* to do something risky: The *drug* he chooses may be cocaine or Cytoxan; the *risk* he chooses to incur may be motivated by the pressure of peers or the pressure of cancer. In either case, the drug may kill him. Some deaths attributed to illegal drug use may thus be accidents (for example, inadvertent overdose); some may be indirect suicides (playing Russian roulette with unknown drugs); and some may be direct suicides (deliberate overdose).

Reforming Drug Policy: Deforming the Market

Because all criticisms of drug control policies are aimed at the way particular drugs are distributed, proposals for reform correspond to the categories described above. I shall summarize each posture vis-à-vis drug controls by identifying the characteristic strategies of its proponents:

1. Criminalizers ("Do you want more crack babies?"): Keep type 3 substances in category 3; expand categories 3, 2b, and 2c, and constrict categories 1 and 2a; drug offenders are both criminals and patients, who should be punished as well as (coercively) treated.
2. Legalizers ("The war on drugs cannot be won."): Remove certain type 3 substances, such as heroin, from category 3 and transfer them to category 2b or 2c (make the manufacture and sale of heretofore prohibited substances a government monopoly); drug abusers are sick and should be (coercively) treated in government-funded programs.
3. Free marketeers ("Self-medication is a right."): Abolish categories 2b, 2c, and 3, and place all presently restricted substances in category 2a; drug use is personal choice, neither crime nor illness.

I disagree with both the drug criminalizers and the drug legalizers: with the former, because I believe that the criminal law ought to be used to protect us from others, not from ourselves; with the latter, because I believe that behavior, even if it is actually or potentially injurious or self-injurious, is not a disease, and that no behavior should be regulated by sanctions called "treatment."[28]

As we have seen, there are three distinct drug markets in the United States today: (1) the legal (free) market; (2) the medical (prescription) market; and (3) the illegal (black) market. Because the cost of virtually all of the services we call "drug treatment" is borne by parties other than the so-called patient, and because most people submit to such treatment under legal duress, there is virtually no free market at all in drug treatment. Try as we might, we cannot escape the fact that the conception of a demand for goods and services in the free market is totally different from the conception we now employ in reference to drug use and drug treatment. In the free market, a demand is what the customer wants; or as merchandising magnate Marshall Field put it, "The customer is always right." In the prescription drug market, we seem to say, "The doctor is always right": The physician decides what drug the patient should "demand," and that is all he can legally get. Finally, in the psychiatric drug market, we as a society are saying, "The patient is always wrong": The psychiatrist decides what drug the mental patient "needs" and compels him to consume it, by force if necessary.

Merchants thus *advertise*—to create a demand for the goods they want to sell. Tylenol, for example, is advertised to *customers*. Physicians *prescribe*—to open a drug-market otherwise closed to persons and thus make specific drugs available to them. Penicillin, say, is prescribed to *patients*. And psychiatrists *coerce*—to force mental patients to be drugged as they, the doctors, want them to be drugged. Haldol is forcibly injected into *psychotics*.

However, the foregoing generalizations—valid until recently—no longer hold. Drug manufacturers have begun to advertise prescription drugs to the public. While this practice reveals the hitherto concealed hypocrisy of prescription laws, it introduces increasingly serious distortions into the drug market. For example, tobacco—a legal product— cannot be advertised on television, but Nicorette—an illegal product— can be. (Nicorette is a nicotine-containing chewing gum available by prescription only.) Here are some other current examples of prescription drug advertisements aimed at the public:

For Estraderm, an estrogen patch for women: "Now the change of life doesn't have to change yours."[29]

For Minitran, a transdermal form of nitroglycerin: "Everything you asked for in a patch . . . for less."[30]

For Seldane, an antihistamine: "You've tried just about everything for your hay fever. . . . Have you tried your doctor?"[31]

For Rogaine, an anti-baldness drug: "The earlier you use Rogaine, the better your chances of growing hair."[32]

The advertisement for Rogaine goes beyond simply alerting the customer to the availability of a prescription drug about which he might not be aware: It offers him cash for going to see a doctor and demanding the drug. In a coupon at the bottom of the page, a smaller caption tells the reader: "Fill this in now. Then, start to fill in your hair loss." The coupon is worth $10 "as an incentive" to see a doctor. Because many of the prescription drugs advertised to the public are very expensive, the logic of this practice suggests that drug companies may be tempted to offer increasingly large sums to would-be patients, in effect to bribe them to solicit a prescription from their physician.

Naturally, drug companies defend the practice. "The ads," they say, "help educate patients and give consumers a chance to become more involved in choosing the medication they want."[33] But that laudable goal could be better served by a free market in drugs. In my opinion, the practice of advertising prescription drugs to the public fulfills a more odious function, namely, to further infantilize the layman and, at the same time, undermine the physician's medical authority. The policy puts physicians in an obvious bind. Prescription laws give doctors monopolistic privilege to provide certain drugs to certain persons, or withhold such drugs from them. However, the advertising of prescription drugs encourages people to pressure their physicians to prescribe the drugs they *want*, rather than the drugs the physicians believe they *need*. If a doctor does not comply, the patient is likely to take his business elsewhere. A professor of medicine at Columbia University tells *Time* magazine, "There is no question that certain physicians are being influenced to issue prescriptions that they would not otherwise write."[34] Missing is any recognition of the way this practice reinforces the role of the patient as helpless child, and of the doctor as providing/withholding parent. After all, we know why certain breakfast food advertisements are aimed at young children: Because while they cannot buy these foods for themselves, they can pressure their parents to buy the advertised cereals for them. Similarly, the American people cannot buy prescription drugs, but they can pressure their doctors to prescribe the advertised drugs for them.

The Fiction of Drug Abuse Services

American law, medicine, and public opinion regard not only involuntary confinement in a mental hospital but also involuntary confinement in a drug treatment program as bona fide medical treatments: "Civil commitment is frequently used with addicts who are arrested for criminal activity; with criminal charges pending, the addict can be coerced into treatment and retained long enough to receive the benefits of a treatment program."[35] Thus, perhaps the most important function of our fashionable drug treatment rhetoric is to distract us from the fact that the drug user wants the drug of his choice, not the drug treatment the authorities choose for him. We are flooded with news stories about addicts robbing people to get money to pay for drugs. But who has ever heard of an addict robbing a person to get money to pay for drug treatment? Q.E.D.

If we were to view the whole package of illegal drug use plus legally coerced drug treatment from a free-market perspective, we would see the drug abuser's behavior as his existential and economic demand for the drug of his choice—and the drug prohibitionist's so-called services as deceptive and coercive meddling deliberately mislabeled as "therapy." Indeed, so long as the drug counselor (or whatever he is called) acts as a paid agent of the state (or some other third party in conflict with the self-defined interests of the drug user), we would have to define his intervention as interference not only in the life of his nominal client, but in the free market in drugs as well. All this, and more, Frederic Bastiat had warned against in the early ninteenth century. "To rob the public," he observed, "it is necessary to deceive it. To deceive it, it is necessary to persuade it that it is being robbed for its own benefit, and to induce it to accept, in exchange for its property, services that are fictitious or often even worse."[36]

If ever there were services that are fictitious or even worse, they are our current publicly financed drug treatment services. The wisdom of our language reveals the truth and supports the cogency of these reflections. We do not call convicts "consumers of prison services," or conscripts "consumers of military services"; but we call committed mental patients "consumers of mental health services," and paroled addicts "consumers of drug treatment services." We might as well call drug traffickers—conscripted by the former drug czar William Bennett for beheading—"consumers of guillotine services." After all, Dr. Guillotin was a doctor, and Mr. Bennett used to teach ethics.

To be sure, persons drafted as convicts, conscripts, and "chemically dependent persons" all receive certain services, such as food, shelter, clothing, and anti-drug propaganda. The provision of such "services" is then used to mask the fact that the beneficiaries would prefer being left alone by their benefactors. Like the mythologizing of personal problems as mental diseases, so the mythologizing of illegal drug use as a disease has been overwhelmingly successful. In 1991, the federal government will spend *more than $1 billion on drug treatment research*. Enthusiasm for such "research" is not diminished by the fact that, according to a General Accounting Office report released in September 1990, "researchers know little more about the best way to treat various drug addictions than they did 10 years ago."[37]

THE WAR ON DRUGS AS A WAR ON PROPERTY

Although it is obvious that the American drug market is now completely state controlled, most people seem at once unaware of this fact and pleased with it, except when they want a drug they cannot get. Then they complain about the unavailability of that particular drug: For example, cancer patients complain that they cannot get Laetrile; AIDS patients, that they cannot get unapproved anti-AIDS drugs; women, that they cannot get unapproved chemical abortifacients; terminally ill patients in pain, that they cannot get heroin; and so on. It seems to me

that just as the Soviet people must now suffer the consequences of their
war on private property, we shall have to suffer still more wrenching
personal and national tragedies as the consequences of our War on
Drugs.

Sadly, the very concept of a closure of the free market in drugs is
likely to ring vague and abstract to most people today. But the personal
and social consequences of a policy based on such a concept are anything
but abstract or vague. Every aspect of our life that brings us into contact
with the manufacture, sale, or use of substances of pharmacological
interest to people has been utterly corrupted. The result is that, in all
the complex human situations we call "drug abuse" and "drug abuse
treatment," the voluntary coming together of honest and responsible
citizens trading with one another in mutual trust and respect has been
replaced by the deceitful and coercive manipulation of infantilized people by corrupt and paternalistic authorities, and vice versa. The principal
role of medical, and especially psychiatric, professionals in the administration and enforcement of this system of chemical statism is to act as
double agents—helping politicians to impose their will on the people
by defining self-medication as a disease, and helping the people to bear
their privations by supplying them with drugs. This is a major national
tragedy whose very existence has so far remained unrecognized.

The War on Drugs has many grave consequences. In this discussion
I can touch on only a few of them. Perhaps the most obvious consequences of drug prohibition are the explosive increase in crimes against
persons and property and the corresponding increase in our prison
population. Both phenomena are typically attributed to "drugs," a misleading locution for which the media bears an especially heavy responsibility. I shall not belabor the fact that drugs do not—indeed, cannot—
cause crime. Suffice it to repeat that crime is an act; that the criminal
actor, like all actors, has motives; and that drug prohibition provides
powerful economic incentives for both the trade in prohibited drugs and
crimes against persons and property.

The United States vs. Drug-tainted Property

One of the most ominous and least publicized consequences of the
War on Drugs is the government's use of the Internal Revenue Service
and of the international banking system to detect and apprehend persons
engaged in the drug trade, along with its practice of confiscating property
from persons accused of drug offenses even when they are innocent.

These measures illustrate that the War on Drugs is, *literally*, a war on property—waged by the U.S. government with the enthusiastic support of the Supreme Court. The leading Supreme Court decision supporting the charade of the so-called civil forfeiture procedure—legitimizing the government's seizure of the property even of innocent persons connected to drug-related offenses—merits brief mention.

In 1971, the Pearson Yacht Leasing Company of Puerto Rico (called the "appellee" in the decision) rented a yacht to two Puerto Rican residents. Subsequently, the police found *one marijuana cigarette* on board the yacht, charged the lessees with violation of the Controlled Substances Act of Puerto Rico, and seized the yacht.[38] The lessor (the yacht-leasing company) sued to recover its vessel. The case reached the Supreme Court, which held that, even though the lessor was innocent, the seizure was legal. I will briefly summarize how the Court reached this remarkable conclusion.

The Court acknowledged that the "appellee was in no way . . . involved in the criminal enterprise carried on by [the] lessee and had no knowledge that its property was being used in connection with or in violation of [Puerto Rican law]."[39] Nevertheless, the Court—led by Justice William Brennan, one of its leading liberals—ruled against the yacht company, holding that "statutory forfeiture schemes are not rendered unconstitutional because of their applicability to the property interests of innocents, and here the Puerto Rican statutes, which further punitive and deterrent purposes, were validly applied to appellee's yacht."[40]

Justice William O. Douglas dissented—not on principle, but because he felt the punishment was disproportionate to the (nonexisting) crime:

> Only one marihuana cigarette was found on the yacht. We deal here with trivia where harsh judge-made law should be tempered with justice. I realize that the ancient law is founded on the fiction that the inanimate object itself is guilty of wrongdoing. But that traditional forfeiture doctrine cannot at times be reconciled with the requirements of the Fifth Amendment.[41]

Note that Justice Douglas cavalierly sidesteps the legitimacy of the core issue, namely, the prohibition of marijuana. Instead of engaging in a principled argument, he magnanimously offers to return the yacht to its rightful owners.

A closely related case, in which the Supreme Court ruled unanimously that the government could dispossess a person of his property *even after he had been acquitted* on a related criminal charge (of gun law, rather than drug law, violation), deserves to be mentioned in this connection. In 1977, Patrick Mulcahey was apprehended by agents of the Bureau of Alcohol, Tobacco, and Firearms and charged with dealing in firearms without a license. Although Mulcahey had no license, a jury acquitted him, perhaps because it felt that he had been entrapped. Following Mulcahey's acquittal, the United States moved to "forfeiture of the seized firearms." [42] The Court held that

> an acquittal on criminal charges does not prove that the defendant is innocent; it merely proves the existence of reasonable doubt as to his guilt. . . . [T]he substantive criminal provision under which Mulcahey was prosecuted, does not render unlawful an *intention* to engage in the business of dealing in firearms without a license; only the completed act of engaging in the prohibited business is made a crime. . . . Because the par. 924(d) forfeiture proceeding brought against Mulcahey's firearms is not a criminal proceeding, it is not barred by the Double Jeopardy Clause. [43]

The crux of the matter is Congress's power to define punishment as a "remedial act." With the transforming of de facto punishments into sanctions de jure "intended to be civil and remedial, rather than criminal and punitive,"[44] our rights to liberty and property vanish. Mental patients have, of course, long been the beneficiaries of such remedial sanctions, being incarcerated though innocent of crime. Civil commitment skirts the prohibition against *preventive detention* by permitting "mental patients," *accused* of being "dangerous," to be deprived of their liberty. This is accomplished by calling the legal procedure for incarcerating the victim "civil," and the place of confinement a "hospital."[45] In the same way, the federal forfeiture laws skirt the prohibition against *punishing innocent persons* by permitting "drug criminals," *accused* of "having used or intending to use" their property to commit or facilitate a drug law violation, to be deprived of their property.

The Fourth Amendment protection against unreasonable searches and seizures is thus neatly nullified by calling the legal procedure for confiscating the property "civil," and the economic loss imposed on the victim a "storage fee." People suspected of drug-related offenses have thus been deprived of their boats, cars, houses, and money, which they may or may not be able to regain after they prove their innocence, by which time the effort may be counterproductive. One victim of this civil deprivation-of-property procedure, whose boat worth $7,600 was seized and kept for three and a half months, got it back "upon payment of $4,000 in storage and maintenance charges."[46] Another had his brand-new $140,000 fishing boat seized after Customs Service agents found 1.7 grams of marijuana in a crewman's jacket pocket. "Customs officials admitted that Mr. Hogan [the owner] knew nothing about the marijuana. But they held his boat long enough for him to miss the halibut season (a $30,000 loss), and at first demanded that he pay a $10,000 fine for failing to keep drugs off his vessel."[47] Similar horror stories abound.[48]

During the past half-dozen years, civil forfeiture has become a huge federal business, and a huge federal boondoggle. According to a 1991 report of the General Accounting Office, the inventory of property seized by the Federal Marshalls Service "grew from 2,555 items at the start of the 1985 fiscal year, to 31,110 by December 31, 1990"—by which time the service was "mismanaging more than $1.4 billion in commercial property seized from drug dealers."[49] Although not offered in connection with the drug laws and their enforcement, a remark made by Jefferson scholar Forrest McDonald is apposite here: "The Government of the United States [now] interferes on a level in ordinary people's lives in a way they [the Founding Fathers] would have regarded as the most vicious form of tyranny imaginable. George the Third and all of his ministers could not have imagined a government this big, this intrusive."[50]

Every Man Has a Right to Eat as He Pleases

In 1884, protesting the arguments of (alcohol) prohibitionists, Dio Lewis—a physician and temperance reformer—declared, "Every man has a right to eat and drink, dress and exercise as he pleases. I do not mean moral right, but legal right."[51] The profound truth of this simple statement is reflected, I believe, in an important inference that we ought to—but never do—draw from the Prohibition Amendment.

The men who drafted the Volstead Act, which provided for enforcement of the Eighteenth Amendment, wanted to prohibit the consumption of alcohol; however, they did not outlaw *it*. They were not interested in whether people transported bottles of chemicals from one place to another, yet *that* is what they outlawed. I infer from this that, deep in their hearts, they and their constituents realized that a competent adult in the Land of the Free has an inalienable right to ingest whatever he wants. It should be unnecessary to add (but our current drug scapegoating justifies my adding) that there was no question, during Prohibition, of randomly testing people to determine if there was any ethanol in their system, or of searching their homes for alcohol, or of imprisoning them for possessing alcohol, or of involuntarily treating them for the disease of unsanctioned alcohol use.

DRUG CONTROLS AS CHEMICAL STATISM

The contemporary legal justification of drug controls rests heavily on the traditional Judeo-Christian equation of murder and suicide as two species of *homicide*, combined with the modern and peculiarly Western tendency to view both as due to abnormal mental states. Although murder and suicide both result in death (as do many other human behaviors), they are as different from one another as rape and masturbation. The one someone else does *to* you; the other you do *for* yourself. Drug abuse, like food or sex abuse, can injure or kill only the abuser; and of course it rarely does that. However, drug law abuse—the criminalization of the free market in drugs—injures and kills users and so-called abusers alike. Many have already been killed by impure drugs, the adulteration of a criminalized product ("dope"); by bullets fired, in the course of gang wars, for instance, by persons engaged in the illegal trade in drugs ("pushers"); and by AIDS, owing to the absence of a free market in clean hypodermic syringes and needles ("drug paraphernalia"). Many more will surely be killed in the name of this holy war that promises to purify America and make it drug-free.

The Fable of the Bees vs. the Medical Model

The close connection we now tend to draw between suicide and murder, between drug abuse as harm to self and harm to others, is a manifestation of what is often called the "medical model": the viewing of behavior—especially socially disturbing behavior—as if it were a disease or the product of a disease. This absurd but nonetheless popular perspective on bad habits—on which our drug controls and much else in our contemporary struggle with lack of self-discipline and self-responsibility rest—is, in effect, an inversion of our traditionally moral perspective on behavior. The latter perspective Hobbes stated, simply and forcefully, when he declared, "Of the voluntary acts of every man, the object is some *good to himself*."[52] Indeed, what else could be their object? Yet it pains us now to acknowledge this.

Try as we might to hide from ourselves the bitter truth about the influence of our societal perspective on behavior in these matters, we shall have to rediscover it or perish. Such painful learning by collective experience seems to be a characteristic feature of the free market and of the nearly reflexive human revolt, born out of an innate combination of dependency and paternalism, against it. However, overcoming our predicament with respect to the market in drugs will require just such relearning.

In this connection, consider the illuminating title of Bernard de Mandeville's epoch-making work *The Fable of the Bees: Or Private Vices, Publick Benefits*.[53] By cannily characterizing the market as a mechanism for turning *private vices into public virtues*—benefits, as he put it—Mandeville (1670–1733), a Dutch-born British physician-satirist, succeeded not only in giving a satisfactory account of its psychosocial underpinnings, but also in making it socially acceptable. Mutatis mutandis, abolishing the free market—in drugs or other goods or services deemed "dangerous" or "sinful"—reverses the process Mandeville described. Replacing personal efforts at self-control with impersonal laws coercing others, sumptuary laws prohibiting private pleasures create a mechanism for turning *private virtues into public vices*. This is precisely the lesson we draw from what communism has wrought in the Soviet Union, and is the lesson we ought to draw—but so far have stubbornly refused to draw—from what drug controls have wrought in the United States.

The Case for Chemical and Economic Statisms

Our individualist-libertarian and collectivist-redemptionist impulses—each robust in our political traditions—are, of course, at odds with one another and need to be constantly reconciled. In 1917 this ambivalence emerged as the principal ideological conflict of our age, pitting the United States and the Soviet Union against one another in a bitter antagonism. While the intensity of this conflict as an international struggle for power now appears diminished, its future as a domestic conflict within the American soul remains unpredictable. What is clear is that our justificatory images for chemical statism (command pharmacology) and for economic statism (command economy) are much the same, as the following schematic syllogisms illustrate.

Under conditions of economic insecurity, inexorable under capitalist exploitation, freedom is a meaningless concept. The precondition of true freedom is economic security, which can be assured only by government ownership of the means of production and state control of the market in goods and services. Ergo, only in a communist society, based on command economy, can there be true freedom.

Under conditions of chemical insecurity, inexorable under narco-terrorism, freedom is a meaningless concept. The precondition of true freedom is pharmacological security, which can be assured only by government ownership of pharmaceutical production and state control of the market in drugs. Ergo, only in a therapeutic state, based on command pharmacology, can there be true freedom.

These are marvelously persuasive arguments. If the first were not, fewer people would accept it in communist countries as providing moral and political legitimacy for the policy of state control of the market in goods and services; and if the second were not, fewer would accept it in the United States as providing legitimacy for the control of the market in pharmaceutical goods and services. There is only one thing wrong with these arguments, namely, that they are erroneous. Nothing can alter the fact that, like disease and death, insecurity and risk are intrinsic to the human condition. The state cannot protect us from any of them. The most the state can do is provide us with a social environment in which we can protect ourselves from the various risks that life poses. We, in turn, must learn to protect ourselves and others we care for, by cultivating our intelligence, prudence, and self-discipline.

Although the state cannot protect us from the risks of life, it can easily create an economic and legal environment in which we are deprived of the goods and drugs we crave. Perfect economic and pharmacological security is not to be had in this world. However, states whose citizens acquiesce in policies ostensibly aimed at protecting them from their own anti-social and/or unhealthy dispositions can easily bring about crushing economic and pharmacological deprivation for all but a corrupt elite.

Toward Politics qua Therapy

In recent years, there has been no shortage of critics of big government, on both sides of the rusted Iron Curtain. But words are cheap. Mikhail Gorbachev criticizes communism but continues to practice it where it counts, maintaining state control of the means of production. Similarly, George Bush criticizes opponents of the free market but continues to practice state interventionism where it counts, maintaining and even intensifying state control of medicine and especially the trade in drugs. And sadly, there seems to be little recognition of this, even within the ranks of anti-statists. Paul Johnson, for example, writes of the disenchantment with messianic politics and asks, ''Was it possible to hope that the 'age of politics,' like the 'age of religion' before it, was now drawing to a close?''[54]

But so long as human nature remains what it is, neither religion nor politics will disappear. Hence, Johnson's question is poorly framed. We might better ask, ''Is it possible to hope that the 'age of politics qua nationalism,' like the 'age of politics qua religion' before it, is now drawing to a close?'' To which I would answer, The ''age of politics qua nationalism'' is already past, having been replaced by the ''age of politics qua therapy.''

When all is said and done, what has made the United States a safe haven for the weak and the oppressed? Due process—a lofty tradition of according *persons* genuine legal protection against accusations of wrongdoing. But the American political system accords no similar legal protection to *drugs*. The state may call a person dangerous, but it cannot deprive him of liberty unless it can prove him guilty of a crime (or incriminate him as mentally ill). Similarly, the state may—and can—call a drug dangerous and remove it from the market, and there is nothing any of us can do about it. Thus, all that the therapeutic demagogues need to do is declare a particular drug to be the embodiment of transcendent disease-producing evil and, presto, we have the perfect modern medicomythological scapegoat. This *pharmakos* (Greek for scapegoat) is not a person, so why should it have any rights? It is an ominous threat, causing deadly dangerous diseases, so what rational person would come to its defense?

In 1889, Emile Zola aroused the world when he cried, ''*J'accuse!*'' But Dreyfus was a man, a human being for whom people could feel compassion. Today, the orchestrators of universal sympathy feel compassion for animals, plants, the ecosystem, the whole universe. But who can feel compassion for ''crack''?

2

The American Ambivalence: Liberty vs. Utopia

Mississippi will drink wet and vote dry so long as any citizen can stagger to the polls.

—Will Rogers[1]

Ever since Colonial times, the American people have displayed two powerful but contradictory existential dispositions: They looked inward, seeking to perfect the self through a struggle for self-discipline; and outward, seeking to perfect the world through the conquest of nature and the moral reform of others. The result has been an unusually intense ambivalence about a host of pleasure-producing acts (drug use being but one) and an equally intense reluctance to confront this ambivalence, embracing simultaneously both a magical-religious and rational-scientific outlook on life. In his important work on the intellectual origins of the Constitution, Forrest McDonald notes that the colonists displayed a Puritan devotion to so-called sumptuary legislation, that is, to laws prohibiting "excessive indulgence" in frivolous pleasures, such as gambling. Yet the Framers also believed "that the protection of property was a (or the) fundamental purpose for submitting to the authority of government."[2] McDonald does not acknowledge that these beliefs are mutually irreconcilable.

As the nation grew more populous and powerful, this peculiar national heritage of unresolved ambivalence became a veritable national treasure. Combined with our historically unparalleled diversity as a people, the mixture—not surprisingly—yields a uniquely vague and uncertain national identity. What makes a person an American? Or, to put it in more precise political-philosophical terms: What is the basis for our union as a people? It cannot be the English language, because too many Americans do not speak the language or speak it very badly, and because too many non-Americans speak (more or less) the same language. It cannot be the Constitution, because too many Americans do not know what it says and, if they did, would repudiate it. I submit that, lacking the usual grounds on which people congregate as a nation, we habitually fall back on the most primitive yet most enduring basis for group cohesion, namely, scapegoating.[3] Hence the American passion for moral crusades, which, thanks to the modern medicalization of morals, now appear as crusades against disease. This is why so many Americans believe there is no real difference between the effort required to combat the devastation caused by polio and that caused by heroin.[4]

In short, we must not underestimate the demagogic appeal that the prospect of stamping out evil by suitably dramatic means has always exercised, and will continue to exercise, on the minds of men and women. The Romans, barbarians that they were, had circuses where they watched gladiators kill one another. Our circuses—splashed across the front pages of newspapers and magazines, and flashed unceasingly on television screens—entertain us with our own civilized, and of course scientific, spectacles. We are shown how "bad" illicit drugs injure and kill their victims, and how "good" psychiatric drugs cure them of their nonexistent mental illnesses.

MAKING THE WORLD SAFE FROM SIN

If a person prefers not to question a phenomenon, it is futile to answer his nonexistent query. Such, precisely, is our situation today with respect to drugs. Instead of pondering the so-called drug problem, people know—as Josh Billings would say—"everything that ain't so" about it.[5] Accordingly, they flit from one absurd explanation to another, without ever stopping long enough to hear what they are saying and then, appalled, stop talking and start thinking.

Former First Lady Nancy Reagan: "Any user of illicit drugs is an accomplice to murder."[6]

Former drug czar William Bennett: "It [drug abuse] is a product of the Great Deceiver. . . . We need to bring to these people in need the God who heals."[7]

New York State Governor Mario Cuomo, described while visting a school: "Pupils and teachers waving banners gathered at the school's entrance and the band played the national anthem as Governor Cuomo walked through the door. Cuomo praised the children for taking a stand against drugs, which he called 'the devil.' . . . 'Thank you from the bottom of my heart,' Cuomo said. . . . 'Anybody who does not believe in the devil, think about drugs.' "[8]

These remarks can easily be multiplied. I choose them because they exemplify the nature of public discourse about drugs in the United States today. Looking at the contemporary American drug scene, it is difficult to escape the conclusion that, notwithstanding the contrary evidence of impressive scientific and technological achievements, we stand once again knee-deep in a popular delusion and crowd madness: the Great American Drugcraze. As in the persecutory movements that preceded it, harmless persons and inanimate objects are once again demonized as the enemy, invested with magically dangerous powers, and thus turned into scapegoats whose denunciation and destruction become self-evident civic duty.[9] During the Middle Ages, Nancy Reagan's "drug users" and Mario Cuomo's "devils" were witches and Jews—the former typically accused of abusing children; the latter, of poisoning wells.

America: Redeemer Nation

To understand America's protracted struggle against drugs, we must situate the current anti-drug hysteria in the context of this nation's historical penchant for waging moral crusades. Since Colonial times, the New World was perceived—by settlers and foreign observers alike—as a New Promised Land, a place where man, corrupted in the Old World, was reborn, uncorrupted. This vision inspired the colonists, informed the Founders, burned brightly in the nineteenth century, was clearly exhibited during the earlier decades of this century—first in a great war to make the world safe for democracy, then in an even greater war to make it safe from German and Japanese nationalism—and is now plainly manifest in the war to make the world safe from dangerous drugs.[10] Perhaps more than any recent president, George Bush embodies our self-contradictory quest for a free society *and* a utopian moral order. Giving his inaugural address in January 1989, Bush stressed two themes: the free market—and the war against it. "We know," declared the president, "how to secure a more just and prosperous life for man on earth: through free markets . . . and the exercise of free will unhampered by the state." Then, hardly pausing, he declared drugs to be the nation's chief domestic problem, and pledged, "This scourge will stop."[11]

Formerly, the conviction that America's manifest destiny was the moral reformation of the world was couched in clerical terms, as a fight against sin (drinking as "intemperance"); now, it is couched in clinical terms, as a fight against disease (drug use as "chemical dependency"). The medieval well-poisoning imagery, brought up to date, remains irresistible: General Manuel Noriega is a "narco-terrorist" who sends us cocaine to infect our children; we, in turn, launch Operation Just Cause, invade Panama, kidnap its head of state, and bring him to the United States for a fair trial. Although in his magisterial work, *Redeemer Nation*, Ernest Lee Tuveson does not mention drugs or drug controls, his book can be read as a sustained historical critique that pulls the rug of rationalizations from under the feet of the drug warriors. "To assume," Tuveson cautioned, "that what is good for America is good for the world, that saving the United States is saving mankind, is to open up a large area of temptation. . . . The danger in all this is evident."[12]

Comstockery: Setting the Stage for the War on Drugs

There was a time, not long ago, when America was at peace with drugs—when the trade in drugs was as unregulated as the trade in diet books is today; when people did not view drugs as presenting the sort of danger that required the protection of the national government; and when, although virtually all of the drugs of which we are now deathly afraid were freely available, there was nothing even remotely resembling a "drug problem." It would be a mistake to assume, however, that in those good old days Americans minded their own business. Far from it. Then they hounded themselves and their fellows with the fear of another dangerous pollutant threatening the nation, namely, pornographic books, magazines, and pictures. Inasmuch as the turn-of-the-century war on obscenity preceded, and in part paved the way for, the twentieth-century War on Drugs, let us begin by taking a brief look at print controls or media censorship.

Censorship—that is, the prohibition of uttering or publishing "dangerous," "heretical," "subversive," or "obscene" ideas or images—is an age-old social custom. In fact, appreciation of the moral merit of the free trade in ideas and images is a very recent historical acquisition, limited to secular societies that place a high value on individual liberty and private property. In many parts of the world today, there is no press freedom and the very idea of opposing the right of the church or of the state to control information is considered to be subversive.

The reason for censorship is as obvious as the maxims celebrating the power of ideas are numerous. If the pen is mightier than the sword, we can expect sword-holders to want to sheath their adversaries' swords. As Justice Oliver Wendell Holmes, Jr., put it, censorship rests on the realization that "every idea is an incitement."[13] Perhaps he should have specified "every interesting idea," for a dull idea is not. By the same token, every interesting drug is an incitement. And so is everything else that people find interesting, whether it be dance, music, gambling, or sport. For a number of reasons, among them an increasing tempo of immigration and population growth, in the 1880s Americans began to feel besieged by a pitiless enemy determined to destroy the very soul of their nation. The scriptural serpent surfaced once again, put on the mask called "obscenity and pornography," and suddenly books like *Fanny Hill* and pictures of seminude women became dire threats to the welfare of the nation. So the country declared war on obscenity and soon had a censorship czar committed to stamping out smut. That czar was Anthony Comstock, whose heroic exploits so amused George Bernard Shaw that he made the czar's last name a part of the vocabulary of American English. A "comstock," according to *Webster's*, "is a ludicrous prude, esp. in matters relating to morality in art," and "comstockery [is] prudery; *specif.*: prudish concern in hunting down immorality, esp. in books, papers, and pictures."[14]

I am not going to dwell on Comstock's amazing achievements. The following episode should suffice to illustrate the power he wielded and the similarities between the war on obscenity at the beginning of this century and the War on Drugs at the end of it. As William Bennett's efforts were hampered by drug pushers, Anthony Comstock's were hampered by smut pushers, among them Margaret Sanger, the pioneer feminist and birth control advocate. Clearly, Comstock's anti-obscenity crusade and Sanger's right-to-sex-information crusade were on a collision course.

To provide women with what we now call sex education, Sanger wrote a series of articles for the socialist newspaper *Call*. The publication was stopped, however, when Comstock "announced that an article on gonorrhea violated the bounds of public taste."[15] This further inflamed Sanger, who decided to confront Comstock by publishing all the then available contraceptive information in a magazine appropriately titled *The Woman Rebel*. Comstock was ready. The magazine was banned by the Post Office and, on August 25, 1914, Sanger "was indicted by the federal government on nine counts that could bring a jail sentence of

45 years.''[16] Her lawyers wanted to get her off on a technicality, but Sanger refused, preferring to flee to England. In 1915 Comstock died, and the following year the government dropped its charges against Mrs. Sanger.

Margaret Sanger had money, fame, and power, and survived the war on obscenity essentially unscathed. Others were not so lucky. In 1913, two years before his death, Comstock offered this catalog of his exploits: ''In the forty one years I have been here, I have convicted persons enough to fill a passenger train of sixty-one coaches, sixty coaches containing sixty passengers each and the sixty-first almost full. I have destroyed 160 tons of obscene literature.''[17]

Comstock was at once a symbol and shaper of his age. Federal prosecutor William P. Fiero's declaration, in pleading for the conviction of an obscenity trafficker, was a telling symptom of Comstock's influence. ''The United States,'' Fiero asserted, ''is one great society for the suppression of vice.''[18] How prophetic was that plea! Vice, sin, sickness, addiction, dependency, codependency—the United States is one great society for the suppression of them all. Heywood Broun and Margaret Leech, Comstock's biographers, wrote perceptively of the disastrous legacy that Comstockery conferred on the nation:

> In a wide and growing curve, over the frenzied protests of the adherents of Jefferson, the tendency toward centralization has grown. The lottery laws, the Mann Act, the Pure Food Act, the Narcotics Act, the Prohibition Amendment—in these can it be suggested that the obscure drygoods salesman who went crusading against impurity played any part?[19]

Note that the Comstock laws prohibited only ''the transportation of obscene matter in the mails.''[20] Producing and possessing obscene materials were perfectly legal. The distinction is crucial. Suppose that an artist wanted to paint a picture of a nude woman. He could do so legally. He could gaze at the picture to his heart's content. He could overdose on obscenity. He could show the picture to his friends. He could sell it to them, and they could buy it from him. He could even take it across state lines to show it or sell it. Today, a person cannot do any of these things with any controlled substance grown in his own garden or synthesized in his own laboratory.

Deplorable though they were, the Comstockian anti-obscenity statutes were intended to protect the public only from the (ostensibly) harmful acts of others. The extension of the reach of the interventionist state from protecting people from *moral self-harm* or *vice* (by means of print censorship) to protecting them from *medical self-harm* or *illness* (by means of drug censorship) is a momentous transformation that has not received the critical scrutiny it deserves. On the contrary, academics and intellectuals now speak and write as if providing such protection has always been within the province of state intervention. Drug prohibitionists thus proudly proclaim that protecting people from themselves is just as legitimate a goal for criminal as well as civil law as protecting people from others. Accordingly, trying to save people from their own drug-using proclivities is considered to be ample warrant for depriving individuals of life, liberty, property, and any or all constitutional protections that obstruct this lofty goal.

THE WAR ON DRUGS

After the turn of the century, having enjoyed the blessings of two centuries of free trade in medical care, America succumbed to the lure of European "progress," a/k/a government regulation.[21] Ever since then, the United States has waged a War on Drugs. The hostilities began with minor skirmishes before World War I, grew into guerilla warfare after it, and now affect the daily lives of people not only in the United States but in foreign countries as well.

The Food and Drugs Act of 1906

Before 1907, all drugs could be sold and bought like any other consumer good. The manufacturer did not even have to disclose the contents of his concoction. Hence the name *patent medicine*, the adjective alluding to the fact that the composition was a trade secret, protected by a patented name.

Although there is no evidence that the American consumer ever complained about the free market in drugs, there is plenty of evidence that his self-appointed protectors complained bitterly and loudly. The first landmark event in the federal regulation of drugs (and foods) was the Food and Drugs Act of 1906.[22] What did Congress intend to achieve with this seemingly laudable legislation? To protect people from the sale of "adulterated" or "misbranded" foods or drugs, that is, "assur[ing] the customer of the identity of the article purchased, not of its usefulness."[23]

I say Congress's aim in enacting this legislation was *seemingly* laudable because, while it is desirable that people know what drugs they buy, forcing manufacturers by law to list the ingredients of their products is an unnecessary infringement on the free market—the foot in the door of paternalistic-statist protectionism. If Great American Drugs, Inc., wants to market a mystery product, there is no reason why the government should prevent it from doing so. And if I want to buy such a pig in a poke, why should the government prevent me from making that choice? People who want to be informed about the drugs they buy and use would abstain from purchasing mystery products, and market forces would then create a supply of truthfully labeled drugs. In short, there is no need to prohibit the *non-disclosure* of the contents of medicinal (or other) products. It is enough to prohibit *false disclosure* and to punish it, as fraud, by both criminal and civil penalties. As for nondisclosure, it would be "punished" by the invisible hand of the market.[24]

The truth is that behind Congress's ostensible aim of combating drug misbranding lay its growing antagonism to the habit of pharmacological self-pleasuring, manifested by the act's specifically mandating the listing on the label of what were then the main ingredients of Americans' favorite nostrums: alcohol, hypnotics, and sedatives. The relevant lines of the Food and Drugs Act read as follows:

> That for the purposes of this Act an article shall also be deemed misbranded: . . . if the package fails to bear a statement on the label of the quantity or proportion of any alcohol, morphine, opium, cocaine, heroin, alpha or beta eucaine, chloroform, cannabis, chloral hydrate, or acetanilide.[25]

It is implicit in this sentence that, back then, Congress took for granted the legality of a free market in drugs, including cannabis, cocaine, heroin, and morphine. Accordingly, Congress did not intend to abridge the drug manufacturer's right to freedom of speech (including his right to make exaggerated or false therapeutic claims for his product) or the consumer's right to economic freedom (including his right to buy any medicinal product he might choose and enjoy the benefits, or suffer the harms, of his choice). Thus, the government had no authority to prosecute the drug manufacturer for making "misleading claims" about his product. Making such claims was then still considered to fall within the realm of the seller's free speech and the buyer's responsibility to heed the warning of caveat emptor.[26] Correlatively, the buyer could not sue the drug manufacturer for damages when the product he decided to buy and ingest disagreed with him.

Although in some respects the Food and Drugs Act of 1906 was a salutary piece of legislation because it increased the consumer's power to make an informed choice in the market, its enactment enabled the federal government to enter an arena where the utmost vigilance was required to contain its power. However, such a paranoid posture toward therapeutic state paternalism was by that time quite unfashionable.

United States v. Johnson, 1911

In 1911 the Supreme Court decided to hear the case of *United States v. Johnson*, brought on the basis of the 1906 Food and Drugs Act. The opinion of the Court in this matter is one of the most important and most interesting documents in the annals of American drug laws. The facts were briefly as follows.

The defendant, Dr. O. A. Johnson, was charged with the interstate shipment of allegedly "misbranded medicines," specifically, of articles "labeled respectively 'Cancerine tablets,' 'Antiseptic tablets,' 'Blood purifier,' 'Dr. Johnson's Mild Combination Treatment for Cancer,' " and others. The labels made extravagant therapeutic claims for the products—for example, that Dr. Johnson's Blood Purifier was "an effective tonic . . . utterly destroying and removing impurities from the blood."

These claims were patent nonsense. Most people knew, or should have known, that they were hyperbole to sell the product. Nevertheless, three members of the Court wanted to uphold Mr. Johnson's conviction, on the grounds that the product he was selling was *worthless* and that he *knew* it was worthless. "Why," asked some of the justices, "should not worthless stuff, purveyed under false labels as cures, be made contraband of interstate commerce—as well as lottery tickets?" What a deliciously ironic analogy! In 1911 our Supreme Court justices recognized that advertisements for medicines and for lottery tickets were equally misleading. Today, selling misbranded lottery tickets is perfectly legal: For "a dollar and a dream," the New York State lottery system promises the buyer the chance to win millions. But selling (or buying) truthfully labeled (illegal) drugs is not: Cough syrup, truthfully labeled as containing one-eighth of a grain of codeine per teaspoon, is an illegal product (unless both patient and pharmacist receive permission from a licensed physician for effecting the transaction).

Why did a majority of the U.S. Supreme Court hold, as recently as 1911, that not only is selling cocaine, heroin, and other "dangerous drugs" a constitutionally protected right, but so is making false claims about their therapeutic efficacy? Because the Court presumably believed that property rights and personal rights cannot endure without a marketplace governed by the principle of caveat emptor. According to this principle, the government is required to protect buyers only from products that are mislabeled in the sense that the contents are falsely identified. If a person wants to buy a bottle of aspirin, the government must protect him from vendors who might sell him a bottle labeled "aspirin" but containing arsenic. By the same token, this principle requires the government to leave the buyer alone to make his own decision. If you claim that vitamin C cures cancer or the common cold, and if I choose to believe you and want to buy vitamin C, I ought to be left free by the government to believe or disbelieve you and act accordingly. It is not the duty of the drug manufacturer, the pharmacist, the physician, or the state to protect people from the consequences of acting on *false beliefs*. If it were, where would that leave religions and those who teach religious beliefs?

In its ruling in the *Johnson* case, the Court reemphasized the rationale that animated Congress to enact the Food and Drugs Act of 1906. "The purpose of the statute," declared Justice Holmes, "is to secure pure food and drugs. . . . [The statute does not] refer to claims for curative properties of such drugs." He then added this significant comment: "[The] claim that a beneficial result will follow the use of a prescribed drug [cannot be] an existing fact, but is a forecast concerning a future event and is in the nature of things an expression of an opinion." In addition, concerning the manufacturer's or seller's right to make claims about the therapeutic efficacy of his product, Holmes stated, "It is a postulate, as the case comes before us, that *in a certain sense* the statement on the label was false, or, at least, misleading."[27] Of course. Is not the art of salesmanship that of promising hope? Does it not invariably entail claiming more merit for the good or service advertised than it "actually" (as if that could be objectively ascertained) possesses? Is there an advertisement for a car or a cosmetic that, *in this sense*, does not represent a form of mislabeling? However, this type of misbranding had nothing to do with the 1906 Food and Drugs Act. "We are of the opinion," wrote Justice Holmes, "that the phrase is aimed not at all possible false statements, but only at such as determine the identity of the article, possibly including its strength, quality and purity."

In short, the purpose of the Food and Drugs Act was to guarantee truthful information about what is in the bottle, not about what will happen to the user who ingests its contents.

The Harrison Act (1914) and Its Aftermath

In 1914, Congress enacted another landmark piece of anti-drug legislation: the Harrison Narcotic Act.[28] Originally passed as a record-keeping law, it quickly became a prohibition statute. In the course of the next seven years, by a curious coincidence of history—if, indeed, it is coincidence—in Russia the Soviet Union replaced the czarist empire, while in the United States the free market in drugs was replaced by federal drug prohibition possessing unchallengeable authority. Excerpts from two key Supreme Court decisions quickly tell the story.

In 1915, in a test of the Harrison Act, the Court upheld it but expressed doubts about its constitutionality: "While the Opium Registration Act of December 17, 1914, may have a moral end, as well as revenue, in view, this court, in view of *the grave doubt as to its constitutionality* except as a revenue measure, construes it as such."[29] Yet, only six years later the Court considered objection to federal drug prohibition a taboo. In *Whipple v. Martinson* the justices declared,

> There can be no question of the authority of the State in the exercise of its police power to regulate the administration, sale, prescription, and use of dangerous and habit-forming drugs. . . . The right to exercise this power is so manifest in the interest of public health and welfare, that it is unnecessary to enter upon a discussion of it beyond saying that it *is too firmly established to be successfully called in question.*[30]

In 1914, trading in and using drugs was a right. In 1915, limited federal drug controls were a constitutionally questionable tax revenue measure. By 1921, the federal government had gained not only complete control over so-called dangerous drugs, but also a quasi-papal immunity to legal challenge of its authority. Thus has the *rejection of one of our most basic constitutional rights become transformed into reverence for one of our most baneful therapeutic-religious dogmas.*

Once ignited, the fire of "progressive" drug protectionism spread and soon enveloped the whole country, transforming the Harrison Act into the legislative embodiment of the "moral principle that taking narcotics for other than medicinal purposes was harmful and should be prevented."[31] That threw the monkey wrench *medicinal purpose* into the machinery of the trade in drugs; this undefined and undefinable concept has haunted us ever since. In 1920, drug prohibitionists won another major victory: America was, at last, alcohol-free—if not de facto, then at least de jure. Since 1924, when Congress made it illegal to manufacture, possess, or sell heroin, America has been free from heroin as well—if not in practice, then at least in theory.

The prohibition of heroin even for medical uses was, and has remained, a uniquely American phenomenon. In 1925 at the Third Opium Convention in Geneva, the manufacture of heroin, approved for sale only as a cough medicine, was restricted to European and Japanese firms. (This convention represents a truly bizarre moment in the annals of international trade agreements, the United States in effect requesting other nations to prohibit it from manufacturing a medicinal product widely used throughout the civilized world. In my opinion, this unilateral heroin-disarmament policy—like Prohibition—symbolized America's delusive commitment to playing the role of the drug-pure nation.) In 1926 the famed Bayer Company—then a part of the German giant, I.G. Farben Works—produced *1.6 tons of heroin.*[32]

In retelling this tale, it is impossible to overemphasize that, although initially the drug laws were intended to protect people from being "abused" by drugs *others wanted to sell them*, this aim was soon replaced by that of protecting them from "abusing" drugs *they wanted to buy*. The government thus succeeded in depriving us not only of our basic right to ingest whatever we choose, but also of our right to grow, manufacture, sell, and buy agricultural products used by man since antiquity.

The Dual Aims of Drug Controls

The initial aim of prescription laws was to protect uninformed patients from using powerful ("dangerous") drugs. The laws were not intended to protect the drug user from his own desire to use a particular drug (opiates becoming the first exceptions). Thus, until the 1940s, lay persons could obtain most prescription drugs (except opiates) without a prescription; and pharmacists and physicians, who had unlimited access to prescription drugs, could use such drugs to medicate themselves as they saw fit. Today, politicians and drug experts mouth the platitude that the solution to the drug problem lies in drug education and job training. But the former can yield only a better informed person, and the latter a more employable one. Surely, doctors know enough about drugs and have enough employment. Yet we now view a physician who prescribes a controlled substance for his own personal use not as an educated person exercising autonomous choice, but as a hapless victim of the disease of drug abuse—and as a criminal, to boot.

The distinction I draw here—between the government's using force *against others* to protect us from being harmed by them, and its using force *against us* to protect us from harming ourselves—goes to the heart of both the evil and the failure of drug prohibition. The following hypothetical scenario illustrates this point. Suppose that in 1907 a dairy farmer discovered that one of his cows had tuberculosis. In compliance with the Food and Drugs Act, he would have been forbidden to sell its milk or meat; however, there was nothing in the law to prevent him from drinking the milk or eating the meat. Change the date from 1907 to 1987, replace the milk with marijuana, and the farmer becomes a criminal for the mere possession of the targeted substance.

This, in brief, is the story of how the government succeeded in depriving us of our right to drugs. To be sure, the government did not simply do this to us. We did it to ourselves, too. Fearful of the responsibility of having free choice in a free pharmaceutical market, we colluded with physicians and politicians to have the state put us under its medical-tutelary protection. The cost of this protection, in rights as well as dollars—although negligible at first—quickly became oppressive. The results of a *Washington Post*/ABC News poll taken in September 1989 are illustrative:

> 62 percent of the respondents were willing to give up "a few" freedoms in order to curb drug use; 67 percent would allow police to stop cars at random to search for drugs; 52 percent would allow the police to search without court order the homes of people suspected of selling drugs, even if some homes were searched by mistake; 71 percent would make it against the law to show the use of illegal drugs in the movies.[33]

These responses show us the unadorned visage of the current American zeitgeist, and not merely with respect to drugs.[34] Note that most of the respondents "would make it against the law to show the use of illegal drugs in the movies." This is a truly remarkable preference in view of the fact that nearly every American movie shows the use of guns, legal and illegal. The result is that we live in a society in which people have legal access to loaded guns but not to sterile syringes—an incongruity I interpret as signifying that the American people fear yielding to their own temptations more than they fear being victimized by those who would prey on them, as predators or as protectors.

TEMPERANCE VS. PROHIBITION

We have long regarded our two most popular psychoactive drugs—alcohol and tobacco—with the utmost ambivalence. Throughout the nineteenth century, the prohibition of alcohol (though not of tobacco) was often advocated and occasionally practiced on a local level. However, there was no question of the federal government's involvement in such an effort—it would have been seen as incompatible with the spirit and letter of the Constitution. Unlike today, most people then still appreciated the difference between temperance and prohibition, that is, between controls from within and controls from without, between self-discipline and coercion by the criminal law.

Vices Are Not Crimes

Lysander Spooner's *Vices Are Not Crimes*, his memorable *cri de coeur*, rests on his using the words *vice* and *crime* in their literal senses. "*Vices*," he declared, "are those acts by which a man harms himself or his property. *Crimes* are those acts by which one man harms the person or property of another."[35] However, nothing is easier than interchanging these terms metaphorically in order to persuade people that such figures of speech represent truth, and to create social policy based on and justified by such officially sanctioned falsehoods. Thus, in 1906 it was illegal to operate a lottery, but it was legal to sell and buy heroin; today it is the other way around. Formerly, gambling was considered to be both a vice and a crime; now, operating a lottery is considered to be a public service (indeed, it is a state monopoly, like the postal service), and playing the lottery is regarded as neither a vice nor a crime. (It is regarded as a disease only if the player loses too much money; then he suffers from "pathological gambling.") My point is simply that neither participating in the drug trade nor using drugs (legal or illegal) need be interpreted as constituting vice, crime, or disease.

Although we now shamefully neglect and obscure the differences between vice and crime—and hence the differences between peaceful persuasion and government coercion—these differences form the pillars on which a free society rests. Conversely, denying these distinctions (by metaphorical bombast, sloppy thinking, or political propaganda making use of both) is the decisive step in transforming self-restraint into the restraint of others, temperance into prohibition, persuasion into persecution, the moral ideals of individuals into the immoral madness of crowds. All this Spooner saw clearly and described eloquently:

> No one ever practices a vice with any . . . criminal intent. He practices his vice for his own happiness solely, and not from any malice toward others. Unless this clear distinction between vices and crimes be made and recognized by the laws, there can be on earth no such thing as individual right, liberty, or property; no such things as the right of one man to the control of his own person and property, and the corresponding and co-equal rights of another man to the control of his own person and property.[36]

This view—neither novel nor radical prior to the twentieth century—was consistent with the fact that, in those days, the only way a person could protect and preserve his health was by self-discipline. If he debauched his body, neither the medical profession nor the state could be of much help to him. Only in post–World War II America can people drink, smoke, and use drugs to their hearts' content; claim to be suffering from alcoholism, tobacco dependence, and drug addiction; demand treatment from the state and damages from the companies that sold them the substances they craved; and enjoy the approval of a society eager to authenticate their excuses as the valid complaints of victim-patients, and their expectations as the rightful demand for "health care rights."

Lest the reader think the distinction between vice and crime is elementary, and that it is an exaggeration to say we have lost not only our right to drugs but also our language for expressing the idea clearly, consider the following example. In a report revealingly titled "Temperance: An Old Cycle Repeats Itself," the *New York Times* uses the word *temperance* to describe behavior that is no more than compliance with our draconian drug laws. After being informed that middle-class drug use is diminishing, we are warned that, "if such temperance takes hold and drug use falls to very low levels in the middle class, some experts fear politicians will turn their backs on poor people who may still desperately need publicly financed drug treatment services."[37] When middle-class (white) persons obey the drug laws, they are "temperate"; when lower-class (black) persons violate them, they need "drug treatment services." This misuse of language illustrates that we no longer even care to distinguish between temperance, a personal virtue, and law-abiding behavior, a civic duty.

Not surprisingly, this progressive-protective kind of covert racism packaged as sophisticated medical-social science is supported by a respected drug expert. David Musto declares that our current drug policies represent "the third temperance movement in American history" and predicts its demise in ten or twenty years "with a wild backlash." But Musto is mistaken: Ours is a *prohibition movement, not a temperance movement.* Moreover, for the first time in our history of waging war on drugs, we now call avoiding prolonged incarceration in prison "temperance." This is a moral tragedy, and here is why.

A person does not feel virtuous for performing a particular act when the alternative is forbidden by law. For example, a person with a tendency to obesity who successfully diets feels proud of his achievement, which serves as a continuous reminder of his powers of self-discipline. If obesity ("food addiction") were treated as a criminal offense, like drug addiction, then non-obese persons would simply be law-abiding rather than self-disciplined. Obscuring this distinction is like throwing sand into the gears of self-discipline. Herein lies one of the many undesirable consequences of prohibiting sumptuary behavior on the ground that it is necessary to protect people from making themselves ill.

Regarding the delayed consequences of indulging in bad habits, Spooner wisely observed, "Vices are usually pleasurable, at least for the time being, and often do not disclose themselves as vices, by their effects, until after they have been practiced for many years; perhaps for a lifetime."[38] This familiar fact points to the drug prohibitionist's hidden agenda, namely, that under the guise of trying to protect others from self-harm, he is trying to protect himself from others' becoming a burden on him. Although Spooner wrote long ago and addressed himself only to the social problems posed by alcohol, his remarks fit our present situation perfectly:

> But it will be said, again, that the use of spirituous liquors tends to poverty, and thus to make men paupers, and burdensome to the tax-payers; and that this be sufficient reason why the sale of them should be prohibited. . . . [But] if the fact that the use of liquors tends to poverty and pauperism, be a sufficient reason for prohibiting the *sale* of them, it is equally a sufficient reason for prohibiting the *use* of them; for it is the *use*, and not the *sale*, that tends to poverty. The seller is, at most, merely an accomplice of the drinker. And it is a rule of law, as well of reason, that if

the principal in any act is not punishable, the accomplice cannot be.[39]

Evidently, it never occurred to Spooner that Americans would actually persecute their fellow citizens for what they *eat* or *drink*. But, then, neither did he imagine that vices would be renamed diseases.

America Embraces Therapeutic Paternalism

During the first two decades of this century, several protectionist programs—prohibiting alcohol, providing "pure" food and drugs, limiting access to certain pharmaceuticals—converged and reinforced one another. Each of these programs was, of course, defined as a "reform," ruling out opposition. And each was based on the belief, rapidly gaining ground in the country, that the world was becoming too complicated for ordinary people to manage without the active support of the protectionist state, whose duty should be to safeguard people from the hazards of putting the wrong things in their mouths or bodies. With this view firmly planted in the American mind, an avalanche was loosened that no one could stop. It still has not hit bottom.

As respect for the right to drugs diminished, enthusiasm for drug controls increased. Both Right and Left embraced Prohibition. The Left, intoxicated with anti-capitalism, discovered that alcoholism is a disease caused by the free market. At its 1912 annual meeting, the American Socialist Party endorsed a resolution concerning the "liquor question," affirming that "alcoholism is a disease of which capitalism is the chief cause. . . . To abolish the wage system with all its evils is the surest way to eliminate the evils of alcoholism and the traffic in intoxicating liquor."[40] The Right, intoxicated with religion, stuck to its theme that alcoholism is a sin. Declared the Reverend Josiah Strong, coeditor of the magazine *The Gospel of the Kingdom*, in 1914: " 'Personal Liberty' is at last an uncrowned, dethroned king, with no one to do him reverence. . . . We are no longer frightened by that ancient bogey —'paternalism in government.' We affirm boldly, it is the business of government to be just that—paternal."[41] This credo is now recited as if it were an irrefutable scientific (medical) principle. Dr. Forest S. Tennant, medical adviser to the National Football League, explains, "We use a strictly medical definition of drug addiction. . . . When human lives are at stake, a little totalitarianism is not such a bad thing."[42] We have come a long way since the time when the government was, in theory at least, our servant rather than our master.

Let us briefly reconsider our escalating effort, from 1914 to the present, to curb personal choice vis-à-vis drugs. At the beginning of the century, our principal drug problem was that people drank too much; the solution was Prohibition. Then the banning of booze became the problem; the solution was repealing Prohibition. Then the problem became that people bought many drugs not because they needed them to become healthier, but because they wanted to use them to feel better. This was defined as a medical problem; the solution was giving physicians (and pharmacists) monopolistic control over the trade in drugs—especially those drugs deemed to be pleasure-producing. This led to the abuse of prescription drugs and then efforts to combat it by fresh countermeasures such as triplicate prescriptions for certain "controlled substances," monitoring and prosecuting doctors for "overprescribing," and an orgy of escalating quasi-therapeutic repressions. "Fanaticism," George Santayana sagely observed, "consists in redoubling your effort when you have forgotten your aim." Exactly so: The more hopeless our drug problem becomes, the more stubbornly we cling to the myth that drugs pose a threat to every man, woman, and child in the world, and the more certain we are of our duty to combat drug abuse by coerced treatment and criminal penalties at home, and by armed intervention and economic sanctions abroad. Truly, we are the redeemer nation, our centuries-old ambivalence toward alcohol seemingly entitling us to assume the role of moral savior not merely of our own people, but of people everywhere.

Once the United States entered World War I, victory for national prohibition was assured. Although the fighting stopped on November 11, 1918, Congress—having set in motion the War Prohibition Act—outlawed the manufacture and sale of beer and wine after May 1, 1919, and of all intoxicating beverages after June 30, 1919. As a result, America actually went dry under the War Prohibition Act on July 1, 1919, rather than on January 16, 1920, when the Eighteenth Amendment took effect. With the triumph of national prohibition finally assured, the Anti-saloon League raised its sights even higher. Prohibition in America was just the beginning. The United States's mission was to lead the world to worldwide prohibition. "Redeemed by prohibition," declared the Reverend A. C. Bane, "America will 'go over the top' in humanity's greatest battle. . . . [S]truggling with the same age-long foe, we will go forth with the spirit of the missionary and the crusader to help drive the demon of drink from all civilization."[43]

In retrospect, it is hard to know what to marvel at more: the arrogance or the naiveté displayed by these enthusiasts. In an address to the Anti-saloon League's convention in Washington, D.C., in 1917, the Reverend Sam Small predicted that national prohibition would usher in the day when "you and I may proudly expect to see this America of ours, victorious and Christianized, become not only the savior but the model and the monitor of the reconstructed civilization of the world in the future."[44]

This role of universal religious-therapeutic saviorship seems to fit America's collective spirit so perfectly that we have preserved the play intact, merely modernizing it. We have replaced the actors: liquor with cocaine, Christianity with Medicine. And we have intensified the struggle by equipping the combatants with more powerful weapons: temptations more irresistible than man has ever known ("crack"), and treatments more effective than man has ever dreamed of ("programs" for chemical dependency). All this took time, of course—almost threescore years and ten.

From 1906 when the first anti-drug legislation was enacted, until 1933 when President Franklin D. Roosevelt was inaugurated, federal agencies inspected food and ensured proper drug labeling. During Prohibition, bootleggers gave back to the American people what Congress had taken away from them. And, throughout it all, prescription laws remained permissive rather than prohibitory, physicians needing to fear no penalties for prescribing whatever analgesics, hypnotics, or sedatives their patients wanted or asked for (except opiates).

DRUG REGULATION DURING THE NEW DEAL

Franklin Delano Roosevelt is usually credited with two major achievements: (1) saving the country from its domestic enemy, big business, during the Depression; and (2) saving it from its foreign enemies, the Germans and the Japanese, during World War II. To fight big business, Roosevelt gave America big government; to fight the war, he gave it the atomic bomb. Overshadowed by these dramatic events, Roosevelt's role in the War on Drugs is all but forgotten.[45] Yet the first business he set out to bust was the "monkey business" of merchandising medically "worthless" drugs. Of course, he failed to get rid of such drugs; but he succeeded in socializing the pharmaceutical market and undermining the legitimacy of self-medication.

FDR as Anti-drug Warrior

Although libertarians and conservatives are well aware of Roosevelt's efforts to undermine America's free-market economy, they seem to be unaware of how far-reaching his success was in laying the groundwork for abolishing the free market in drugs. The various drug-regulatory measures enacted during the prewar years of Roosevelt's presidency—especially the Food, Drug, and Cosmetic Act of 1938—led inexorably to the present situation of virtually complete state control of the drug economy, which I call "chemical statism" (drug socialism).

Moreover, while free marketeers generally believe that "it was President Franklin D. Roosevelt who was directly responsible for the abandonment of most of the principles of economic liberty on which this nation was founded,"[46] there is no agreement on why this happened, only on when it happened. Among the explanations usually advanced are the Depression and Roosevelt's personality—both no doubt relevant. I would add another reason that is closely related to our present concerns, namely, the Eighteenth Amendment. Prohibition failed to prevent Americans from drinking, but succeeded in accustoming a whole generation to the criminalization of what, prior to 1920, had been an important and legitimate free-market enterprise. Although Prohibition, *the law*, was repealed, *the idea* of drug prohibition remained imprinted on the national consciousness and henceforth found expression in the progressive criminalization of self-medication. Generation after generation of Americans thus became inured to state supervision of their drug use, much as generation after generation of Soviet citizens became inured, after 1917, to state supervision of their economic affairs. Indeed, perhaps the most important (and certainly the most invisible) cost of the War on Drugs has been the indoctrination, through chemical statism, of the American people into socialism as the correct system for regulating the market in drugs.

What rankled Roosevelt and his rationalist advisers—fittingly called "brain trusters"—was that, despite the drug-labeling laws, the American people continued to "waste" millions of dollars on "worthless" patent medicines. From a free-market point of view, these medicines were not worthless; if they had been, people would not have spent their hard-earned money on them. Moreover, from the consumer's point of view, these medicines were self-evidently useful; most of them contained generous portions of alcohol, providing a legal source of liquor during a period when the government criminalized liquor truthfully labeled as such. To Roosevelt's chagrin, the FDA was powerless to interfere, its authority being limited to ensuring truthful labeling.

Once again in American history, under the guise of protecting the American people, muckraking journalists—though jealous of their own precious freedom to say and publish what they will—instigated the government to divest people of their freedom to sell, buy, and advertise products as they saw fit. With unemployment rampant at home and the alleged virtues of socialism touted abroad, pharmaceutical "exploiters" of the sick became convenient targets of social criticism.[47] In his study on drug legislation during the New Deal, Charles Jackson notes, "Almost invariably each [muckraking] book found in the advertising industry the ultimate villain" for the supposedly pernicious free market in drugs.[48] Ironically, it was a mishap connected with the first effective modern antibiotic, sulfanilamide—a toxic solvent used in its preparation having caused the deaths of nearly one hundred persons—that lent popular support to further tightening state regulation of the drug market.[49]

The Food, Drug, and Cosmetic Act of 1938

James Harvey Young—the author of two major texts on twentieth-century American quack medicines, and an enthusiastic supporter of chemical statism—notes the "deficiencies" of the 1906 law and then observes that with Roosevelt's election "there was a dramatic change," making the imposition of far-reaching drug-regulatory measures feasible.[50] Young correctly attributes much of the impetus behind these changes to the Roosevelt brain trusters—especially Rexford Tugwell, a professor of economics at Columbia University whom Roosevelt appointed assistant secretary of agriculture:

> [Tugwell] was frank to say that he believed in a planned economy. He had spent two months in Russia. . . . In a book published in May 1933, Tugwell had stated, "it is doubtful whether nine-tenths of our sales effort and expenses serve any good social purpose." He was soon to assert that "property rights and financial rights will be subordinated to human rights."[51]

As the brain trusters saw it, among all of the articles lacking a "good social purpose" that Americans were eager to buy, patent medicines stood near the top. This was understandable. After all, the brain trusters were academics and intellectuals who believed in scientific medicine and had no use for quackery. Tugwell was determined to implement his rationalist-messianic vision: "Whole categories of proprietary products which Dr. Wiley's law [of 1906] had not touched were covered in the Tugwell bill. . . . [They were to be banned as adulterated if they were] *dangerous to health* when used according to directions on the label."[52]

Who can be *for* drugs that are dangerous to health? Thus was still another "uncontested term" (as Richard M. Weaver called words that brook no disagreement) added to our lexicon of drug controls.

In 1938, Tugwell's brainchild—the Federal Food, Drug, and Cosmetic Act—became law.[53] In effect, this act disqualified both patients and doctors as legitimate judges of what should count as "therapeutic." Instead, what mattered was statist medical science: Government bureaucrats became the final arbiters of what counted as a therapeutic drug and as legitimate medical treatment in general. As a result, the patient lost his right to drugs traditionally available in the free market; the doctor lost his freedom to medicate his patient as he saw fit, subject only to his patient's consent; and the medical profession lost its integrity as an organization independent of the political vagaries of populist politics. At the same time, by expanding the list of prescription drugs and augmenting the physicians' prerogatives to grant or deny the public access to drugs, the government enhanced the power of the medical profession as a state-licensed monopoly.

Remarkably, some prophetic pessimists foresaw that Roosevelt's drug control laws—ostensibly aimed at protecting the public—were, in fact, "aimed at abridging the 'sacred right' of self-medication. . . . People would have to visit a physician to get medicine they could otherwise purchase without a professional fee, at the local drugstore."[54] Alarmed, a poor woman in North Carolina wrote to her senator, "If any one has a sick headache would it be a violation of the law to make a cup of thyme tea for relief? The poor can't have a Doctor for every minor scratch."[55] But even the worst pessimists could not have anticipated that possessing and ingesting marijuana, which grew wild like mushrooms, would become both a disease and a crime. Clearly, the common people did not want drug controls and were never consulted. Who were the people who pushed for chemical statism and who *were* consulted? In addition to the muckraking journalists, support for federal drug controls came mainly from women's groups, the American Medical Association, and influential physicians such as famed Harvard neurosurgeon Harvey Cushing, who was a personal friend of the Roosevelts.[56]

The irony about Roosevelt's War on Drugs is that people did not think of it then, and do not think of it now, as a war on drugs and seemingly forgot that the federal government had no legitimate authority to control our drug use. To be sure, people knew and generally approved of Roosevelt's determination to diminish the power of the states and increase the power of the federal government; however, they did not realize he was replacing federal alcohol prohibition with federal drug prohibition—without the blessing of a constitutional amendment. In vain did Rufus King protest, in the 1970s, that *"ultimately*, it must be recognized that the federal government has no rightful place in the drug-*use* picture at all. . . . The U.S. system is, after all, a *federal* system."[57]

From Patent Medicine to Official Medicine: Legitimizing Quackery

It is all but forgotten today that the early prescription laws were not used to punish physicians for prescribing, or patients for taking, "too many" drugs. In fact, before the enactment of the Federal Food, Drug, and Cosmetic Act in 1938, a consumer could buy any nonnarcotic "prescription" drug he wanted, *without a prescription.*[58] Of course, if a person did not know what drug to use and wanted to get a prescription, he could consult a physician for his advice and obtain a prescription; but he did not need the doctor's permission to purchase the drug he wanted.

Although the 1938 revisions of the FDA regulations were drafted by brain trusters, their aim was anything but making the consumer more brainy vis-à-vis drugs: The new regulations mandated that indications for prescription drugs "appear only in such medical terms as are not likely to be understood by the ordinary individual."[59] The *prohibition of misbranding patent medicines* was thus replaced by the *requirement of mythicizing prescription drugs*. As a result, virtually all effective medicines were placed beyond the reach of the consumer; the physician, entrusted with the keys to the pharmacopoeia, was interposed between the patient as drug buyer and the pharmacist as drug seller; and the patient was encouraged to distrust his own judgment regarding drugs, deprecate his self-responsibility for the drugs he took, and view the mere act of self-medication as a sort of medical sin. Rationalist academics, physicians given monopolistic control over drugs, the progressive press, and the public reeling from the Depression all welcomed the government's paternalistic concern for the health and welfare of the public. Anyone who dared to object to these reforms was dismissed as a defender of quackery.

But what is quackery? *Webster's* defines it, not very helpfully, as "acts, arts, or pretensions of a quack; charlatanry"; and it defines *quack* (in the sense relevant here) as "a boastful pretender to medical skill; hence a charlatan." These definitions remain discreetly silent about who judges whether the actor pretends to medical skills or actually possesses them. A better definition of *quackery* is that it is the name we attach to any method of healing deemed ineffective or invalid by an official medicine whose judgment is supported by the power of the state. In short, quackery is medical heresy. If the U.S. government refused to recognize any particular system of medical healing as scientifically valid (and all others as not real medicine), just as it refuses to recognize any particular system of religious beliefs as divinely true (and all others as false), then quackery would and could be no more of a problem than is heresy. The formal recognition of a single system of medical healing creates a state-sanctioned monomedicine similar to the state-sanctioned monotheisms with which we are only too familiar.

The fact is that quackery is not only here to stay, but is the hallmark of our modern therapeutic states. So long as there are people who want to believe in a "scientific" medicine legitimized and supported by the state, there will be quackery—just as so long as there are people who want to believe in a "true" religion legitimized and supported by the state, there will be heresy. The best we can hope for is avoiding, as much as possible, the politicization of religion and medicine. With respect to religion, we have deliberately sought this goal. With respect to medicine, we have deliberately evaded it. Today, after almost a century of struggle against quackery, we have more quackery than ever. A congressional committee on health fraud found "that Americans spend 9 billion dollars a year on fraudulent cures for arthritis and cancer alone."[60] Other examples abound.

In a cover story on the weight-loss industry, the reporter for *Newsweek* asks, "Where does science stop and snake oil begin?" A silly question. If a person consumes more calories than his body burns, he gains weight; and if he consumes fewer, he loses weight. All the rest is "snake oil." Anyone with minimal education ought to know that. So what? The punch line in the story, so far as our present interest is concerned, is this: "Federal law prohibits the Food and Drug Administration from policing the $3 billion-a-year food-supplement industry."[61] This conclusion leaves *Newsweek* unhappy that the government tolerates a free market in the medical-magical absurdities of weight reduction. But medical-magical absurdities are all around us. Which ones should be targeted for prohibition? For example, should the government let "cryonics firms," for a mere $100,000, freeze your corpse, while your dead body waits for medical science to discover the secret of eternal life?[62]

The foregoing examples of quackery may be sensational, but are trivial. Their significance—economic, legal, and political—pales in comparison with the significance of the quackeries that now count as bona fide medical practices.[63] I submit that the War on Drugs itself is a gigantic quackery. In its name, pharmacological information is falsified and then called "drug abuse treatment"; morphine is withheld from dying patients willing to pay for it, and yet methadone is provided gratis to "addicts"; "demand reduction" of illegal drugs is urged, and overprescribing of neuroleptic drugs is encouraged (especially for psychiatric patients and old people in nursing homes);[64] giving condoms to teenagers is touted as a means of combating the AIDS epidemic, but sterile hypodermic syringes and needles are banned, furthering the spread of AIDS.[65] (Consider that 20 percent of hospital admissions of elderly patients are for complications resulting from drug interactions; and more than 50 percent of fresh AIDS cases in the United States are attributable to contaminated needles.)

Sovietizing the Drug Market

In 1939, emboldened by Tugwell's successful efforts to increase the government's powers to restrict access to drugs, the FDA proposed banning saccharin. This gave rise to an amusing episode in the otherwise bleak and baneful progression of the politicization of drug controls. What the FDA did not count on was that Roosevelt was a regular user of saccharin, which was then the only noncaloric sweetener. "Anybody who says saccharin is injurious to health is an idiot," declared the commander in chief of the therapeutic state; and saccharin was safe.[66] Today, the Food and Drug Administration is no longer so hamstrung by presidential preferences. In a single month (November 1990), the agency proposed to ban more than a hundred ingredients in nonprescription diet drugs. Why? Because it "question[ed] the ingredients' effectiveness." One of the agency's targets was guar gum, a harmless high-fiber plant extract used in many low-calorie products. The FDA wants to ban guar gum because, it claims, the gum presents a "choking hazard." What is a choking hazard? It is a scare term coined by the FDA to report that, among millions of persons who use products containing guar gum every day, there have been "17 nonfatal choking cases."[67] The FDA is also eyeing popular laxatives, such as Metamucil, as possible choking hazards.

Although Young—who is in complete sympathy with Roosevelt's "progressive" drug reformers—ridicules the opponents of therapeutic statism, he deserves credit for reminding us of the crucial issues that were then so fatefully decided:

The enactment of this [Tugwell's 1938] bill... meant nothing less than the end of the "constitutional right" of self-medication, which, along with freedom of religion and the press, had been "jealously guarded" since the foundation of the republic. And this tolled the death of proprietary medicines.... Drug stores would be "sovietized." ... [There was heard] the oft-repeated cry of imminent czarism.[68]

The "reactionaries'" predictions were prophetic, down to the reference to "czarism." The Roosevelt-Tugwell team's battle against self-medication proved to be a decisive victory in the battle to turn America into a bona fide therapeutic state. Unlike for liquor during Prohibition, no prominent American came to the defense of self-medication. Mark Twain was dead. Mencken was growing old and evidently had no interest in this issue. In vain did the producers of pills and potions protest that their remedies were not a whit less effective than the physicians' officially legitimized interventions: " 'Why not,' inquired the attorney for the United Medicine Manufacturers, 'require that a sign be put over all doctors' doors saying, 'I do not cure'? "[69] It was too late. Roosevelt was at the helm of the ship of state, and the fervor of his therapeutic bureaucrats carried the day. Young concludes, "To demonstrate that *self-medication was not yet* [sic] *safe*, [FDA chief Walter G.] Campbell showed the Senators a series of graphic posters, with bottles, labels, advertisements, death certificates attached."[70]

During the late 1930s, law after law was enacted giving ever more power to the FDA to tighten the noose around the necks of drug manufacturers, drug distributors, and drug users. True to type, the reformers insisted that the purpose of their prohibitions was "to make self-medication safer and more effective... [and] to protect the vast multitude which includes the ignorant, the unthinking, and the credulous who, when making a purchase, do not stop to analyze."[71] For liberal consumer advocates, these changes were and continue to be a necessary and welcome adaptation to an increasingly complex world, with which the average citizen—with plenty of money in his pockets but not enough brains in his head to make his own choices—is no longer able to cope without the assistance of a corps of self-appointed Ralph Naders. Mary Bennett Peterson hits the nail on the head when she writes, "Consumerism looks upon the consumer as largely unprotected and upon the very quantity and variety of available goods and services as complicating choice."[72] Indeed, the devout consumer-advocate sees his "client" as a child or mental patient who needs paternalistic protectors to make decisions for him, in his own "best interest." This explains why Ralph Nader and the whole American consumer protection movement have been so supportive of organized psychiatry, endorsing the most intrusive and injurious involuntary psychiatric interventions as bona fide medical treatments.[73]

Thus, in America today the principle of caveat emptor, especially with respect to substances labeled "drugs," is a despised anachronism. Instead of cherishing this principle as the emblem of the consumer's autonomy, we disdain it as no longer socially appropriate, preferring instead to view certain personal choices as the symptoms of mental diseases. Recalling the mood of the Great Depression and the momentum of the Roosevelt-Tugwell anti-drug legislative program, Charles Jackson—though wholly supportive of drug controls—cogently remarks, "It was inadequate to growl indignantly about the 'right of self-medication.' 'The phrase itself sounds synthetic,' commented *Printer's Ink*. 'The man who buys a box of pills seldom feels that he is . . . a crusader in the cause of human liberty.' "[74]

In 1939 war broke out in Europe, and in 1941 the United States formally entered the struggle, keeping the government as well as the people busy struggling against military rather than medical dangers. However, once that interruption was over, the war for chemical statism could reassume its rightful place on the American political scene. Henceforth, the war to make the world safe from dangerous drugs was used unashamedly as a pretext for enlarging the scope and power of the centralized national government. The aim of this struggle soon became the complete destruction of the right to self-medication, correctly perceived as the emblem of heretical independence from the warm embrace of the therapeutic state. The post–World War II phase of the War on Drugs has now raged for more than four decades, longer than World War I, World War II, the Vietnam War, and the War in the Gulf combined; its proud victories are scattered all around us, there for anyone to see who cares to look.

THE MIRAGE OF A HOLY/HEALTHY UTOPIA

The War on Drugs is a moral crusade wearing a medical mask. Our previous moral crusades targeted people who were giving themselves sexual relief and pleasure (the drives against pornography and masturbation). Our current moral crusade targets people who are giving themselves pharmaceutical relief and pleasure (the drive against illicit drugs and self-medication). Although the term *drug abuse* is vague and its definition variable, by and large it is the name we give to self-medication with virtually any interesting and socially disapproved substance. Why is self-medication a problem? Because, for the reasons discussed above, we view it as both immoral and unhealthy.

And so we arrive back at our point of departure: the essentially religious, redemptive nature of the American dream of a world free from dangerous drugs. This aspiration arose, as Tuveson suggested, from a peculiarly American mix of devotion to both religious and secular utopianism.

> The real importance of the elements of secular progress is that they have stirred up and made possible the militancy of Christianity *in this world*, which is to produce the *holy utopia*. . . . The new "benevolent and reformatory" movements [are] designed to bring human conduct and institutions into conformity with the *idea of right*.[75]

It is this longing for a holy utopia that leads to the fateful obliteration of the distinction between vice and crime, and the tragic transformation of the virtue of temperance into the vice of prohibition. In a society such as ours—religious by tradition, secular by law, and forever striving toward a free political order—this is a terrible folly, for reasons Lysander Spooner articulated perhaps better than anyone else:

> [E]verybody wishes to be protected, in his person and property, against the aggressions of other men. But nobody *wishes* to be protected, either in his person or property, against himself; because it is contrary to the fundamental laws of human nature itself, that any one should wish to harm himself. He only wishes to promote his own happiness, and to be his own judge as to what will promote, and does promote, his own happiness. This is what every one wants, and has a right to, as a human being.[76]

However, what Tuveson termed our collective striving for a "holy utopia" is the superglue that reconciles and unites in an intoxicating embrace of intolerance the diverse personalities and politics of Nancy Reagan and Jesse Jackson, George Bush and Charles Rangel, William Bennett and Ralph Nader. If our love of the Constitution and gratitude for our heritage cannot keep us united as a nation, then hatred of "dangerous drugs" must do the job.

3

The Fear We Favor: Drugs
as Scapegoats

Be wary then; best safety lies in fear.

—William Shakespeare[1]

Timeo ergo sum. [I fear, therefore I am.]

—Maurice Vienne[2]

When Franklin Delano Roosevelt declared, "The only thing we have to fear is fear itself,"[3] he uttered an inspired piece of political rhetoric, reassuring a depressed nation in the classic tradition of a Platonic philosopher-king. More wisely, Seneca, the great Stoic philosopher, offered exactly the opposite advice: "If you wish to fear nothing, consider that everything is to be feared."[4] Christianity carried this counsel further still, exalting the sinfulness of the world into justification for a pervasive *contemptus mundi*, or contempt for the world. Once the aim of life became the avoidance of perpetual torment in hell, fearing temptations—and hence oneself—became the central preoccupation of the devout believer. Jean Delumeau speaks of medieval Christians as "haunted by truly metaphysical fear . . . [the] most saintly individuals [being] often those who most deeply feared themselves."[5]

However, it would be naive to attribute a fearful attitude toward life to religion. It is the other way around: Religion is one of its products.

To be sure, for millennia, the talent to be afraid—a fundamental feature of human nature, with obvious protective functions—was exploited by religion. Now it is exploited by many other institutions as well, especially by medicine, and especially with the threat of harm from allegedly dangerous drugs, such as cocaine, heroin, marijuana, and peyote.

Yet, as any educated person ought to know, coca, hemp (marijuana), psychedelic mushrooms, and the opium poppy are naturally occurring plants whose products have been used, safely and beneficially, since ancient times—marijuana and opium, for analgesia and sedation; coca, for enhancing endurance; peyote, for inducing unusual experiences. Moreover, people have always been allowed to use these substances by and for themselves, making self-medication (like feeding oneself) the most elementary human right. The question we ought to ask is this: Why has the use of these ancient drugs become a matter of special social and political concern only in the twentieth century, and why especially in the United States?

As Mary Douglas and Aaron Wildavsky aptly observe, "Plenty of real dangers are always present. No doubt the water in fourteenth century Europe was a persistent health hazard, but . . . it became a public preoccupation only when it seemed plausible to accuse Jews of poisoning the wells."[6] Similarly, drugs became a public preoccupation only when it seemed plausible to accuse them of poisoning people—especially "kids." In 1937 Harry J. Anslinger, the nation's first "drug czar" (the term had not yet been invented), declared, "How many murders, suicides, robberies, criminal assaults, hold-ups, burglaries, and deeds of maniacal insanity it [marijuana] causes each year, especially among the young, can only be conjectured."[7] Only a few years earlier, such a statement would have been dismissed with scorn and ridicule.

THE "DANGEROUS DRUG" AS SCAPEGOAT

Suppose a social historian in the days when it was popular to accuse Jews of poisoning wells decided to study that phenomenon. Surely, it would have been a mistake for him to assume that the wells were, in fact, poisoned; that the culprits were invariably Jews; and that, in order to advise the authorities about how best to reform Jew-control policies, he would have to examine the "physiological and psychological effects" of the poisoned waters. In fact, until modern times, water was a notoriously unsafe beverage, the source of water-borne infections. (Water is still unsafe in many parts of the world.) This is why Jesus turned water into wine—not vice versa—and why people drank much beer and wine, gave alcoholic beverages to children, and often avoided drinking water altogether.[8]

The point is that—just as, in medieval Europe, drinking water from *any* source was dangerous, and the matter had nothing to do with Jews— so, now the use of *any* drug is dangerous, and the matter has nothing to do with drug traffickers. Obviously, no drug is dangerous so long as it remains outside the body; and every drug—even the seemingly most innocuous, such as aspirin or vitamin A—is potentially dangerous, for certain persons, in certain doses. This simple fact is ignored by virtually all contemporary scholars and commentators addressing the subject of drug controls. For example, David Musto makes the very prejudgment I have just described when he declares, "Reasonable regulation of drug use requires knowledge of physiological and psychological effects."[9] Not necessarily. To be sure, the person who intends to use a particular drug needs to be familiar with its effects. But do politicians (qua politicians) need to know pharmacology? Not really. After all, they must know by now that tobacco is more harmful than marijuana.[10] Nevertheless, marijuana is prohibited, but tobacco is not. Musto does not acknowledge, or does not believe, that "drugs" are scapegoats. Instead, donning the mantle of the value-free, academic historian-psychiatrist, he validates the objective reality of "dangerous drugs," lends legitimacy to the view that the truthful labeling of drugs is insufficient protection for the consumer, and supports the prevailing statist prejudice that every civilized nation *must* criminalize the trade in "narcotics."

Musto's views exemplify the currently "correct" position on drugs: All drug law reformers share Musto's basic prejudice, namely, the belief that while the customary protections of criminal and civil law, combined with the principle of caveat emptor, may suffice to protect people from making stupid choices with respect to cars and cosmetics, they do not suffice to protect them from making stupid choices with respect to cannabis or cocaine. I reject this view and the arrogant claim that goes with it, namely, that every piece of meddling into our drug use by the coercive medical apparatus of the interventionist state constitutes "drug reform."[11] It is rather the other way around: The claims that "recreational" drug use is dangerous and that coercive state interventions in the drug market are "remedial" are, as Edmund Burke remarked in a very different context, only pretexts for creating "great public evils." Deeply aware of the versatility of evil, he warned,

> Wise men will apply their remedies to . . . the causes of evil, which are permanent, not to the occasional organs by which

they act, and the transitory modes in which they appear. . . .
Seldom have two ages the same fashion in their pretexts and
the same modes of mischief. Wickedness is a little more inven-
tive. Whilst you are discussing fashion, the fashion is gone by.
The very same vice assumes a new body.[12]

I maintain that drug abuse and the War on Drugs are both transitory
modes—pretexts for scapegoating deviants and strengthening the state.
Our official understanding of the drug problem rests on a fallacious
scapegoat-type imagery and a correspondingly erroneous approach to
remedying it. For example, we conceptualize self-medication—say, with
marijuana—as self-poisoning rather than as self-pleasuring, and then
rely on this image of the drug as poison to justify using state power to
punish people who possess marijuana. Although in his important study,
The Scapegoat, René Girard does not refer to drugs as scapegoats, he
remarks—apropos of our scientific progress from the Middle Ages to
the present—that "frequent references to *poisons*" has remained a con-
stant feature of the imagery and rhetoric of scapegoating. "Chemistry,"
he concludes, "takes over from purely demoniac influence."[13] The chemistry that takes over, I would add, is not pharmacological chemistry, but
ceremonial chemistry.

Drug Abuse as Profanation

Prior to 1914, the main ingredients of American patent medicines, in
addition to alcohol, were cocaine and morphine. Now, these drugs are
our favorite scapegoats. In *Ceremonial Chemistry* I tried to show that we
cannot understand the War on Drugs without taking seriously the scapegoat function of so-called dangerous drugs—a suggestion that, because
it presents an obstacle to the arguments of both the opponents and the
supporters of drug prohibition, both have ignored. I contend, however,
that without recognizing the importance of this theme for drug prohibition, there can be no informed discussion of drug controls, much less
an end to the War on Drugs.[14]

The scapegoat's social function of saving the group by its victimization
is clearly articulated in the Gospels. The scene is as follows. Jewish
society feels itself to be in mortal danger: "The Romans will come and
destroy both our holy place and our nation." What is there to do? How
can the community save itself? By sacrificing one of its members. Caiaphas, the high priest, addresses the congregation: "You know nothing

at all; you do not understand that it is expedient that one man should die for the people, and that the whole nation should not perish."[15]

Like a Jew defiling the Torah, or a Christian the Host, an American using an illicit drug is guilty of the mystical crime of profanation—a transgression of the strictest and most feared taboo. The drug abuser pollutes himself as well as his community, endangering both. This is why, while to the secular libertarian the drug abuser commits a "victimless crime" (that is, no crime at all), to the normally socialized person he is a dangerous defiler of the sacred. Hence, his incapacitation is amply justified. After all, what greater good is there than saving the family, the clan, the nation, indeed the whole world from certain destruction?

Caiaphas, Girard remarks, "is the incarnation of politics at its best, not its worst. . . . [He] is the perfect sacrificer who puts victims to death to save those who live. . . . [E]very real cultural *decision* has a sacrificial character."[16] The etymology is thought-provoking: The English word *decide* comes from the Latin *decidere*, which originally meant to cut the victim's throat.[17]

Risk Management by Scapegoating

Life is full of risks. Faced with risks, we must make decisions. When the danger is great and imminent, we must stop thinking and start acting. Suppose you are driving down a divided highway and see a driver, confused or drunk, coming straight at you. You must try to pass him on the right or the left or drive off the road. Whichever you do, you must do it quickly. The longer you hesitate, the greater the chances that you will collide head-on with the approaching vehicle and die.

On the collective level, a danger so acute precludes individual initiative and puts us at the mercy of those who hold the levers of power in their hands. But this is not the sort of danger that the temptation to use a particular drug poses. Being tempted by drugs is precisely the sort of danger that is amenable to—and indeed requires—personal choice and action. Yet it is precisely this sort of danger that the modern scapegoater deliberately miscasts as a threat not only imminent and immense, but aimed at the group rather than the individual: We are faced with nothing less than a "drug epidemic." Perishing in an epidemic of, say, the plague has assuredly nothing to do with temptation. Neither, in this imagery, is becoming a victim of the drug epidemic a matter of temptation. Accordingly, the scapegoater's advice for the individual is to avoid the scapegoat like a tabooed object; and his recommendation for the poli-

tician is to commit the state to waging a holy war against it. In the War
on Drugs, the grand themes of taboo, scapegoating, and redeemership—
traditionally religious, now medical—thus recombine and reemerge in
a novel pseudo-therapeutic form. A recent decision of the Supreme
Court illustrates this thesis.

In 1989, two members of the Native American Church in Oregon were
fired from their jobs and denied unemployment benefits because they
participated in the sacramental rite of ingesting peyote. They sued their
employer for reinstatement and benefits, arguing that their dismissal
violated their First Amendment right to free exercise of religion. The
Oregon courts held that ingesting peyote violated the criminal laws,
whose observance took precedence over the Indians' religious rights.
The case went to the U.S. Supreme Court, which ruled that "prohibiting
Native Americans from using peyote in their religious rituals does not
violate their constitutional right to free exercise of religion."[18] Although
this case received a good deal of press coverage, to my knowledge not
a single commentator connected the prohibition of this particular religious practice—at this particular time in our history—with the War on
Drugs. Instead, the critics simply repeated the cliché that the ruling is
"disastrous for the free exercise of religion."[19] The irony that these "drug
offenders" had been working as "drug rehabilitation counselors" apparently was also lost on the pundits as well as the public.

The Method in the Drug-War Madness

The irrationality of the War on Drugs—by which I mean its rationality
as scapegoat persecution—is so pervasive that it may be invisible for
that very reason. The virtuousness or wickedness of the scapegoat is
unimportant: Empty syringes are taboo, but loaded guns are not. What
is important is whether the person or object is authoritatively defined
as a "drug-related danger." The following drug law policy allows no
other explanation.

Although law enforcement authorities complain that drug offenders
clog the criminal justice system—and although persons arrested for drug
offenses constitute a minuscule part of those who are de facto guilty of
drug law violations—nevertheless, the government *literally imports* innocent foreigners for the sole purpose of turning them into drug criminals. I do not refer here to celebrity scapegoats such as Manuel Noriega,
or to the extradition of so-called drug lords. Instead, I refer to a practice
that has received virtually no press coverage.

Commercial airline flights between South America and Europe often make unscheduled refueling stops in San Juan, Puerto Rico. When this sort of thing happens in international aviation, passengers either stay on board or are taken to a transit lounge to await reboarding their flight. However, the U.S. Customs Service and the Drug Enforcement Administration (DEA) have seized this opportunity to search the passengers and their baggage. Sometimes they find illegal drugs. The "guilty" passenger is then taken off the plane, charged with drug smuggling, and given a long prison sentence (often as much as twelve to fifteen years). This exercise "costs the U.S. taxpayer approximately $20,000 per year for the imprisonment, plus the cost of the trial which could be in the tens of thousands of dollars."[20]

Mr. Jorge Aguilar-Pena, a Colombian citizen, was caught in such an unscheduled stop on a Lufthansa flight from Bogotá to Zurich. He was carrying a few ounces of cocaine. For this he received a four-year prison sentence—almost double the sentence recommended by the U.S. Sentencing Commission. The judge gave the extra time "because he wanted to deter future smugglers—a wholly ridiculous notion since Aguilar wasn't even trying to come to the U.S., much less smuggle here."[21]

The view that the prohibited drug is a scapegoat also helps to account for the paradox that, with respect to drug controls, the conservative anti-drug warrior and the liberal consumer advocate are in complete agreement. The former, exemplified by William Bennett, insists on miscasting the mere possession of an allegedly dangerous drug as a threat to the entire society; the latter, exemplified by Ralph Nader, insists on miscasting the entire adult population as children needing parental protection. Because neither can support his position with reasoned argument, both rely on paternalistic coercion, buttressed by semantic flag waving: Who can be *for* children using cocaine? Who can be *against* consumer protection? While everyone agrees on these platitudes, there is no agreement at all among Americans on what counts as a dangerous drug or what constitutes the consumer's best interest.

The most obvious option is to accept the subject's own definition of a dangerous drug and his best interest. However, when we are confronted with deviant behavior, we no longer do that; instead, we impose our definitions of reality on the deviant. In view of this, the honest thing to do would be to acknowledge that our (conventional) values exert a paramount influence on our perception of the risks from which (in our opinion) the drug user or the endangered consumer needs protection. Some people do that. Most prefer to scapegoat the nonconformist, making risk, as Douglas and Wildavsky observe, "an ideal target for criticism. It is immeasurable and its unacceptability is unlimited. . . . There can never be sufficient holiness or safety."[22]

That such an alarmist posture toward (certain) drugs is a useful tactic for anyone who wants to use drug controls to strengthen the therapeutic state is obvious. The alleged dangerousness of drugs justifies the medical-political persecution of both drug sellers and drug users—of the former, in terms of law enforcement, of the latter, in terms of drug treatment. All this requires the coercive apparatus of the state, which costs money that must be confiscated from the people. Yet even if the most wildly inflated estimates of illegal drug use in the United States are true, the fact remains that the overwhelming majority of Americans do not use illegal drugs at all; and of those who do, most use marijuana in a way that endangers neither them nor others. Nevertheless, most Americans support the War on Drugs, confirming Randolph Bourne's insight that "war is the health of the State. It automatically sets in motion throughout society those forces for uniformity, for passionate cooperation with the Government in coercing into obedience the minority groups and individuals which lack the larger herd sense."[23]

WHO SHALL GUARD THE MEDICAL GUARDIANS?

Like all public health measures, drug controls tend to be regarded as unselfish, public-spirited legislation, their sole aim being the improvement of the health of the population. However, because self-interest is intrinsic to the human condition, this is, prima facie, an absurd assumption. It is also totally inconsistent with the historical evidence.[24] For example, the 1906 Food and Drugs Act was actively supported by large food and drug producers—not because they were interested in promoting public health, but because they wanted to restrict competition by cartelizing their industries. The story of margarine regulation is illustrative.

Margarine, an artificial product made from processed vegetable fats, was invented in 1869 as a substitute for butter. It was (or could have been) cheaper than butter, tasted good, and gained immediate consumer acceptance. To protect their dairy industries, states with dairy interests undertook to counteract free and informed consumer choice: They imposed special taxes on margarine and banned coloring it yellow. By 1902, thirty-two states had banned coloring margarine, "the phrasing of the statutes convey[ing] the clear impression that margarine was an unhealthy, low-quality imitation of butter."[25] Discriminatory taxes on margarine remained in effect until the 1950s.

The Guardians' Hopeless Task

Long ago, we decided that our collective hands were unfit to handle drugs, and thus we entrusted the regulation of the drug market to a corps of increasingly numerous guardians. I contend that the guardians against dangerous drugs cause more harm than good, not only because that is a talent all guardians possess by nature or acquire by practice, but also because we expect them to satisfy mutually contradictory needs, namely, the needs of both a *market-oriented system of individual rights* and a *health-oriented system of medical obligations*. Although this particular conflict weighs especially heavily on guardians entrusted with protecting public health, similar inconsistencies are familiar to legal scholars—for example, the conflict between the *market-generated rights morality of capitalism* and the *compassion-generated mercy morality of Christianity*.[26] A few examples will help to illustrate our dilemma of the conflicting demands of individual rights and duties anchored in the economic-legal matrix of the market, and the demands of medical needs and obligations anchored in the collectivist-compassionate matrix of theology-therapy.

The laws that deny healthy people "recreational" drugs also deny sick people "therapeutic" drugs. This is partly because some of the same drugs—including our favorite scapegoat drugs, cocaine, heroin, and marijuana—have both recreational and therapeutic uses, and partly because certain drugs believed to be therapeutic for serious diseases (and sometimes available abroad) have not (yet) been approved by the FDA as both effective and safe, the two basic criteria drugs must meet under present U.S. law. However, with enough political clout, special interest groups often prevail and determine both diagnostic and therapeutic policy. The ability of gay activists to influence psychiatric nosology as well as FDA policy is an example.

In 1973, under pressure from homosexuals, the American Psychiatric Association declared that homosexuality was no longer a mental illness. Similarly, in May 1990, the Food and Drug Administration approved— under the policy known as "expanded access" or "parallel track"—the use of certain anti-AIDS drugs, even though they had not met "the same criteria that drugs used for other diseases have to meet."[27] Drug regulations thus selectively reward and punish people on the basis of sexual preference. This inequality before the law—clearly a political and constitutional issue of the first rank—is nevertheless not so regarded. Instead, it is disguised as an ethical-therapeutic method of drug distribution, called a "compassionate release system." But a bureaucratic system that can "compassionately release" a drug can also cruelly withhold it.[28] This illegality and injustice deserves the name *affirmative drug action*— an appropriate emblem for the American therapeutic state today.

The collision between the demands of our new health-oriented morality and our traditional rights-oriented legality leads to especially ironic results when we mix our drug laws with the ethical perplexities posed by pregnancy. No one would deny that, other things being equal, it is healthier for a fetus to be gestated by a woman who does not drink or have diabetes than by one who drinks or has diabetes. It is also healthier for a fetus to be born alive as a baby than dead as an abortus. However, we do not punish a diabetic woman for having a child (even if both she and her husband have juvenile diabetes), because we judge her behavior on the basis of our rights-based system of law and morality; but we do punish a pregnant woman for "using drugs" (as a drug trafficker), because we judge her behavior on the basis of our health-based system of law and morality. Thus, in Kentucky a woman was convicted "of abusing her unborn child by taking drugs during pregnancy";[29] in Florida a woman "was sentenced to 14 years' probation and participation in a drug treatment program" because she delivered cocaine to her baby through the umbilical cord, and her conviction was upheld by the Fifth District Florida Court of Appeals;[30] and in Minnesota the state "has amended its definition of criminal child neglect to include prenatal exposure to controlled substances."[31] By May 1990, "at least 50 women have been charged with crimes for their behavior during pregnancy. . . . [The women were arrested] for a new and independent crime: continuing their pregnancy while addicted to drugs."[32] Only twenty-odd years ago, abortion was illegal; now a pregnant woman who uses a prescription drug may be prosecuted and punished if she does not get an abortion.

When Protections Fail

Many modern medical interventions—initially hailed as sensationally beneficial—proved to be disastrously harmful. These tragic episodes offer dramatic proof, if any were needed, that reliance on the protection of the medical profession and of the state is a dangerous substitute for reliance on oneself and the principle of caveat emptor. Horrifying examples abound: oxygen for premature infants, causing them to go blind; X-ray irradiation of the thymuses of "sickly" children, giving them cancer of the thyroid; radioactive waters for tired and impotent adults, resulting in their being poisoned with radioactivity; severing the healthy frontal lobes of "schizophrenics," making them permanently brain-injured.

The belief that it is the duty of a state-controlled and state-funded medicine to discover and provide effective treatment for every disease that affects human beings (and animals and plants as well) is relatively recent. It would probably surprise most people to learn that not one cent of public money was spent on developing the Salk and Sabin vaccines. Fifty years ago, neither the American people nor their government viewed the battle against diseases—even against a contagious disease such as polio—as the state's job. The research that led to the development of the polio vaccines was supported by the National Foundation for Infantile Paralysis, a private health organization founded by FDR in 1938, and was financed by funds from the March of Dimes.[33]

However, after World War II, the belief that it is the duty of the state to fund every aspect of medicine—research, education, health care delivery—quickly hardened into dogma, unquestioned even by conservatives. The result is a characteristically American crowd madness, comprised of a self-contradictory combination of pharmacological phobia and pharmacological hubris. The phobia, which we mistake for a real threat, makes us believe that "dangerous drugs" cause "epidemics" and "plagues"; while the hubris, which we confuse with real science, makes us believe that a narcotic prescribed by a doctor (methadone) is a cure for addiction to a narcotic purchased on the black market (heroin)—and that as-yet-to-be-discovered drugs will cure every human malady, from AIDS to mental illness.

Our pharmacological arrogance has engendered two specific types of blunders, both on a gigantic scale. One blunder is the belief that the tragedies of human existence are diseases, susceptible to treatment—specifically, psychiatric treatment. The other is the belief that every discovery in chemistry and physics must have therapeutic applications, even though many of the cures so generated are nothing more than sophisticated-sounding con jobs. Radium cures are a classic example.

In 1898 the Curies discovered radium—and, presto, doctors hailed radium as a miracle cure for a variety of ailments, among them "rheumatism, gout, syphilis, anemia, epilepsy, multiple sclerosis, . . . hypertension, and metabolic disorders."[34] In 1912 Harvard Medical School opened its Huntington Memorial Radium Hospital and began to advertise "radium ward beds for $3 a day." A year later, "radium therapy was a well-established medical subspecialty," its practitioners supposedly interested in (what they thought were) radium's physiological powers (rather than its anti-tumor effects). Radithor, a mixture of radium 226 and radium 228 in distilled water, "was advertised as an effective treatment for over 150 'endocrinologic' diseases, especially lassitude and sexual impotence."[35] Most of the people who took Radithor developed radium poisoning: They became chronically ill, were horribly disfigured, and died a few years after having given testimonials of miraculous recoveries. This story is important because doctors hailed Radithor, the press praised it, and the public loved it. The moral to be drawn from all this, therefore, is that eliminating the public's faith in miracle cures, and the health professionals' self-interested willingness to exploit that faith, is nothing but a pipe dream.

Merchandising Fear

In their cross-cultural study of risk, Douglas and Wildavsky ask, "What are Americans afraid of?" They answer, "Nothing much, really, except the food they eat, the water they drink, the air they breathe, the land they live on, and the energy they use."[36] The authors forgot to add that we are also afraid of AIDS, drugs, suicide, and mental illness. In fact, dangerous drugs constitute one of the fear industry's best-selling products. (The other is mental illness, the two being typically yoked together as cause and effect.)

There are some good reasons for our collective hypochondriasis. Thanks to advances in medicine and public health, we are now healthier than we have ever been. Hence, like the person who fears poverty more after he has made some money than when he had none, we fear illness more now that we are healthy and live a long life than we did when life was beset by illness and death came at an early age.

Obviously, fear of the unknown is part of the human condition. Hence, people have always been afraid of something; and arousing and allaying fears has always been a profitable enterprise. When life was short and uncertain, which was the case until recent times, merchandising fear was a priestly monopoly: It was the clergyman's job to arouse and allay people's fears about their lives in the hereafter. After the Enlightenment and the Industrial Revolution, when everyday existence became a little more secure and death came a little later, the politician entered the fear business: It became his job to arouse and allay people's fears about their prospects here on earth. In the nineteenth century, with the advent of modern medicine, the physician joined the team: Charged with provoking and pacifying people's fears about diseases, he quickly rose to be the dominant player in the fear market.[37] Finally, in our own day, the consumer advocate and the psychiatrist have joined the flourishing fear business: the consumer advocate's job being to alarm and reassure the masses; the psychiatrist's, to cater to the fears of individuals. Conducting these symphonies of fear and reassurance is the media—especially television. The whole thing makes Roosevelt's famous slogan about our having nothing to fear but fear itself look like a classic case of whistling past the graveyard.

Risks: Assumed vs. Imposed

Since mid-century, we have become more knowledgeable than we have ever been about how our environment—both human and inanimate—can protect as well as imperil our health. Thus, our very consciousness of health risks and health protections has become a fresh source of anxiety, the more so because the government has systematically misled and confused people about two altogether different types of drug-related dangers: (1) those we *assume* by choosing to ingest drugs (recreational or therapeutic); and (2) those that are *imposed* on us, against our will or without our knowledge, by the introduction of toxic chemicals into the environment (by private industry or the state).[38] For their part, the people let themselves be blinded by a paternal state—because they are infantile and are encouraged to believe that they can master the chemical dangers they face by means of some simple individual or collective action. Anti-drug slogans such as "Just say no!"; anti-drug ads such as the TV spot showing an egg frying in a pan, accompanied by the legend, "This is your brain on drugs"; anti-drug laws such as those against hemp, renamed "marijuana"; and prohibitions of sterile syringes, renamed "drug paraphernalia"—these are just some of the glaring examples of such misguided efforts at risk management.

In addition, we are endangered by state-supported health education programs that, instead of providing accurate information, are a bottomless source of deception and misinformation. To be sure, the state has always been a source of grave danger to its own people—traditionally, by getting them maimed and killed in wars. While the danger of war has by no means disappeared, armed conflict is less popular than it used to be. The principal danger to our health to which the state now subjects us is probably environmental pollution, especially by radioactive wastes produced by the nuclear weapons industries. In short, concern about chemicals that might get into our bodies is well justified. But the War on Drugs misdirects our attention from what we should fear and what we should do about it.

There are some 45,000 chemicals in commercial use today.[39] The air we breathe, the liquids we drink, the meat, fruit, and vegetables we eat are full of chemicals, most of which we cannot see or smell. In addition, we are exposed to radioactive and other chemical wastes produced by our government and placed in American waters and soil by our government—the same government that tells us that Peruvian peasants endanger us by growing coca.[40] But coca does not endanger the Peruvians or befoul their land, whereas radioactivity endangers us and befouls our land where

> just 50 years ago several Indian tribes wandered and foraged . . . and 6,000 farmers from the towns of Hanford, Richland, and White Bluffs [Washington] grew fruit in orchards irrigated from the Columbia. But after the Manhattan Project expropriated 570 square miles of land in 1943, plutonium and its lasting legacy, nuclear waste, became Hanford's crop.[41]

The Hanford reprocessing plants were deadly polluters on a vast scale: By 1985, "the cumulative volume of liquid wastes discharged to the environment from [this plant alone] . . . surpassed 200 billion gallons—enough fluid to cover the isle of Manhattan to a depth of over 40 feet."[42]

At the very moment when our government proclaims "zero tolerance" of drugs, the Nuclear Regulatory Commission proposes that "mild radioactive waste [be disposed] . . . in municipal dumps or ordinary incinerators or even recycled into consumer products." If adopted, the policy could result in the recycling of radioactive waste "into toys, jewelry, and other common objects. . . . The commission said that an activity that increases the risk of death by one in 100,000 would be 'of little concern to most members of society.' "[43] Extrapolated to the population of the United States, that would come to 2,500 extra deaths, plus 2,500 cases of protracted painful illnesses per year—all directly attributable to the government's policy of imposing risks on us against which, unlike the risks of illegal drugs, we cannot protect ourselves by means of personal self-discipline.

From a moral point of view, perhaps the most scandalous aspect of our drug control policies is that while we protest against poor foreign farmers' growing crops smuggled into our country, we send them—with the approval of our government—American-made chemicals so toxic that they cannot be sold in the United States. Chemical manufacturers export "up to 150 million pounds of these blacklisted products worth more than $800 million, about one fourth of U.S. pesticide production."[44] The World Health Organization estimates that, as a result, "agricultural workers in developing countries suffer 3 million cases of acute pesticide poisoning annually."

In short, although it is true that, in a certain sense, cocaine and heroin are dangerous drugs, this truth has been so radically wrenched from its proper pharmacological and social context that it has become a big lie. I say this because of all the potentially dangerous chemicals in our environment, none is more difficult to avoid than a radioactive element in the air, water, or soil—and none is easier to avoid than cocaine or heroin.

The Perils of the Preventive Function of Government

Calvin Coolidge is remembered mainly for his legendary taciturnity. As one story about him has it, the first lady feeling indisposed, the president went to church without her. Back in the White House, Mrs. Coolidge inquired what the minister spoke about. "Sin," replied Coolidge. "What did he have to say about it?" his wife pressed. "He said he was against it," explained the president.[45]

In a fundamental sense, *that* is what the War on Drugs is about. And that is what makes it so revolting morally and so risky politically. It is one thing for President Coolidge to say that a minister delivered a sermon against sin—a laconic redundancy rendering the statement humorous. It is quite another thing to arm the priest with the power of the state and let him wage war on sin and sinners. Seemingly anticipating the medical-remedial ambitions of the modern secular state, John Stuart Mill warned against this very danger in his classic essay *On Liberty*:

> The preventive function of government, however, is far more liable to be abused, to the prejudice of liberty, than the punitory function; for there is hardly any part of the legitimate freedom of action of a human being which would not admit of being represented, and fairly too, as increasing the facilities for some form or other of delinquency.[46]

Mill could not have put it better were he addressing our freedom of action with respect to drugs. It is self-evident that free access to a particular drug, like free access to any object, increases our opportunities for abusing it. But again the statement is redundant, for "freedom of action" means the freedom to act wisely or unwisely, to do right or wrong.

In some ways, we were better off in the old days, when sin was sin and the sinner was punished qua sinner. To be sure, the consequences were usually unpleasant, but the business was at least on the up-and-up. Now, sin is secular and medical. It is sickness, especially sickness considered to be self-inflicted—exemplified by the deleterious consequences of drug abuse. As a result, terms such as *illness* and *treatment* have become elasticized and politicized. Although it is perfectly apparent that this is the case in the definition of what counts as the disease of drug abuse, it makes no difference: Doctors, judges, journalists, civil libertarians, everyone accepts that deviant drug use is disease. Do I exaggerate? Consider the sorts of drug-using behaviors the World Health Organization classifies as drug abuse:

Unsanctioned Use—Use of a drug that is not approved by a society or a group within that society . . . e.g., certain psychedelics.

Hazardous Use—Use of a drug that will probably lead to harmful consequences for the user. . . . This category includes the idea of risky behavior, e.g., smoking 1 pack of cigarettes a day.[47]

Prohibiting the use of "not approved" drugs and classifying the defiance of the ban as a disease is, of course, politically indistinguishable from prohibiting the reading or writing of "not approved" books and classifying the defiance of the ban as a disease. I have said enough about this pernicious nonsense elsewhere and merely note it here. But consider some tragicomic conundrums to which the prohibition of medically unsanctioned use of prescription drugs logically leads.

Suppose that a man injures his back, visits his physician, and receives a prescription for thirty Valium tablets to ease his muscle spasm. He takes the pills for a few days, feels better, and stops the medication. He has fifteen Valium tablets left. Six months later, he has a fight with his wife, cannot go to sleep, and takes Valium as a sleeping pill. He has no prescription for Valium as a hypnotic, making this an instance of "medically unsanctioned drug use." Or suppose that six months later, just for the fun of it, he takes a drink and a Valium. Is such a person a drug criminal and a drug abuser?[48] In the United States, in 1991, the answer is yes. In April 1988, a nurse-captain in the Air Force had her wisdom teeth removed and, to relieve the pain, received a prescription for Tylox (which contains oxycodone and acetaminophen). On September 26, 1990, pregnant and suffering from an infected hematoma, "she took the last two Tylox pills from the 1988 prescription." As a result, she was court-martialled and sentenced to six months in jail plus dismissal from the Air Force and forfeiture "of all pay and allowances, which could amount to $35,000 to $40,000 annually."[49]

Still, the view that the concept of disease is now a political category as much as it is a medical category continues to be considered heretical. My point is simple, but runs counter to contemporary conventional wisdom. It is that some illnesses are *medical* (for example, cancer of the prostate), some are *legal* and *political* (for example, criminal insanity, unsanctioned drug use), and some are *mental* (for example, agoraphobia).[50] Luckily, the physician who espouses this modern heresy is no longer murdered, he is only marginalized. However, eliminating legitimate opposition to the modern coercive-therapeutic ethic makes it easy to mask the War on Drugs as, de jure, a combined public health and criminal law measure, while, de facto, allowing it to flourish as a holy war of scapegoat persecution and collective self-purification. Such an enterprise, as we know from history, is not only of great ideological and economic value to the scapegoaters, but is also practically unopposable, effective resistance to it requiring precisely the sorts of *political* checks and balances that are lacking against the therapeutic state. Indeed, the very existence of checks and balances against the alliance of medicine and the state—similar to those created by the Founders against the alliance of church and state—are now regarded as "unscientific," and hence irrational and inappropriate.

4

Drug Education: The Cult of Drug Disinformation

Everything has a slogan, and of all the bunk in America, the slogan is the champ. . . . Congress even has slogans: "Why sleep at home, when you can sleep in Congress?" "Be a Politician—no training necessary!" . . . "Join the Senate and investigate something."

—Will Rogers[1]

Nancy Reagan's slogan, "Just say no to drugs," is not as funny as Will Rogers' coinages; but then, a sense of humor is not a virtue anyone would dare attribute to this former first lady. Actually, as a slogan, "Just say no to drugs" is simply witless, in both senses of that word: It is at once humorless and stupid, leaving unsaid to what drugs, in what doses, and under what circumstances one ought to say no. But that is just the point. The meaning of this message does not lie in its words alone; instead, it lies in its value as a ritual incantation that might as well be set to music, such as typically accompanies the text of a national anthem or religious hymn.

THE MISCHIEF OF THE IMMORAL DRUG MAJORITY

In 1979 when Ronald Reagan ran for the presidency, he did so as a Conservative, with a capital C. The liberals were hippies who smoked marijuana, got abortions for their girlfriends, and neglected their children. Such, at least, was the image into which conservative Republicans cast liberal Democrats. In contrast, Conservatives—exemplified by Ronald and Nancy Reagan—stood for morality, tradition, and family values. Those claims will, in my opinion, go down in history as the most transparent hypocrisies of the Reagan presidency. For whatever ugliness was committed in the name of drugs by President Reagan's predecessors, it was the Reagans who, through the repetition of a moronic anti-drug slogan, taught American children to spy on their parents and denounce them to the police.

President Reagan claimed that he stood not only for family values, but also for less government. As an abstract proposition, he surely would have agreed that a person's loyalty to his family is more important and should be more enduring than his loyalty to a temporarily expedient government policy. But talk is cheap. When the Reagans' vaunted family values were put to the test of practical politics, when old-fashioned allegiances came in conflict with the pursuit of personal self-aggrandizement, their noble professions were brutally belied by their ignoble policies. They embraced one of the most characteristic and most despicable practices of the great socialist states of the twentieth century: turning children against their parents in a holy war against enemies of the state. The identity of the enemy who justifies this contemptible tactic has varied from one totalitarian ideology to another. In *national* socialism, the enemy was the Jew; in *international* socialism, it was and still is the profiteer; in *medical* socialism, it is the drug trafficker. The true nature and behavior of these scapegoats are unimportant. What is important is that the state be able to persuade people the threat is so serious that all efforts at self-defense are justified; in our present case, this translates to the danger of drugs justifying the destruction of parental authority and its replacement by the state as parent.

Drugs: A Pretext for Subverting Family Loyalties

In August 1986, after listening to an anti-drug lecture, Deanna Young, a "blonde, blue-eyed junior high school student [in California] walked into the police station carrying a trash can bag containing an ounce of cocaine . . . [and] small amounts of marijuana and pills. By sunrise, her father and mother had been arrested and jailed."[2] Mrs. Reagan rushed to congratulate Ms. Young. "She must have loved her parents a great deal," she told the press.

Ms. Young's patriotism was rewarded by Hollywood as well. Nine major production companies were vying to acquire the rights to her story. One film producer attributed the high interest in the story to its being the reverse of the usual scenario: "The *normal* situation is parents trying to keep young people off drugs."[3] Thanks to Nancy Reagan, parents denouncing their children to the police was already *normal* in the American family in the 1980s.

The Bush administration endorsed and intensified the effort to enlist "kids" in the War on Drugs. Betraying one's own parents was not enough; better to betray one's friends as well. In May 1989, "federal drug chief [William Bennett] instructed students [in a high school in Miami] . . . to tell on their friends. . . . 'It isn't snitching or betrayal to tell an adult that a friend of yours is using drugs and needs help. It's an act of true loyalty—of true friendship.' "[4] Bennett is untroubled about the moral implications of such a practice or the potentialities for its abuse. He told the *New York Times* "he was not worried that students would make false allegations about their peers' drug use."[5]

Although children denouncing their parents for illegal drug possession has become commonplace, no one seems disturbed about it. In fact, as the War on Drugs escalates, ever younger children are turning their "sick" mothers and fathers over to a kinder and gentler American state for "help." After a twelve-year-old girl in Fremont, California, turned her parents in to the police for growing marijuana and using cocaine, a spokesman for the Fremont police declared, "She did the right thing. We don't see this as turning in parents. We would rather view this as someone requesting help for their parents and for themselves."[6] The media report this as if it were as ordinary as a weather forecast for a sunny summer day: "Parents used to turn their children in to authorities when they caught them using drugs. Today, the tables have turned—children are blowing the whistle on their parents. In California, seven children in the last three months [August–October 1986] have informed on their parents for drug abuse."[7] In September 1989 an eight-year-old Illinois boy turned in his mother and her friend. They were promptly arrested on cocaine and marijuana charges. " 'My mom's selling and using coke and marijuana,' the boy told [the police]. 'It ain't right.' The boy's father said the boy had listened to Bush's talk on drugs last week."[8]

President Bush's self-advertisement as the "(drug) education president" has required certain sacrifices, but not on his part, of course. In September 1989 (a year before Saddam Hussein offered a more challenging opportunity for President Bush to posture as the savior of mankind), the president's entourage decided on staging a photo opportunity to dramatize his heroic struggle against drugs. DEA agents lured an eighteen-year-old high school senior to Lafayette Square, across the street from the White House, and used him "as a prop in an anti-drug speech [by Bush] . . . to dramatize how easy it is to buy drugs in the nation's capital."[9] Bush's popularity rose to a new high. The teenager was arrested and sentenced to ten years in prison.

Casualties of the Children's Drug Crusade

As illegal drug use becomes equated with illness, and its coercive control with treatment, the people caught up in this crowd madness—as anyone familiar with linguistics might expect—lose not only their common sense but their sense of humor as well. An eight-year-old girl takes an unopened can of beer to her third-grade classroom in Richmond, Virginia, for "show and tell." She is promptly suspended and ordered to "undergo counseling for illegal possession of alcohol. It was a can of Billy Beer . . . and was kept at home, unopened, as a collector's item."[10]

This sort of drug education is not merely asinine; it is positively subversive of the values we ought to instill in children. Instead of teaching young people to be self-reliant, we encourage them to rely on corrupt authorities; instead of teaching them to be grateful to their parents and supportive of their friends, we incite them to betray parents and friends and disdain ordinary human decencies. A sixteen-year-old high school sophomore gives her friend two Midol tablets to ease her menstrual discomfort. A teacher sees them and reports them to the principal, who publicly humiliates the "drug trafficker" by suspending her "for five days for carrying over-the-counter medication in her purse."[11] Note that the newspaper report describes the guilty student's behavior as "dispensing over-the-counter medication—a remarkable choice of words in these 1990s when talk-show hostesses routinely refer to every shameless act of exhibitionism as "sharing." But no, this gift of two Midol tablets was not an act of one young woman sharing a drug useful for menstrual cramps with another. It was the violation of "the district's drug policy [which forbade] carrying medications of any kind." The suspended teenager complained to the press that "she has carried Midol in her purse for two years and never knew she was breaking the rules." Her mother complained that "the district is overreacting. . . . 'The punishment should fit the crime. And in any event, this wasn't a crime.' "[12] Quite the contrary. This is a perfect example of the type of ordinary human decency that the bureaucrats who run our public schools now classify and punish as a crime.

Consider, for a moment, where our ad hoc, unprincipled approach to rights and wrongs has gotten us. Intoxicated with the rhetoric of drug wrongs, we deny a sixteen-year-old woman the right to have Midol in her purse at school and share it with a friend. But, intoxicated with the rhetoric of abortion rights, feminists and liberal Americans insist that, should she become pregnant and want an abortion, she should have a right to it—free (paid by the taxpayer) and without the knowledge or consent of her parents. Also, contrast the Midol episode with the fact that, because they are imbued with the mythology that inner-city youths need self-esteem rather than self-discipline, the educational bureaucrats look the other way when children carry knives and guns to school.

Lest the critical reader dismiss all this as too absurd to be *really* believed by Americans, let us recall that Mrs. Reagan believes in astrology, and Mr. Reagan in the medical mythology of personal nonresponsibility for premeditated crime. Indeed, former President Reagan has made it clear that he believes in responsibility for good deeds only. For bad deeds, someone or something other than the actor is responsible. Did he ever blame a specific Soviet leader for the misfortunes of the people in the Soviet Union and the Eastern bloc? Never. He blamed an abstract "evil empire." I believe this explains why Ronald Reagan comes across as such an amiable person: He never blames anyone. Two brief examples illustrate this point.

In his autobiography, Mr. Reagan relates how, when he was a child, his mother explained to him that his father was not simply a man who liked to drink, but "had a disease called alcoholism." He also tells us that he still prays for his would-be assassin, John Hinckley.[13] The idea that Hinckley is not responsible for his crime is not a passing fancy of Mr. Reagan's. It is his carefully considered and firmly held belief. As soon as the president recovered from his acute chest wound—long before Hinckley's (non)trial—Mr. Reagan hurried to tell the American people that "He [Hinckley] is a very disturbed young man. . . . I hope he'll get well, too."[14] Like the president with a bullet wound in his chest, Hinckley was "sick" and needed to "get well."

These vignettes—together with our reflexive rejection of personal responsibility for alcoholism, drug use, crime, and similar misbehaviors—are ominous signs that we have let our concern about drug abuse displace our concern about matters of elementary morality. The merchandising of a new drug-detection device is illustrative. The kit, called DrugAlert, consists of three aerosol cans with which a parent can detect whether his child is "on drugs." To use this tool, the parent need only "wipe a piece of paper on a surface that drugs might have touched, then spray the paper with the chemicals," and—presto—cocaine turns the paper turquoise; marijuana, reddish brown.[15] Does this kind of parental behavior invade the child's privacy? "Sure, it's an invasion of privacy," the manufacturer acknowledges, "but so is a thermometer. . . . [P]arents need any tool they can get to protect their kids from drugs."[16] Unfortunately, the test is far from foolproof: It picks up over-the-counter antihistamines as cocaine. Too bad. But better safe than sorry.

THE SCANDAL OF DRUG EDUCATION

The belief that our drug regulations rest on a rational, scientific basis is one of the root causes of our drug problem. On the contrary, they rest on pseudoscience, create pseudomedical diagnoses, and employ pseudotherapeutic interventions. As the theological state formerly was a bottomless source of disinformation about everything from cosmology to medicine, so now the therapeutic state is a rich source of disinformation about sex, drugs, and AIDS. Thus, sex education is a campaign of religious and medical disinformation in the service of promoting the acceptance of traditionally stigmatized sexual practices and justifying a war on sexual differences. Drug education is a campaign of pharmacological disinformation in the service of justifying the government's War on Drugs. And AIDS education is a campaign of epidemiological and economic disinformation in the service of justifying the expenditure of virtually unlimited government funds on activities ostensibly aimed at combating AIDS. The results are monumental boondoggles. After $450 million of federal funds had been squandered on so-called AIDS education, a survey of the residents of the nation's capital revealed that "33% did not know that blood transfusion can transmit AIDS, 39% did not know that sharing needles can transmit AIDS, 16% thought toilet seats can transmit AIDS, and 28% thought drinking glasses can carry AIDS."[17]

The truth is that we have simply exchanged one puritanical-prohibitionist posture for another. In 1890, an unmarried female high-school student who became pregnant would have been so cruelly ostracized that she would have been driven to the brink of suicide, but she enjoyed legally unrestricted access to cocaine (in Coca-Cola). Today, the situation is reversed. A high school student caught with crack is so cruelly punished that he may be driven to the brink of suicide, but his or her nonmarital sexual and procreative behavior is accepted and even rewarded (with free condoms, and financial support for mother and baby).

The Fruits of Pharmacological Disinformation

After decades of carpet bombing the American consciousness with drug laws and drug lies, the people are showing unmistakable signs that they have learned their lessons. According to a 1990 *USA Today* poll, about 25 percent of Americans surveyed said they would report their child to the police if he were found selling cocaine; 56 percent believed that "addicts are victims"; 34 percent called for increased drug education; and 62 percent said they would approve a tax increase for drug education.[18]

From parents denouncing their children, children denouncing their parents, and students denouncing each other, it is only a small step to people denouncing neighbors and even strangers they suspect of using illegal drugs. This public-spirited act is now encouraged in many American communities. In 1990, Chattooga (Georgia) County's major newspaper, *The Summerville News*, added "drug coupons" to its pages, inviting readers "to fill in the names of suspected drug users and send them to the sheriff."[19] In Anderson County, South Carolina, the sheriff put up billboards that read: "Need cash? Turn in a drug dealer." Informers were promised 25 percent of the assets seized from any dealer they helped arrest.[20]

Although it is ridiculous to call our now fashionable anti-drug propaganda "drug education," syndicated columnist Anna Quindlen is virtually the only public figure to question the practice of treating *children* as if they could, or ought to, know what drugs *adults* should or should not use. "They are the children," she writes, mocking one of the popular anti-drug advertisements, "who come into the kitchen, look at an egg frying, and say with certainty, 'That's your brain on drugs.' "[21] To encourage children to use language so mindlessly is a depraved thing for adults to do because, as Quindlen sagely observes, "some [of these children] will discover that people use drugs and booze because they seem to make you feel better," and the children will then "reject the message but remember the permission—even the invitation—to be intolerant of human weakness."

Under the pretext of protecting our children from poisonous drugs, we thus systematically fill their minds with poisonous ideas and call it "education." The slogan "Just say no to drugs" does not educate by imparting information; it commands by reiterating a catch phrase. Of course, children should not go around using crack. They also should not go around killing people, but we do not call communicating that command "murder education."

To be worthy of the name, drug education would have to be premised on taking drugs seriously and treating children honestly. In turn, this would require that we acknowledge the obvious similarities between eating and drug taking, "food use" and "drug use." In fact, the same agency of the federal government—the Food and Drug Administration (FDA)—monitors the purity and safety of the foods we eat and of the drugs we take. Accordingly, if we treated children with respect, we would recognize that telling them "Just say no to drugs" makes about as much sense as telling them "Just say no to food"—a phrase that sounds more like an incitement to anorexia nervosa than an encouragement of good eating habits. In short, the aim of real drug education ought to be to encourage not drug avoidance, but good drug-using habits, that is, using drugs knowledgeably, responsibly, and with self-discipline.

We cannot, as the title of a popular Broadway play proposed, stop the world and get off. Hence, everything we do, or do not do, is a statement we make about ourselves, a clue to our role—real or pretended—in the game of life. Eating or not eating meat, drinking or not drinking alcohol, smoking or not smoking marijuana, each is a statement people make about themselves. This fact explains the important role food and drug taboos play in religions. In this light, consider the following remarkable feature of the 1988 presidential race.

Presidential Politics: Pushing Anorexia Pharmaceutica

On March 18, 1988, under the heading "Candidates' Survival Guide," *Newsweek* magazine presented a tabular summary of "How they make it to the next photo opportunity."[22] Listing Democrats and Republicans in alphabetical order, the table supplied information about eight items of behavior, among them, "Medication." The following is the list of entries in that category, exactly as printed:

Michael Dukakis: "a glass of white wine, as often as once a week."
Richard Gephardt: "occasional beer."
Albert Gore: "none."

Jesse Jackson: "doesn't smoke or drink; occasional aspirin."

Paul Simon: "none."

George Bush: "occasional Margarita or vodka Martini at end of day."

Bob Dole: "occasional half glass of white wine."

Pat Robertson: "none."[23]

This list is prima facie evidence of the pharmacological crowd madness affecting contemporary American society. To appreciate the sanctimonious absurdity of our leading politicians' aversion to recreational drugs (especially alcohol), consider the views of two of our greatest presidents. "Were I to commence my administration again," said Thomas Jefferson, "the first question I would ask respecting a candidate would be, 'Does he use ardent spirits?' "[24] More afraid of the teetotaler than of the alcoholic, Jefferson—a connoisseur of wine—suggested this drug test to avoid the threat posed by the moral meddler. Lincoln was similarly afraid of and opposed to the anti-alcohol fanatic. In 1842, in an address to a temperance society in Springfield, Illinois, he declared, "I believe, if we take habitual drunkards as a class, their heads and their hearts will bear an advantageous comparison with those of any other class."[25] On the basis of their responses summarized above, none of the presidential candidates would have passed the Jefferson-Lincoln drug test.

- All of the candidates treat beer and wine (beverages ordinarily consumed during a meal) as "medication."
- Jesse Jackson believes that not drinking and not smoking are instances of not taking medication.
- Three out of eight candidates claim to use no drugs whatever.
- None of the candidates smokes or admits to smoking.
- Only George Bush acknowledges drinking hard liquor, and he qualifies it by emphasizing that he does so only "occasionally" and only "at the end of the day."
- Only Jesse Jackson acknowledges using an over-the-counter medication.

THE ANTI-DRUG CRUSADERS: A CAST OF CHARACTERS

The propaganda campaign we call "drug education" consists, for the most part, of simplistic slogans urging complete—and, if taken literally, impossible and senseless—drug avoidance. What sorts of persons stoop so low as to endorse and expound such wretched pseudoscientific pieties and outright lies? Here we can observe the operation of another of Edmund Burke's maxims. He wrote, "When men of rank sacrifice all ideas of dignity to an ambition without a distinct object, and work with low instruments and for low ends, the whole composition becomes low and base."[26] Indeed, the defective character of our drug educational program attracts drug warriors with defective characters to match.

Father Bruce Ritter

During the 1980s, no one in America was more venerated for saving "kids" from drugs than Father Bruce Ritter, founder of New York's famed Covenant House. So high did Father Ritter rise in the pantheon of child protectors that, in his 1984 state of the union address, President Ronald Reagan paid special tribute to him as an "unsung hero."[27] In fact, Father Ritter was neither unsung nor a hero.

Father Ritter's entry into the drug war should have served as a warning, but the authorities looked the other way. "I became involved with the kids of the neighborhood quite by accident, and, quite frankly, against my will," he writes in his autobiography, which reeks both of his prurient interest in the sex lives of the "children on the street" and of his conceit as their savior.[28] One of the things that made Father Ritter a celebrity was his method of securing housing for his "kids": He stole the apartments of alleged drug abusers. "To get the space I needed was simple," he writes. "I just kept taking over more and more of the apartments in my tenement. Most of them, as I mentioned, were occupied by junkies, dealers, and speed freaks. . . . It was kind of, if you will, muscular Christianity. The Holy Spirit made me do it."[29]

With this divinity defense as his shield, and with his resolve to fight drugs as his spear, Father Ritter rode forth and, for two decades, preyed on male children as the objects of his sexual desire. In December 1989 a young male prostitute finally succeeded in exposing Father Ritter for the fraud he was. After the whole sordid mess became public, John Cardinal O'Connor acknowledged that "he and other board members . . . had been derelict in carrying out their duties. 'Obviously, we failed,' he said. 'What we don't know is monumental.' "[30]

That was not true. The board members of Covenant House knew— or could have known—a good deal about Father Ritter, inasmuch as he had boasted of dispossessing people of their apartments. But the victims were dehumanized as "drug abusers," and those charged with guarding the guardians tacitly approved. The final unmasking of America's most

celebrated priest–drug warrior was sensibly summed up by syndicated
columnist John McLaughlin. "For those who admired Father Ritter,"
McLaughlin wrote, "the hypocrisy of the sanctimoniousness" comes as
a particularly bitter betrayal, because "Ritter was uncompromising in
his denunciation of those who treat children as sexual prey."[31]

President John F. Kennedy

It is not hypocrisy, however, that distinguishes Father Ritter from his
unsavory fellow anti-drug warriors. Most prominent anti-drug figures
have preached water but drunk wine. However, few prominent persons
were more accomplished drug hypocrites than President John F. Kennedy, whose use of controlled and other questionable chemicals goes
back to his Senate days when he secured the services of the eminent
quack Max Jacobson.[32] Jacobson's specialty was injecting drug cocktails
of his own secret formula into celebrities who wanted to enhance their
sexual prowess. Jack Kennedy's involvement with "Max," as he was
known among his clients, became public only after President Kennedy
was dead; and Jacobson, having lost his patron, was quickly targeted
for investigation of his shady medical practices and stripped of his
license.[33]

Recent Kennedy biographies tell us a good deal more about the drug
habits of the president and various members of the Kennedy family.
For example, C. David Heymann relates, "On his [Jacobson's] second
day at the White House, he was confronted by an agitated Jackie Kennedy. She had discovered a vial of Demerol in the President's bathroom.
Further investigation revealed that a Secret Service man had supplied
her husband with the unauthorized drug."[34] Another episode, at once
hilarious and sinister, was told to Heymann by Mary Meyer, sister-in-
law of *Washington Post* publisher Ben Bradley:

> In July, 1962, while visiting the White House, Mary took Ken-
> nedy into one of the White House bedrooms and she produced
> a small box with six joints in it. They shared one and Kennedy
> laughingly told her that they were having a White House con-
> ference on narcotics in a couple of weeks. They smoked two
> more joints. . . . He [Kennedy] admitted to having done cocaine
> and hashish, thanks to Peter Lawford.[35]

Betty Ford

One of our most famous drug educators, of course, is Betty Ford. Her career as a chemical dependency expert began in 1978, when she was hospitalized for what was first described as a "problem with medication." That story was soon changed to her having become addicted to "certain prescription drugs." The final revision, which she disclosed to the press on April 21, 1978, was this: "I'm addicted to alcohol."[36] That confession transformed her, virtually overnight, from addict to expert on addiction.

Soon, Mrs. Ford was the famed founder of the prestigious Betty Ford Center, a lofty perch from which, at last, she could look down on people as sickos. "I'm almost sorry," she writes in her autobiography, "for people who *haven't* been alcoholic, because I know things a person who's never been sick doesn't know."[37] Mrs. Ford is no mere figurehead at her clinic, either. She herself "counsels patients." What are her and her colleagues' qualifications? Being repentant sinners, a/k/a recovering addicts: "Two-thirds of the staff and five of the center's seven board members, is recovering from addiction."[38]

Kitty Dukakis

A more recent but less successful entrant in the Great American Drug Derby is Kitty Dukakis. Her story is too pathetic to parody, though it cries out for it.

Mrs. Dukakis began taking amphetamines in 1956, when she was nineteen years old. In 1963, she married Michael Dukakis and lived with him for eleven years without his suspecting that she was "on drugs." When he discovered that she was, it was not because her behavior was in any way abnormal; on the contrary, her behavior became abnormal only after she was deprived of the drug. What happened in 1974 was that Mr. Dukakis accidentally "stumbled on her cache of pills." Then, according to *Time* magazine, Mrs. Dukakis "told him the truth: I was chemically dependent."[39] Three months later, having switched doctors, she was back on amphetamines and continued "the charade for eight more years until her husband noticed a stray bill from the doctor who was writing her prescriptions."[40] But Kitty Dukakis's tale of double deception—deceiving her husband about both her using drugs and telling the truth—dragged on. In 1987, when Mr. Dukakis was running for the presidency and when no one suspected Mrs. Dukakis of "drug abuse," she suddenly decided to come out of the closet. Why? Because, she told *Time* magazine,

> "I've had a long enough period of recovery. . . . I feel strongly about my recovery, and one of the tenets of recovery is to help other people." There were no rumors about Kitty Dukakis and no apparent political need to go public. . . . Her bravery should not be minimized, nor should the extent of her former drug problem be exaggerated.[41]

Subsequent events proved the untruth of Mrs. Dukakis's statement and the naiveté of *Time* magazine's flattering characterization of her behavior. Having anointed herself as a "recovered drug addict," Mrs. Dukakis began her short-lived new career as lecturer on drug abuse, modestly accepting five-figure fees for sharing her wisdom with her audience.[42] What she delivered for the money was, according to *People* magazine, not much, except to let people see her chain-smoking and pity her. For example, it did not go unnoticed that before lecturing, Mrs. Dukakis made it a condition of her appearance "that she would not take any questions of a personal nature—an odd ground rule for a lecture on the very personal problem of alcoholism."[43]

Before long, Mrs. Dukakis was addicted to the delusion that she was an expert whose views were very much in demand. "Wrapping up a frenetic schedule that included 13 appearances in 22 days, she plaintively asked an aide: 'Are you sure there aren't any more speeches?' "[44] Being paid more than $150,000 in a few weeks for knowing nothing about drugs and saying everything about them that was false is likely to intoxicate the subject, and is sure to produce a hangover. For Mrs. Dukakis, it did both. Even before she broke down again—it doesn't seem to me that she ever "recovered" from anything, so that term is misleading—she was described as chain-smoking and looking tense. No wonder. A mere "eight days out of rehab," she began lecturing again and signed a book contract with a prestigious publisher for which she collected a $175,000 advance. But she could not escape from the truth. "I'm afraid," she told a reporter, "that deep down I'm nothing."[45] That is much too harsh. Mrs. Dukakis is something. Everyone is. I am quite certain, however, that she is neither of the two things she most passionately believed she was and wanted to be, namely, drug addict and expert on drug addiction. But how could she know this as long as Mr. Dukakis kept reinforcing her false belief in the reality of these mythical conditions and her special calling for them? And why should he not do just that, when—

poor codependent that he is—he needs to believe this Santa Claus story even more than his wife does? "As she has now discovered," explained the then governor of the Commonwealth of Massachusetts to the press in February 1989, "whether it comes in a bottle or is a solid, if you are chemically dependent, you are chemically dependent."[46]

There is a melancholy footnote to the story. During the summer of 1990, Kitty Dukakis's book was published and she was a celebrity again.[47] Aptly dubbed the "icon of America's addiction to addictions" by Maureen Dowd of the *New York Times*, Mrs. Dukakis now offered further proof of her Olympian stature as a drug abuser and all-purpose addict. During her supposed recovery from addictions, she had consumed (if she is to be believed) not only ethyl alcohol, but also rubbing alcohol, hair spray, vanilla extract, nail polish remover, aftershave, and mouthwash.[48] She also tells us that she has made "suicide attempts . . . [but] never meant to kill herself."[49]

Evidently, Mrs. Dukakis has acquired still another addiction, namely, to truth telling—provided the truth she tells is different from year to year and sordid enough to get her on television talk shows. Predictably, once again the talk-show hosts and hostesses loved (or pretended to love) her valiant struggle against the dread disease of addiction, and especially her hard-won insight into the correct diagnosis of her chronic illness, its true cause, and its scientific cure. The latest diagnosis: manic-depression. Its cause: "her imperious mother . . . herself addicted to diet pills," and her discovery that her mother was an adopted illegitimate child. The cure: lithium.[50]

THE MORAL BANKRUPTCY OF DRUG EDUCATION

It is time that we asked ourselves what, in truth, is the enterprise we call "drug education"? I submit it is the name we give to the state-sponsored effort to inflame people's hatred and intolerance of other people's drug habits, which is as indecent as it would be to inflame people's hatred and intolerance of other people's religious habits and call it "religion education." While this unspeakable ugliness has failed to stem our collective appetite for psychoactive drugs, legal and illegal, it has succeeded in thoroughly misinforming us about the pharmacology of drugs, the nature of drug use, our own drug history, and the drug-using customs of other people.

Drug Abuse: What Disease? What Treatment?

Other people's bad habits have long been the psychiatrist's and psychoanalyst's favorite disease. Accordingly, when I first addressed the subject of drug abuse, I suggested that we keep in mind that "bad habits are not diseases."[51] To illustrate what happens if we forget that warning, let us briefly consider an amusing example of the drug expert's enormous, yet typically unrecognized, cultural blind spot about drugs.

The classic psychoanalytic contribution to our subject—entitled "The Psychoanalysis of Pharmacothymia (Drug Addiction)"—was published in 1933. Its author, the Hungarian psychoanalyst Sandor Rado, devoted more than twenty pages to an exposition of the severe "psychopathology" of the person suffering from the disease of "pharmacothymia," to reach this conclusion: "By easy transitions we arrive at the *normal person* who makes daily use of stimulants in the form of coffee, tea, tobacco, and the like."[52] Today, nicotine abuse is considered to be our number-one public health problem.

Regarding the treatment of drug abuse, it is easy to cite an equally authoritative and amusing example. In a 1991 interview in *Psychiatric Times*, Yale professor of psychiatry Herbert D. Kleber, M.D., deputy director of the Office of National Drug Control Policy, was asked what he considered to be the major accomplishments of the federal government's drug program. He answered, "When President Bush took office, the federal budget [for drug control] was $5.5 billion; it is now in excess of $11 billion. . . . The federal treatment budget, for example, has been increased from $850 million to more than $1.6 billion over the past three years."[53] The reporter for *Psychiatric Times* then inquired if the treatment—"inpatient drug abuse treatment in particular"—is effective. Kleber's response: "In terms of the question of effectiveness, there is an inadequate data base. When we have met with the people who operate these facilities, I have told them that it's difficult to come out in support of their programs because they have not documented their efficacy."[54] Kleber also admitted that for "the pharmacologic treatments for drug abuse . . . there is no hard evidence yet," and reassured the reporter that "in the past few years, we have increased the [drug abuse] treatment budget for the Bureau of Prisons from $2 million to $22 million."[55] In short, nondiseases—especially if their victims can be incarcerated and treated against their will—are at once easily treatable and untreatable, which makes them especially attractive to politicians and psychiatrists.

The Problem of the Drug Abuse Problem

Most Americans are ignorant of the fact that the maniacal pursuit of "good drugs"—expected to make us healthy and live forever—and the maniacal persecution of "bad drugs"—the cause of crime, disease, and every other evil known to man—are peculiarly American social phenomena. Although, in this book, I am not concerned with the attitudes of other peoples toward drugs and drug prohibitions, I think it is important to note that the image of America as a nation of drug abusers is false. Actually, we are less given to self-medication (which we call "drug abuse") than people in many other countries. It is France that has apparently earned the dubious sobriquet of "the most tranquilized country on earth," making the French media ponder "the question . . . how the French can get hold of 3.5 billion mood-changing pills a year, or about 80 pills for every adult."[56] Actually, the answer is simple: The French get their drugs by prescription, from doctors who are not persecuted by their government for prescribing all the Valium and Librium their patients want.

These cultural differences bring to mind the adage "Germans eat to live; the French live to eat." Mutatis mutandis, Americans feel it is morally justifiable to take pills to make oneself healthy, but not to make oneself happy; the French do not feel the urge for a sharp distinction between these justifications. As a result, "young people use relatively few street drugs. . . . Students find it normal to take sedatives and stimulants [prescribed by physicians], and one out of two medical students said they do so before each exam."[57]

Undoubtedly, some Americans "abuse" drugs. However, such a statement asserts an utterly trivial truth. As John Stuart Mill emphasized, "Almost every article which is bought or sold may be used in excess, and sellers have a pecuniary interest in encouraging that excess; but no argument can be found in this, in favor, for instance, of the Maine law [prohibiting alcohol]."[58] Neither can an argument be found in American drug (ab)use for the American laws prohibiting drugs. A brief look at the history of hemp (marijuana) merits our attention in this connection.

Hemp, Cannabis, or Marijuana?

The mischief the American therapeutic state has perpetrated vis-à-vis our relationship to this "drug" begins with its name, which used to be "hemp." I suspect not many Americans know that hemp, cannabis, and marijuana (or marihuana) are three names for the *same plant*—much as six, half-dozen, and twice-three are three names for the same number. The entry under "hemp" in the 1973 *Encyclopaedia Britannica* begins as follows: "*HEMP*, a common name for *Cannabis sativa*, a herbaceous plant of the family Cannabinaceae, which yields fiber, oil, and a crude narcotic drug."[59] The article then goes on to describe the plant along with its history and various uses, discusses "hemp as a drug plant" only briefly, and does not even mention that growing hemp is now (and was in 1973) prohibited by law. To learn that fact we must turn to the entry for "marijuana," where we are referred to the entry for "cannabis," which begins as follows: "*CANNABIS*, a genus of herbaceous plants, including, preeminently, the true hemp plant (*Cannabis sativa*). The crude drug cannabis was obtained originally from the flowering tops of hemp."[60] Most of the entry is devoted to a review of the various international treaties, American laws, and World Health Organization resolutions against hemp, now always referred to as "cannabis."

The hemp-cannabis-marijuana permutation should alert us that underlying our attitudes toward this plant is a powerful name game such as we encounter in many spheres of life, from immigrants being renamed or renaming themselves, to psychiatrists and mental patients renaming human follies and tragedies as diseases.[61] As there are "good" economic and professional reasons for renaming sadness "clinical depression," so there are good reasons for renaming hemp "marijuana." The fact is that hemp qua hemp is one of the most useful plants known to man. During the period between the American Colonies' becoming the United States and the United States' becoming a centralized therapeutic state, hemp was widely used for the manufacture of rope, clothing, and paper, as a source of oil, and as a sedative drug.[62]

The State as Liar: Who Is Fooling Whom?

"Hypocrisy," said La Rochefoucauld, in one of the finest French aphorisms, "is the homage vice pays to virtue." Like most such pithy phrases capturing a facet of human nature in a few words, this remark can be easily amplified. Not all vices invite hypocritical concealment equally. For example, gluttony and miserliness are vices, but their practitioners are rarely, if ever, hypocrites. They do not make careers out of preaching against overeating and squandering money, while secretly gorging themselves with food and dissipating their assets. Persons who make careers out of preaching against drugs, however, often engage secretly in the very activities they rail against in public.

While hypocrisy pervades the human condition, it thrives best where we find laws whose ostensible aim is to protect individuals from themselves rather than from other people, and where the lawmakers claim they want to provide treatment for patients who get diagnosed by being arrested. Thus, formerly, hypocrisy was most flagrant where the authorities set out to protect people from sexual misbehavior. In this century, hypocrisy has been rampant in both communist and capitalist societies, the duplicity characteristic of each system reflecting the dominant ideology's phobic-prohibited target: self-employment and private property in communism; self-medication and private drug trade in capitalist therapeutism.

In Soviet society (to date), hypocrisy pervades economic life and relations: If the state employs you and pays you, you are a patriotic worker—a member of the proletariat—who deserves his income, regardless of how unproductive or useless you are; whereas if you are self-employed and people pay you out of their own pockets because you give them something they want, then you are an unpatriotic profiteer who deserves to be punished by the state for your "obscene profits."[63] This outlook on life and the policy it engenders rest on a Marxist imagery that idolizes the communist state as benevolent parent, and demonizes the individual entrepreneur as a selfish, antisocial person whose sole interest in life is to enrich himself and impoverish everyone else. The result is the politicization of access to goods and services—the political elite living in luxury, and everyone else effectively deprived of ordinary goods and services cheaply and legally for sale in noncommunist countries.

In American society, hypocrisy pervades pharmaceutical life and relations. If the state (official medicine) certifies you as sick and gives you drugs—regardless of whether you need them or not, whether they help you or not, even whether you want them or not—then you are a patient receiving treatment; but if you buy your own drugs and take them on your own initiative—because you feel you need them or, worse, because you want to give yourself peace of mind or pleasure—then you are an addict engaged in drug abuse. This outlook on life and the policy it engenders rest on a medical imagery that idolizes the therapeutic state as benevolent doctor, and demonizes the autonomous individual as a person who is both a criminal and a patient and whose sole aim in life is to be high on drugs and low on economic productivity. The result is the medicalization of drug use—the political elite assured access to the drugs they want from their physician-suppliers, the rest of the people denied drugs cheaply and legally for sale in Third World countries.

5

The Debate on Drugs: The Lie of Legalization

The government offers to cure all the ills of mankind. . . . All that is needed is to create some new government agencies and to pay a few more bureaucrats. In a word, the tactic consists in initiating, in the guise of actual services, what are nothing but restrictions; thereafter, the nation pays, not for being served, but for being disserved.
—Frederic Bastiat (1845)[1]

Less than a hundred years ago, Americans regarded the production, distribution, and consumption of drugs as a fundamental right. Since then, justices of the Supreme Court have added to our previously existing rights a new one: the right to privacy. Remarkably, this right does not apply to ingesting or even possessing, in the privacy of one's own home, a drug the government dislikes. In addition to the right to privacy, our government has given us women's rights, gay rights, minority rights, ethnic rights, Native American rights, prisoners' rights, rights of the ill and disabled, the mental patient's right to treatment, the mental patient's right to reject treatment, the mental patient's right to confinement in the least restrictive setting, and the right to die—none of which existed before 1914.[2] Then, however, Americans had the right to buy and ingest, inhale, or inject any drug they wanted. Clearly, the eagerness of the government to give us fake "rights" is directly proportional to its enthusiasm for depriving us of real rights, in our own best interest.

Why do we now lack a right we possessed in the past? Why did the Founders take the right to drugs so much for granted that they saw no reason even to mention it? No one asks these questions. Yet, the pharmacological properties of drugs have not changed since the eighteenth century; neither has the physiological reactivity of the human organism; nor has the Constitution—which was never amended with respect to drugs, as it had been with respect to alcohol. Why, then, does the federal government control our access to some of mankind's most ancient and medically most valuable agricultural products and the drugs derived from them?

These are some of the basic questions not discussed in debates on drugs. Why not? Because admission into the closed circle of officially recognized drug-law experts is contingent on shunning such rude behavior. Instead, the would-be debater of the drug problem is expected to accept, as a premise, that it is the duty of the federal government to limit the free trade in drugs. All that can be debated is which drugs should be controlled and how they should be controlled.[3]

Like all governments, the U.S. government has always had far-reaching powers to prohibit certain behaviors. However, at least in principle, it has had and still has only limited legitimacy to do so. This is because the government of the United States is supposed to be our servant, not our master; because it is expected to treat us as adult moral agents, not as irresponsible children or incompetent mental patients; and because we possess our inalienable rights as persons, not as the beneficiaries of a magnanimous state. Because the state owns no rights, it cannot give us any rights or "legalize" any acts, whether it be practicing a deviant religion or using a dangerous drug. In other words, American lawmakers can *enact prohibitions* ("illegalize") and can *repeal prohibitions*, but they cannot *legislate permissions* ("legalize").

Nevertheless, the current debate on drugs is premised on the opposite image and vocabulary—reflecting a paternalistic, medical-statist concept of the government. The upshot is that the supporters and critics of the War on Drugs vie with each other in championing state control of the market in drugs. Since we call state control of the production and distribution of goods and services "socialism" (or "communism"), I suggest we call state control of the production and distribution of drugs "chemical socialism (or communism)."

Our ardent embrace of chemical communism seems to me particularly

ironic because never before in history has the issue of the market economy versus the command economy been more sharply polarized than
today; because the ideals of the market are being betrayed not only by
statist liberals but also by conservatives, who claim to be zealous advocates of the free market; and because the items of commerce with
which the virtue of trade is being shamelessly transformed into the
wickedness of trafficking are ordinary plants (or substances derived from
them) that have been used throughout human history. A more obvious
or more stupid attempt to reverse mankind's greatest leap forward—
symbolized by the legend of the Fall—would be hard to imagine.

God, the Scriptures tell us, expelled Man (Adam) from the Garden.
We must grow up or suffer the consequences. This, it seems to me, is
our fate as human beings. The Drug-free Garden Nancy Reagan and
William Bennett want us to reenter is either an infantile illusion or a
concentration camp of the mind. Hitler, let us recall, neither drank nor
smoked, while Churchill spent most of his adult life with ethanol cours-
ing through his veins, and Roosevelt rarely posed for a photograph
without a cigarette (or, more precisely, a jauntily positioned cigarette
holder) between his lips.

DRUG LAWS AND DRUG LIES

As I noted above, the current debate on drugs is premised on the
unquestioning acceptance of the legitimacy of drug laws whose avowed
aim is *to protect legally competent adults from their own decisions to use certain
drugs*. Supporting the *repeal* of such drug laws is not a legitimate option.
Drug legalization is. But what exactly do we mean by this term?

What Is a Legal Commodity?

Because we are the products of nearly a century of medical-statist
infantilization and tyrannization, our language in reference to drugs
reflects our drug control history. When bracketed with the term *drug*,
the meaning of the word *legal* has undergone the same sort of metamorphosis as has the meaning of the word *liberal*.

In the nineteenth century, a liberal was a person who championed individual liberty in a context of laissez-faire economics, who defined liberty as the absence of coercion, and who regarded the state as an ever-
present threat to personal freedom and responsibility. Today, a liberal is
a person who champions social justice in a context of socialist eco-

nomics, who defines liberty as access to the means for a good life, and who regards the state as a benevolent provider whose duty is to protect people from poverty, racism, sexism, illness, and drugs.

Similarly, in the nineteenth century, a legal object or service was something one could purchase on the free market (for example, opium, or a week's stay in a hospital room), whereas an illegal object was something one could purchase on the black market or not at all (for example, pornographic pictures, or an abortion). Also, as I noted earlier, only selling illegal goods and services was prohibited and punished; buying and using them were not. Strictly speaking, then, a legal object is one we can purchase without having to offer a reason for wanting it, and without having to obtain permission from government bureaucrats or medical nannies for buying it. Apricots and aspirin are legal, but amphetamines and antibiotics are not. What do the "drug legalizers" propose? As we shall presently see, they propose one or another scheme of state-supervised, state-funded distribution of presently prohibited drugs. (I deliberately ignore here, as irrelevant to my present argument, regulations controlling access to weapons, whether guns or tanks.) However, such measures are not methods of transforming an illegal product into a legal one; they are methods of bureaucratizing, medicalizing, and policing the market, not of freeing it. We do not call the postal service a "legalized" enterprise; we call it a government monopoly.

It should be noted that many so-called legalizers frankly acknowledge that they are "medicalizers," and even use that term. For example, Baltimore Mayor Kurt L. Schmoke believes "that addiction—all addiction—should lead to the clinic door, not to the jailhouse door";[4] and the Drug Policy Foundation correctly characterizes his position as an "argument for decriminalizing and medicalizing some drugs."[5] However, an important part of my thesis in this book is that medicalization is the problem, not the solution.

What Is Drug Legalization?

Whether used by physicians, lawyers, journalists, or lay persons, the term *drug legalization* has come to mean a "more enlightened" form of *state control of the drug market*. The following proposal—put forward by an attorney, Frederick B. Campbell—captures the legalizers' spirit perfectly:

Legalization would not mean that addictive drugs would be legally available to everyone. The purpose of legalization would be to place better controls on access to such drugs. Addiction would be recognized as a disease or physical affliction. . . . For nonaddicts, the substances would remain illegal in the same way that it is now criminal to sell or use prescription drugs without a prescription.[6]

This is a candid recommendation to control and criminalize the trade in drugs by medicalizing drug distribution. Indeed, Campbell goes so far as to repeat the classic pseudomedical canard, "Curing addicts of addiction is a medical problem, not a law enforcement one." Professing that platitude enables the prohibitionist to ignore the single most important fact about addiction qua disease, namely, that while American medical practice (except for pediatrics and psychiatry) rests on the patient's giving informed consent to the doctor for treating him, addicts are not interested in being cured of a habit they do not want to break. In Orwell's Newspeak, war was peace. In ours, drug medicalization is drug legalization.

The persons now characterized as drug legalizers are, in fact, medicalizers and thus, de facto, paternalistic prohibitionists. The difference between the covert prohibitionist ("legalizer") and the avowed prohibitionist (drug war advocate) is that the former wants to prohibit different substances and punish the drug law violators less severely than the latter. The typical legalizer thus emphasizes that marijuana is less harmful than tobacco or that it is effective for treating glaucoma, and then maintains that therefore its use, at least for certain purposes, should be legal.[7] The position of the American Civil Liberties Union (ACLU) as articulated by Ira Glasser, its executive director, is illustrative: "Legalize the use of marijuana for medical purposes. Stop enforcing the law against marijuana users. Repeal bans on providing intravenous drug users clean needles."[8]

This posture—which is purely expedient, resting on no ethical or political principle whatever—is morally repugnant as well as practically self-defeating.[9] Its advocates acknowledge the government's right, and perhaps even its duty, to prohibit drugs it deems dangerous or lacking medically rational use (as if nonprohibited drugs were not also dangerous, and as if the notion of "medically rational use" were not a hopelessly politicized judgment).

THE DRUG DEBATERS SPEAK

Let us briefly consider some examples of the actual statements of the experts now engaged in the drug legalization debate.

William F. Buckley, Jr., and the *National Review*

Although the *National Review* is an ardent supporter of the free market, a major article in the magazine advocates drug legalization under the title "The Federal Drugstore." This conjoining of words illustrates the catastrophic linguistic slippage epitomized by the now conventional coupling of the verb *legalize* with the noun *drug*.[10] In the article, *drug legalization* is discussed as if the term were synonymous with the sale of psychoactive drugs in federal drugstores—an odd premise for conservatives. In the United States, a legal product is usually sold in stores privately owned and operated. (There are exceptions to this rule, especially with respect to alcohol. However, to refer to gambling in states other than Nevada and New Jersey as "legal" is a tortured and fundamentally misleading use of the term. Lottery gaming, now legal in most states, is a monopoly. Not coincidentally, gambling abuse has become accepted as a bona fide disease—indeed, an addiction.)

It is also fallacious to discuss this subject as if Americans were not interested in buying and using illegal nonpsychoactive drugs—for example, abortifacients, antibiotics, and steroids, just to mention some. To make matters worse, the article proposes that "profits [from federal drugstores] would go to the treatment centers and toward more advertising of the dangers of drug abuse, and indeed of drug consumption."[11] When selling condoms was legalized, were they sold in federal birth control stores? Did the profits from the sale of condoms go to federal treatment centers for curing people from the disease of practicing birth control?

The *Wall Street Journal*

Although the *Wall Street Journal* is also a staunch defender of the free market, with respect to drugs it, too, adopts the language of medical statism. In a long article on drug legalization, we learn that the supporters of legalization maintain it "would be [far better] to let people who insist on using banned drugs obtain them from the government in a regulated fashion rather than from thugs on the black market. . . . Government would use the proceeds for anti-drug education and treatment."[12] Again, nearly every word carries the standard baggage of medical and statist presumptions. Specifically, repeated references to "treatment" in the report betray an astonishingly uncritical acceptance of the view that individuals who purchase, possess, or use illegal drugs are sick. Even in the hypothetical context of drug legalization, with drug users presumably paying for the drugs of their choice, the *Journal* continues to adhere to a statist model of treatment. Drug treatment is always identified as a government-sponsored and tax-supported enterprise, as if nothing else were thinkable or possible. Which, in a sense, is true: Addicts want drugs, not treatment.

The *New York Times*

Not surprisingly, in the pages of the *New York Times* too, the term *drug legalization* means state control of drugs. In a report titled "On the Question of Legal Drugs," Nathan Glazer, professor of sociology at Harvard, ponders this question: "Is it possible to reduce the intensity of the war against drugs . . . by some degree of legalization?"[13] This is very sloppy talk. It makes sense to speak of various degrees of criminalization, but it makes no sense to speak of various degrees of legalization. Murder is more severely criminalized (that is, punished) than a traffic violation; but it would be awkward and wrong to refer to speeding as "more legal" than murder (for they are equally illegal). Like pregnancy, prohibition is a matter of all or nothing. A legally unenforced prohibition is a dead-letter law or a broken promise (indirectly injuring the law-abiding citizen).

So long as Harvard professors of sociology talk this way; so long as the editors of the *National Review* equate drug legalization with the sale of drugs in federal drugstores; so long as the editors of the *Wall Street Journal* do not question that the desire for illegal drugs is a disease; and so long as the former editor in chief of the *New York Times* lavishes praise on Jesse Jackson because "nobody in the country speaks with more passion and clarity [*sic*] about the drug disease [*sic*] than this man"[14]— so long as these are the representative views of our leading opinion-makers, the real legalization of drugs in the United States (like the real legalization of farms and factories in the Soviet Union) will remain nothing more than a foolish fantasy fabricated by people who refuse to take seriously ideas, and the language we use to talk about them.

Congressman Charles B. Rangel

Ostensibly opposing the legalizers, whom they accuse of being "soft on drugs," are the prohibitionists who pledge to stamp out the "drug plague." Congressman Charles B. Rangel, Democrat of New York and chairman of the House Select Committee on Narcotics Abuse and Control, is an exemplary drug prohibitionist. He owes much of his public visibility to his demagogic posturings against drugs. As a professional anti-drug crusader, Congressman Rangel has good reasons to fear a drug peace replacing his beloved War on Drugs. Still, as a prominent black lawmaker, one might expect him to respect the distinction between legal and illegal objects and acts. After all, we now preach the sermon of the free market to the people of formerly communist nations. Against that background, consider Rangel's use of language:

> Just the thought of legalization brings up more problems and concerns than already exist. . . . Has anybody ever considered which narcotic and psychotropic drugs would be legalized? . . . What would the *market price* be and *who* would set it? Would private industry be *allowed* to have a stake in any of this? . . . Will the Government establish *tax-supported* facilities to sell these drugs?[15]

Congressman Rangel has populist support and power, and those are the things that count most in demagogic politics. Why should he *know* that in a market economy there is no "who" to set prices? But if Rangel does not understand this, or does not want to understand it, can we expect people who vote for him to understand it? Moreover, Rangel has access to the media, where he can explain to people that when the state does not prohibit a substance, then its use is, ipso facto, "sanctioned by the government" and this sends "the message that drugs are O.K." Rangel thus maintains that we should not criticize or debate drug prohibition, because doing so is fundamentally subversive. "If we really want to do something about drug abuse," he concludes, "let's end this nonsensical talk about legalization right now."[16] Not for naught did Mark Twain opine that "there is no distinctly native American criminal class except Congress."[17]

Despite such warnings, William F. Buckley, Jr., invited Congressman Rangel to participate in a television debate on "whether the United States would be better off decriminalizing drugs."[18] With great gusto, Rangel disposed of the question and his opponents by pointing out to the nationwide audience that the United States could not legalize drugs even if it wanted to, because "we are bound to honor our drug treaties." Buckley—who acted (or pretended to act) as if his opponent were a debater, not a demagogue—conceded that he was unfamiliar with any such treaty and queried, "Er, Congressman Rangel, what treaties are you referring to?" Unflappably, Rangel replied that "there were quite a few of them," offering "the Psychotropic Drug Treaty of 1987" as an example. That treaty, he patiently explained, "denies its signatories the right to market drugs except for the public health." After the debate was over, Buckley tells us, Rangel was munching a sandwich when a "guest accosted him. 'What about this Psychotropic Drug Treaty of 1987? I never heard of it.' Charles Rangel leaned his head back and laughed uproariously. 'He demanded a treaty, didn't he?' "[19]

Actually, Rangel's memory was better than he realized. In 1988 at Vienna, under the auspices of the United Nations, the United States was indeed one of the signatories of a psychotropic drug treaty.[20] The signing of international drug treaties is a ceremonial affair, however, with virtually no impact on actual policy.[21] The fact that none of the debate panelists except Rangel seemed to know anything about drug treaties, and that Rangel himself thought he had invented a drug treaty when in fact he was citing a real one, is indicative of the level of public discourse on what is supposedly the most important domestic issue of the moment.

THE CASE AGAINST DRUG LEGALIZATION

As their pronouncements show, the drug legalizers' opposition to the drug prohibitionists is so unprincipled that it makes the differences between the two parties illusory. Both groups accept that drugs denominated as dangerous *are* dangerous, and that "drug use" *is* "bad." An article in *Parade* magazine, sloppily titled "Should We Legalize the Illegal?" (as if something legal could be legalized), is illustrative. Largely devoted to a sympathetic expounding of the confused coercive-psychiatric proposals of U.S. District Judge Robert Sweet, the article begins with the statement that Sweet "contends that such drugs as cocaine and heroin should be *legalized* and taxed by the government. . . . The government also would *control prices and distribution*."[22] Although Judge Sweet identifies himself as a "drug legalizer" and is proudly paraded by the legalizers as one of their own, what he means by legalization is even more lawless than what the prohibitionists mean by criminalization.

My earlier observation that the aim of drug laws has undergone a fundamental change, from protecting people from others to protecting them from themselves, is dramatically supported by Judge Sweet's wretched caveat. He proposes not only that "the state set the prices of the legalized drugs and the amounts that could be sold" and not only that "no one without a doctor's prescription would be able to buy a lethal dosage at one time,"[23] but also that "civil-court proceedings [be used] with chronic addicts . . . [to control] this conduct going to extremes."[24] It is ironic that conservative drug legalizers should now naively hail the antilibertarian proposal to medicalize illegal drug use championed thirty years ago by archliberal Justice William O. Douglas. In a ringing opinion in *Robinson v. California*, Douglas declared, "The addict is a sick person. He may, of course, be confined for treatment or for the protection of society. Cruel and unusual punishment results not from confinement, but from convicting the addict of a crime."[25] This is how and where the support for drug legalization qua medicalization dovetails with the support for involuntary mental hospitalization and the deplorable psychiatric coercions that go with it.

Judge Sweet neither defines nor illustrates what sort of conduct would justify the *legal drug* user's psychiatric confinement. That exhibited by Betty Ford? By Kitty Dukakis? By Marion Barry? Or does Judge Sweet intend to reserve the benefits of "civil-court proceedings"—a euphemism for psychiatric incarceration—to poor blacks and women, the favorite beneficiaries of judges for such compassionate treatment? Evidently so, as he asserts that "drug abuse has become an escape for those without a stake in society"[26]—a demarcation that excludes VIP drug abusers such as John F. Kennedy and Betty Ford. Revealingly, in a two-hour-long debate where Judge Sweet proposed psychiatric imprisonment of "addicts" as his idea of drug legalization, not a single panelist challenged him.[27]

Drug Legalization: A Fresh Attack on the Market

As I have shown, professional pundits and journalists now use the term *drug legalization* to mean the statist-medical control of drugs and drug users. "The concept," explains a reporter for *U.S. News & World Report*, "goes by different names—legalization, decriminalization, or narcotics-by-regulation. Whatever it is called, growing numbers of thinkers from both left and right are embracing the idea that the fight against drugs should become a treatment-based effort."[28] But how can the act of choosing to take a drug, legal or illegal, be a disease? How can a person's voluntarily taking an illegal narcotic be a disease (say, "heroin addiction"), and his being ordered by a judge or his deciding on his own to take another illegal narcotic be a treatment ("methadone maintenance")? (Methadone is a strictly "controlled substance," and hence illegal. For a discussion of the illegality of prescription drugs, see Chapter 1.) Characteristically, Judge Sweet recommends "making methadone available to all heroin users who now seek it . . . [and] residential treatment available for anyone who meets a certain defined level of addiction."[29] Such authoritative references to diseases and treatments may sound as if they were facts, and we may pretend they are facts—but they are fictions.

Legal fictions are often important facts of life. Today, we recognize that an individual is either a five-fifths person or not a person at all. However, in 1778, when lawmakers created the fiction of three-fifths persons and inscribed it into the Constitution, people behaved (when it suited their purposes) as if they believed in the reality of such fractional human beings. Now, our lawmakers create the fiction of drug (abuse/addiction/dependency) treatment, and the phrase does yeoman service coercing both drug law offenders and drug law obeyers—the former, to submit to medically sanctioned deprivations of liberty, called "treatment"; the latter, to submit to therapeutically sanctioned expropriation of their labor, called "taxation." During the past ten years alone, federal expenditures on the War on Drugs have grown from about $1 billion to more than $10 billion, "enabling 200,000 more people to be treated."[30] It matters not that "drug treatment" is a fakery compared to which Prince Potemkin's villages were real. We cling more stubbornly to the belief that the drug market must be under state control than the Soviets cling to the belief that the housing market must be under such control. The following plea by public radio storyteller Garrison Keillor is illustrative:

> Tobacco is an obscene branch of capitalism, and so is liquor, and our society would be well served if Congress made the private production of tobacco and liquor illegal and the government bought the distilleries and factories for book value and manufactured these goods as a public service. . . . If you ever visit the Stalinist keep of East Germany [this was written in December 1989], you'll find that the buildings are dreadful, the shops forlorn, the clothing shabby . . . but the cigarettes and alcohol are really okay, about as good as anywhere else. . . . In the field of information and ideas, a free enterprise system seems to work, but it's terrible in the field of addictive substances. *Nationalize Philip Morris.*[31]

Where Garrison Keillor—who enjoyed smoking cigarettes (I assume American cigarettes) for twenty-three years—gets his facts is a mystery.

It is common knowledge that, in the Soviet Union, American cigarettes are a more useful currency than rubles. The claim that cigarettes in the Soviet bloc are "about as good as anywhere else" is every bit as silly as the pre-Gorbachev claim that the communist economic system is superior to the capitalist market system.

The sobering truth is that, although socialism has been discredited in Eastern Europe and the Soviet Union, we still look to it for our salvation from what we call "drugs"—or, for special effect, "crack." Declares Jefferson Morley, a respected journalist: "Crack is a nightmare microcosm of capitalist society."[32] Such remarks, soberly made by thoughtful persons, indicate how profoundly we in America have lost faith in ourselves and look to a therapeutic state to protect us from our own inclinations.

Ethan Nadelmann: Legalization as Taxation

The views of the mainline drug legalizers generally conform to the pattern I have described. For example, Ethan Nadelmann—assistant professor of politics and public affairs at Princeton University and a vigorous spokesman for "drug legalization"—candidly acknowledges that he uses this term to describe a program of more, not less, government control over drugs. In an interview in *Mother Jones* magazine, Nadelmann explains,

> But one thing we can't afford is to have tobacco companies come to dominate the marijuana business. We can't afford to have pharmaceutical companies come to dominate the cocaine business. . . . Look at alcohol advertising. That's pushing. . . . I'd like to see the federal tax on tobacco and alcohol doubled or tripled.[33]

As if he feared that his statist credentials might be endangered by his nominal advocacy of "legalization," Nadelmann never tires of emphasizing that he wants to expand, not reduce, the government's powers to control drug use. Still responding to the question "How to legalize?" he explains,

> Let's say we decide, okay, we're not going to legalize crack; what we will do is legalize 15-percent cocaine. . . . Yes, some people are still going to want to go to the black market . . . and buy crack. You won't be able to prevent that. But let's say 70 percent of the market will be using the legal, less potent substance. That's good, because the government taxes it, regulates it. . . . The object is to undercut the criminal element.[34]

Undercutting the criminal element is a far cry from seriously engaging the problem of drug controls, including especially prescription laws—a subject Nadelmann conveniently avoids.[35]

Eric Sterling: Chemical Statism Über Alles

Another prominent drug legalizer, Eric Sterling—president of the Washington-based Criminal Justice Policy Foundation—is interested in enriching Big Brother, not in empowering "little brother." Conceptualizing the legalization of outlawed drugs as "harm management," Sterling favors "a ban on all drug advertisements, ranging from illegal narcotics to alcohol, tobacco, and even everyday household drugs such as aspirin."[36] This puts the differences between the legalizer and the libertarian squarely before us. The former is interested in the person who wants to make a profit by advertising a legal product; the latter is interested in the free and responsible individual who wants to be in control of his own drug use. The former seeks to curtail the economic opportunities of black-market entrepreneurs by expanding the scope and power of the state; the latter seeks to expand the liberty and responsibility of the individual qua actual or potential drug user. It is unfortunate, but not unexpected, that drug prohibitionists of all types now couch their arguments and conceal their positions in deceitful euphemisms. But, then, these are the 1990s. In Eastern Europe, communists call themselves democratic socialists; in the United States, chemical communists call themselves drug legalizers.

Lester Grinspoon: Taxing Harmfulness

Americans now fear drugs, their children, and even themselves, and look to doctors for protection. Official drug prohibitionists and liberal drug legalizers alike have seized on these weaknesses and have exploited them, their not-so-hidden agenda being to gain political influence. The psychiatrist Lester Grinspoon, a leading advocate of drug legalization, pursues political respectability by packaging drug legalization as a program for combating other people's bad habits.

Donning the mantle of the commander in chief of a command drug-economy, Grinspoon proposes that the government legalize drugs and impose a "harmfulness tax" on them: "[Each drug] would be taxed at a rate that reflects its cost to society, such as direct health care costs and loss in productivity. . . . The 'harmfulness tax' could be established in phases, beginning with alcohol, cigarettes, and marijuana."[37] The message is clear: Control marijuana less, and tobacco more. What also remains unmentioned in debates on drug legalization is that all loyal liberal-despotic psychiatrists—Grinspoon among them—believe in forcing some of the most toxic drugs in our pharmacopoeia down the throats of the most helpless people in the country, rationalizing coercive drugging as the "drug treatment of psychotics."[38] Grinspoon never suggests a harmfulness tax for Haldol.

Blind to the pervasive—public as well as professional—ambivalence toward recreational drug use, and unwilling to see politicians as corrupt rather than caring, Grinspoon has a near-perfect record of mistaken social diagnoses and erroneous prognoses of drug policies. For example, in 1977 he stated,

> Now that marihuana has become so popular among middle-class youth, we are more willing to investigate its therapeutic value seriously; recreational use is spurring medical interest instead of medical hostility. If the trend continues, it is likely that within a decade marihuana will be sold in the United States as a legal intoxicant. Even before that, cannabis-derived compounds... will be available to physicians as prescription drugs.[39]

We are now well past 1987; marijuana is more strictly prohibited than when Grinspoon offered his prediction; and, in general, the recreational drug scene is the exact opposite of what he predicted.[40] On February 12, 1990, the American Bar Association's House of Delegates repealed its eighteen-year-old policy endorsing the decriminalization of simple possession of marijuana by users, noting that "marijuana and other harmful drugs... have become one of the nation's most serious and growing public health problems."[41]

Lastly, Grinspoon's intense anti-capitalist bias makes him completely misinterpret my own continuing critique of drug controls. Unable or unwilling to understand argument based on principle rather than on circumstance, he attributes the motivation of my views to "a general loss of respect for established institutions," and criticizes *Ceremonial Chemistry*'s advocacy of a free market in drugs as "socially ineffectual because of its purely negative content. It defines no positive social function or role for drugs and therefore will probably gain no political constituency."[42]

The Intellectual Bankruptcy of the Legalizers

Astute defenders of our drug laws have quickly seized on the fatal weaknesses in the legalizers' proposals. The counter-critics have focused attention on three specific issues on which the legalizers' position is hopelessly flawed: (1) the inconsistency in permitting the sale of illicit drugs while continuing the prohibition of prescription drugs; (2) the dilemma of the drug manufacturers' liability for the behavior of drug users who injure themselves or others, ostensibly as a result of their drug use; and (3) the problem of suicide, facilitated by access to hitherto illegal drugs.

"Could heroin, cocaine, and speed be sold over the counter like alcohol and cigarettes," asks James B. Jacobs, "while Valium, sleeping pills, some cough medicines, and antibiotics remain available only on doctor's prescription?"[43] Posed rhetorically, his question demonstrates the mindlessness of the legalizers, not the moral legitimacy of drug prohibitions generally or of prescription drug laws in particular.

"Exempting hard drugs from regulation," David C. Anderson cogently points out, "would also increase, perhaps prohibitively, the manufacturer's liability for suicides, overdoses, and any injuries traceable to drug abuse."[44] This, too, is true. However, it illustrates only the absurdities to which our stubborn adherence to the medical model of drug abuse and suicide has led us. There is no more reason to hold Eli Lilly responsible for a person's abusing Seconal or killing himself with it, than there is to hold Exxon liable for a person's abusing gasoline by using it to start a fire for his barbecue or his immolating himself with it. The reason why Lilly is more vulnerable than Exxon is because there is no free market in Seconal as there is in gasoline, and because we regard a sleeping pill as a therapeutic drug rather than as an ordinary commercial product. It is also true, as Anderson adds, that "warning labels probably would not sufficiently protect the producers."[45] Again, this illustrates the enormous power of our anti-drug, anti-responsibility, pro-psychiatry social climate, and proves only that the so-called drug problem cannot be wrenched out of its cultural and legal context. As the Soviets cannot have a free market in goods and services without popular support for the right to private property and without legal respect for contract, so we cannot have a free market in drugs without popular support for the right to drugs as property and without legal respect for contractual relations among consenting adults engaged in the trade in drugs.

Arguing from consequence rather than from principle, the drug legalizers' trump card is the claim that drug prohibition does not work.

But if we argue from principle, then it is moot whether drug prohibition works, because it is problematic what should count as its "working." The very existence and popularity of such a mass movement of scape-goating—uniting a diverse people in a common hatred—may be regarded as evidence that, simply put, it is working.

Finally, I object to a person's defining himself as a "drug legalizer" or a "drug anti-prohibitionist" and then inventing and proposing fresh schemes to "deal with" drug users as deviant Others. The moral essence of the drug anti-prohibitionist program, as I would interpret it, must be the elimination of the legal distinction between the rights and duties of those who use legal drugs, such as coffee, and those who use illegal drugs, such as cocaine. Unlike the current crop of self-styled drug anti-prohibitionists, the real anti-prohibitionists of yore—the men and women who fought against the *prohibition of the self-ownership of blacks*, called "slavery"—kept their eyes on the ball. Convinced that slavery was wrong, their aim was to free the slaves, not to find new justifications for imposing unwanted "help" on them.

All this is contrary to the drug legalizers' view. Declares the National Drug Policy Network, an organization formally dedicated to drug legalization:

> This war is doomed to fail. We need a comprehensive public health approach to drug policy that incorporates the abuse of alcohol and tobacco—the real drug killers in our society—and focuses tax dollars on proven education and prevention strategies. . . . The President's drug strategy is silent on the AIDS crisis among injecting addicts. It is silent on the need to build healthy children and healthy families in our inner cities. It is silent about the desperate need for prenatal and early childhood development programs, literacy and job-training opportunities.[46]

Whether this socialist program is a gospel of salvation or damnation is beside the point; the point is that it has nothing to do with the effort to repeal drug prohibition. Let us remember that the Nineteenth Amendment did not set out to help (much less treat) alcoholics—not because helping alcoholics is not a laudable enterprise, but because it is not pertinent to the repeal of a criminal law. Forging a link between the repeal of a criminal statute and the (compulsory) treatment of persons who use the legalized substance is one of the most sinister features of the therapeutic state. It should also be a clear warning of the reformers' true intentions, and serve as a foretaste of the consequences of their reforms.

6

Blacks and Drugs: Crack as Genocide

Crack is genocide, 1990's style.

—Cecil Williams[1]

No one can deny that, in the tragicomedy we call the War on Drugs, blacks and Hispanics at home and Latin Americans abroad play leading roles: They are (or are perceived to be) our principal drug abusers, drug addicts, drug traffickers, drug counselors, drug-busting policemen, convicts confined for drug offenses, and narco-terrorists. In short, blacks and Hispanics dominate the drug abuse market, both as producers and as products.

I am neither black nor Hispanic and do not pretend to speak for either group or any of its members. There is, however, no shortage of people, black and white, who are eager to speak for them. Which raises an important question, namely: Who speaks for black or Hispanic Americans? Those persons, black or white, who identify drugs—especially crack—as the enemy of blacks? Or those who cast the American state—especially its War on Drugs—in that role? Or neither, because the claims of both are absurd oversimplifications and because black Americans—like white Americans—are not a homogeneous group but a collection of individuals, each of whom is individually responsible for his own behavior and can speak for himself?

BLACK LEADERS ON DRUGS

For the mainline black drug warrior, illegal drugs represent a temptation that African-Americans are morally too enfeebled to resist. This is what makes those who expose them to such temptation similar to slaveholders depriving their victims of liberty. After years of sloganeering by anti-drug agitators, the claim that crack enslaves blacks has become a cliché, prompting the sloganeers to escalate their rhetoric and contend that it is genocide.

Crack as Genocide, Crack as Slavery

The assertion that crack is genocide is a powerful and timely metaphor we ought to clarify, lest we get ourselves entangled in it. Slavery and genocide are the manifestations and the results of the use of force by some people against some other people. Drugs, however, are inert substances unless and until they are taken into the body; and, not being persons, they cannot literally force anyone to do anything. Nevertheless, the claim that black persons are "poisoned" and "enslaved" by drugs put at their disposal by a hostile white society is now the politically correct rhetoric among black racists and white liberals alike. For example, *New York Times* columnist A. M. Rosenthal "denounces even the slightest show of tolerance toward illegal drugs as an act of iniquity deserving comparison to the defense of slavery."[2] Of course, people who want to deny the role of personal agency and responsibility often make use of the metaphor of slavery, generating images of people being enslaved not only by drugs but also by cults, gambling, poverty, pornography, rock music, or mental illness. Persons who use drugs may, figuratively speaking, be said to be the "victims" of temptation, which is as far as one can reasonably carry the rhetoric of victimology. However, this does not prevent Cecil Williams, a black minister in San Francisco, from claiming,

> The crack epidemic in the United States amounts to genocide.
> . . . The primary intent of 200 years of slavery was to break the
> spirit and culture of our people. . . . Now, in the 1990's, I see
> substantial similarities between the cocaine epidemic and slav-
> ery. . . . Cocaine is foreign to African-American culture. We did
> not create it; we did not produce it; we did not ask for it.[3]

If a white person made these assertions, his remarks could easily be interpreted as slandering black people. Being enslaved is something done to a person against his will, while consuming cocaine is something a person does willingly; equating the two denigrates blacks by implying that they are, en masse, so childish or weak that they cannot help but "enslave" themselves to cocaine. Williams's remark that cocaine is foreign to black culture and hence destructive compounds his calumny. Rembrandt's art, Beethoven's music, and Newton's physics are also foreign to black culture. Does that make them all evils similar to slavery?

Another black minister, the Reverend Cecil L. Murray of Los Angeles, repeats the same theme but uses different similes. He refers to drugs as if they were persons and asserts that "drugs are *literally* killing our people."[4] Like other anti-drug agitators, Murray is short on facts and reasoning, and long on bombast and scapegoating. He excoriates proposals to legalize drugs, declaring, "This is a foul breach of everything we hold sacred. To legalize it, to condone it, to market it—that is to put a healthy brand on strychnine. . . . [W]e cannot make poison the norm."[5]

By now, everyone knows that cigarettes kill more people than illegal drugs. But the point needs to be made again here. "Cigarette smoking," writes Kenneth Warner, a health care economist, "causes more premature deaths than do all of the following together: acquired immunodeficiency syndrome, heroin, alcohol, fire, automobile accidents, homicide, and suicide."[6] Many of the conditions Warner lists affect blacks especially adversely. Both smoking and obesity are unhealthy ("poisonous") but "legal" (not prohibited by the criminal law), yet neither is regarded as the "norm."

Up with Hope, Down with Dope

The Reverend Jesse Jackson is not only a permanent presidential candidate, but is also A. M. Rosenthal's favorite drug warrior. Jackson's trademark incantation goes like this: "Up with hope, down with dope." Better at rhyming than reasoning, Jackson flatly asserts—no metaphor here, at least none that he acknowledges—that "drugs are poison. Taking drugs is a sin. Drug use is morally debased and sick."[7] Poison. Sin. Sickness. Jackson the base rhetorician refuses to be outdone and keeps piling it on: "Since the flow of drugs into the U.S. is an act of terrorism, antiterrorist policies must be applied. . . . If someone is transmitting the death agent to Americans, that person should face wartime consequences. The line must be drawn."[8]

It certainly must. The question, however, is this: Where should we draw it? I believe we ought to draw it by categorizing free trade in agricultural products (including coca, marijuana, and tobacco) as good, and dumping toxic wastes on unsuspecting people in underdeveloped countries as bad;[9] by recognizing the provision of access to accurate pharmacological information as liberating drug education, and rejecting mendacious religiomedical bombast as lamentable political and racial demagogy.

Mayor Marion Barry as Drug Hero

In former days, moral crusaders—especially men of the cloth— thundered brimstone and hellfire at those who succumbed to temptation, typically of the flesh. Why? Because in those benighted pre-Freudian days, moral authorities held people responsible for their behavior. Not any more. And certainly not Jesse Jackson vis-à-vis prominent blacks who use illegal drugs. Foreign drug traffickers are responsible for selling cocaine. Washington, D.C., Mayor Marion Barry is not responsible for buying and smoking it. After the mayor was properly entrapped into buying cocaine and was videotaped smoking it, Jackson pontificated, "Now all of America can learn from the mayor's problems and his long journey back to health."[10] A remarkable disease, this illegal drug use, U.S.A, anno Domini 1990: Caused by being arrested by agents of the state; cured by a "program" provided by agents of the state; its course a "journey"; its prognosis—known with confidence even by priest-politicians without any medical expertise—a return "back to health."

Shamelessly, Jackson used Barry's arrest as an occasion not only for sanctifying the defendant (as if he were accused of a civil rights violation) but also for promoting his own political agenda. A priori, the defendant was a good and great man, "entering the Super Bowl of his career." His accuser—the U.S. government—was, a priori, an evil "political system that can only be described as neocolonial." While thus politicizing drugs, Jackson impudently inveighs against his own practice. "Circumstances like these," he babbles, "remind us that the war on drugs . . . should not be politicized. It is primarily a moral crusade, about values and about health and sickness." Having unburdened himself of his pearls of wisdom about politics, moral values, and sickness and health, Jackson comes to his main point: "Behind these gruesome statistics lies the powerlessness of the people who live in the shadow of a national government from which they are structurally excluded. Now more than ever, it is time to escalate the effort to gain statehood and self-government for the district"—and elect Jesse Jackson senator-for-life-or-until-elected-president. Should we not expect political self-government to be preceded by personal self-government, as it normally is in progressing from disfranchised childhood to enfranchised adulthood? Jackson's envy of and thirst for the power of whites is clear enough. His contention that blacks in Washington, D.C., sell, buy, and use illegal drugs because they are "powerless" is thus but another instance of a drug warrior's fingering a scapegoat in the guise of offering an explanation.

Is Jackson, one of our most prominent anti-drug agitators, trying to protect black Americans from drugs or is he trying to promote his own career? Unlike the Black Muslims committed to an ideology of self-help, self-reliance, and radical separatism, Jackson is playing on the white man's turf, trying to gain power by the "enemy's" methods and rules. The War on Drugs presents him, as it presents his white counterparts, with the perfect social problem: Here is an issue on which Jesse Jackson can join—on common ground, shoulder to shoulder—not only such eminent white liberal-democrats as Mario Cuomo and Kitty Dukakis, but also such eminent white conservative-Republicans as Nancy Reagan and William Bennett. Indeed, on what other issue besides drugs could Jesse Jackson and Nancy Reagan—one a black militant struggling up the social ladder, the other a white conservative standing on its top rung— agree? As pharmacological agents, dangerous drugs may indeed be toxic for the body anatomic of the individuals who use them; but as a propaganda tool, dangerous drugs are therapeutic for the body politic of the nation, welding our heterogeneous society together into one country and one people, engaged in an uplifting, self-purifying, moral crusade.

THE WAR ON DRUGS: A WAR ON BLACKS

A Martian who came to earth and read only what the newspaper headlines say about drugs would never discover an interesting and important feature of America's latest moral crusade, namely, that its principal victims are black or Hispanic. (I must add here that when I use the word *victim* in connection with the word *drug*, I do not refer to a person who chooses to use a drug and thus subjects himself to its effects, for good or ill. Being his own poisoner—assuming the drug has an ill effect on him—such a person is a victim in a metaphoric sense only. In the conventional use of the term, to which I adhere, a literal or real victim is a person unjustly or tragically deprived of his life, liberty, or property, typically by other people—in our case, as a result of the criminalization of the free market in drugs.)

However, were the Martian to turn on the television to watch the evening news, or look at a copy of *Time* or *Newsweek*, he would see images of drug busts and read stories about drug addicts and drug treatment programs in which virtually all of the characters are black or Hispanic. Occasionally, some of the drug-busting policemen are white. But the drug traffickers, drug addicts, and drug counselors are virtually all black or Hispanic.

Carl Rowan, a syndicated columnist who is black, finally spoke up. "Racist stereotypes," he correctly pointed out, "have crippled the minds of millions of white Americans."[11] Then, rather selectively, Rowan emphasized that "white prejudice on this point has produced a terrible injustice," but chose to remain discreetly silent about the fact that black leaders are the shock troops in this anti-black drug war. "Blacks," complained Rowan, "are being arrested in USA's drug wars at a rate far out of proportion to their drug use." According to a study conducted by *USA Today*, blacks comprise 12.7 percent of the population and make up 12 percent of those who "regularly use illegal drugs"; but of those arrested on drug charges in 1988, 38 percent were blacks.[12]

Other studies indicate that blacks represent an even larger proportion of drug law violators/victims. For example, according to the National Institute on Drug Abuse (NIDA, the leading federal agency on drug abuse research), "Although only about 12% of those using illegal drugs are black, 44% of those who are arrested for simple possession and 57% of those arrested for sales are black."[13] Another study, conducted by the Washington-based Sentencing Project, found that while almost one in four black men of age 20–29 were in jail or on parole, only one in sixteen white men of the same age group were.[14] Clarence Page dramatized the significance of these figures by pointing out that while 610,000 black men in their twenties are in jail or under the supervision of the criminal justice system, only 436,000 are in college.[15] "Just as no one is born a college student," commented Page, "no one is born a criminal. Either way, you have to be carefully taught."[16]

Page does not say who is teaching blacks to be criminals, but I will: The economic incentives intrinsic to our drug laws. After all, although black Americans today are often maltreated by whites, and are in the main poorer than whites, they were *more maltreated and were even poorer* fifty or a hundred years ago, yet fewer young black males chose a criminal career then than do now. This development is far more dangerous for all of us, black and white, than all the cocaine in Colombia. "Under the nation's current approach," a feature report in the *Los Angeles Times* acknowledges, "black America is being criminalized at an astounding rate."[17] Nevertheless, the black community enthusiastically supports the War on Drugs. George Napper, director of public safety in Atlanta, attributes this attitude to "black people . . . being more conservative than other people. They say: 'To hell with rights. Just kick ass and take names.' "[18] Father George Clements, a Catholic priest who has long been in the forefront of the struggle against drugs in Chicago's black communities, exemplifies this posture: "I'm all for whatever tactics have to be used. If that means they are trampling on civil liberties, so be it."[19] The black leadership's seemingly increasing contempt for civil liberties is just one of the disastrous consequences of drug prohibition. The drug war's impact on poor and poorly educated blacks is equally alarming and tragic. Instead of looking to the free market and the rule of law for self-advancement, the War on Drugs encourages them to look to a race war—or a lottery ticket—as a way out of their misfortune.

Drug Prohibition: Pouring Fuel on the Fire of Racial Antagonism

Clearly, one of the unintended consequences of drug prohibition—far more dangerous to American society than drugs—has been that it has fueled the fires of racial division and antagonism. Many American blacks (whose views white psychiatrists would love to dismiss as paranoid if they could, but happily no longer can) believe that the government is "out to get them" and the War on Drugs is one of its tools: A "popular theory [among blacks] is that white government leaders play a pivotal role in the drug crisis by deliberately making drugs easily available in black neighborhoods."[20] Another consequence of our drug laws (less unintended perhaps) has been that while it is no longer officially permissible to persecute blacks qua blacks, it is permissible to persecute them qua drug law violators. Under the pretext of protecting people—especially "kids"—from dangerous drugs, America's young black males are stigmatized en masse as drug addicts and drug criminals. The possibility that black youths may be more endangered by society's drug laws than by the temptation of drugs surely cannot be dismissed out of hand. It is an idea, however, that only those black leaders who have shaken off the shackles of trying to please their degraders dare to entertain. Thus we now find the Black Muslim minister Louis Farrakhan articulating such a view, much as the martyred Malcolm X did a quarter of a century ago. "There is," says Farrakhan, "a war being planned against black youth by the government of the United States under the guise of a war against drugs."[21] I suspect few educated white persons really listen to or hear this message, just as few listened to or heard what Malcolm X said. And of those who hear it, most dismiss it as paranoid. But paranoids too can have real enemies.

The U.S. Customs Service acknowledges that, to facilitate its work in spotting drug smugglers, the service uses "drug courier" and "drug swallower" profiles developed in the 1970s. Critics have charged that "one characteristic that most of those detained have in common is their race. 'The darker your skin, the better your chances,' said Gary Trichter, a Houston defense lawyer who specializes in such cases."[22] In a ruling handed down on April 3, 1989, the Supreme Court endorsed the government's use of drug profiles for detaining and questioning airline passengers. Although the Court's ruling addressed only airports, the profiles are also used on highways, on interstate buses, and in train stations. In addition, the Customs Service is authorized to request the traveler, under penalty of being detained or not allowed to enter the country, to submit to an X-ray examination to determine if he has swallowed a condom containing drugs. "In Miami, of 101 X-rays, 67 found drugs. In New York, of 187 X-rays, 90 yielded drugs. In Houston . . . 60 people were X-rayed [and] just 4 were found to be carrying drugs."[23] Although the profiles have proved to be of some value, this does not justify their use unless one believes that the government's interest in finding and punishing people with illegal drugs in their possession deserves more protection than the individual's right to his own body.

What do the statistics about the people stopped and searched on the basis of drug profiles tell us? They reveal, for example, that in December 1989 in Biloxi, Mississippi, of fifty-seven stops on Interstate 10, fifty-five involved Hispanic or black people.[24] On a stretch of the New Jersey Turnpike where less than 5 percent of the traffic involved cars with out-of-state license plates driven by black males, 80 percent of the arrests fitted that description. Topping the record for racially discriminatory drug arrests is the drug-interdiction program at the New York Port Authority Bus Terminal, where 208 out of 210 persons arrested in 1989 were black or Hispanic.[25] Still, the anti-drug bureaucrats insist that "the ratio of arrests reflected a 'reality of the streets,' rather than a policy of racial discrimination."[26]

However, in January 1991 Pamela Alexander, a black judge in Minnesota, ruled that the state's anti-crack law—which "calls for a jail term for first-time offenders convicted of possessing three grams of crack, but only probation for defendants convicted of possessing the same amount of powdered cocaine"—discriminated against blacks and was therefore unconstitutional.[27] Her ruling focuses on the fact that crack cocaine and powdered cocaine are merely two different forms of cocaine, and that blacks tend to use the former, and whites the latter. The law thus addresses a difference in customs, not a difference in drug effects. "Drug policy," Judge Alexander concluded, "should not be set according to anything less than scientific evidence." Unfortunately, this is a very naive statement. There is no scientific basis for any of our "drug policies"—a term that, in this context, is a euphemism for prohibiting pharmaceutical and recreational drugs. Warning people about the risks a particular drug poses is the most that science can be made to justify.

In any case, science has nothing to do with the matter at hand, as the contention of the drug enforcers illustrates. Their rejoinder to Judge Alexander's ruling is that "crack is different."[28] In what way? "The stuff is cheap and . . . affordable to kids in the school yard who can't afford similar amounts of powdered cocaine." Behind this pathetic argument stand some elementary facts unfamiliar to the public and denied by the drug warriors. Simply put, crack is to powdered cocaine as cigarettes are to chewing tobacco. Smoking introduces drugs into the body via the lungs; snorting and chewing, via the nasal and buccal mucosae. Different classes tend to display different preferences for different drugs. Educated persons (used to) smoke cigarettes and snort cocaine; uneducated persons chew tobacco and smoke crack. (This generalization is rapidly becoming obsolete. In the United States, though much less in Europe, Asia, and Latin America, smoking cigarettes is becoming a lower-class habit.) These facts make a mockery of the Minnesota legislators' disingenuous denunciation of Judge Alexander's decision: "The one thing we never contemplated was targeting members of any single minority group." It remains to be seen whether the Minnesota Supreme Court, to which the case was appealed, will uphold punishing crack smokers more severely than cocaine snorters.

The enforcement of our drug laws with respect to another special population—namely, pregnant women—is also shamefully racist. Many state laws now regard the pregnant woman who uses an illegal drug as a criminal—not because she possesses or sells or uses a drug, but because she "delivers" it to her fetus via the umbilical cord. Ostensibly aimed at protecting the fetus, the actual enforcement of these laws lends further support to the assumption that their real target is the unwed, inner-city, black mother. Although, according to experts, drug use in pregnancy is equally prevalent in white middle-class women, most women prosecuted for using illegal drugs while pregnant have been poor members of racial minorities. "Researchers found that about 15 percent of both the white and the black women used drugs . . . but that the black women were 10 times as likely as whites to be reported to the authorities."[29]

Drugs and Racism

How do the drug warriors rationalize the racism of the War on Drugs? Partly by ignoring the evidence that the enforcement of drug laws victimizes blacks disproportionately compared to whites; and partly by falling back on a time-honored technique of forestalling the charge by appointing a respected member of the victimized group to a high position in the machinery charged with enforcing the persecutory practice. This is what former drug czar William Bennett did when he picked Reuben Greenberg, a black Jew, as his favorite drug cop.[30] What has Greenberg done to deserve this honor? He chose to prosecute as drug offenders the most defenseless members of the black community. "The tactics Greenberg developed in Charleston [South Carolina]," explained *Time* magazine, "are targeted on the poorest of the poor—the residents of public-housing projects and their neighbors. . . . The projects were 'the easiest place to start, because that's where the victims are.' "[31] Perhaps so. But, then, it must be safer—especially for a black Jewish policeman in South Carolina—to go after blacks in inner-city housing projects than after whites in suburban mansions.

The evidence supports the suspicion that the professional pushers of drug programs pander precisely to such racial prejudices, with spectacularly hypocritical results. Consider the latest fad in addictionology: a racially segregated drug treatment program for blacks. Because the program is owned by blacks, is operated by blacks for blacks, and offers a service called "drug treatment," its owner-operators have been able to pass it off as a fresh "culturally specific" form of therapy. If whites were to try to do this sort of thing to blacks, it would be decried as racist segregation. When black "former drug abusers" do it to fellow blacks, the insurance money pours in: Soon after opening, the clinic called Coalesce was handling three hundred patients at $13,000 a head per month—not bad pay for treating a nonexisting illness with a nonexisting treatment.[32]

BLACK MUSLIMS ON DRUGS

Mainstream American blacks are Christians, who look for leadership to Protestant priest-politicians and blame black drug use on rich whites, capitalism, and South American drug lords. Sidestream American blacks are Muslims, who look for leadership to Islamic priest-politicians and maintain that drug use is a matter of personal choice and self-discipline.

The Black Muslim supporters of a free market in drugs (though they do not describe their position in these terms) arrive at their conclusion not from studying the writings of Adam Smith or Ludwig von Mises, but from their direct experience with the American therapeutic state and its punitive agents decked out as doctors and social workers. As a result, the Black Muslims regard statist-therapeutic meddling as diminishing the person targeted as needing help, robbing him of his status as a responsible moral agent, and therefore fundamentally degrading; and they see the medicalization of the drug problem—the hypocritical defining of illegal drug use as both a crime and a disease, the capricious law enforcement, the economic incentives to transgress the drug laws, and the pseudotherapeutic drug programs—as a wicked method for encouraging drug use, crime, economic dependency, personal demoralization, and familial breakdown. I have reviewed the enduring Black Muslim principles and policies on drugs, as developed by Malcolm X, elsewhere.[33] Here I shall summarize only what is necessary to round out the theme I develop in this chapter.

Black Muslims demand, on moral and religious grounds, that their adherents abstain from all self-indulgent pleasures, including drugs. Accordingly, it would be misleading to speak of a Black Muslim approach to the "treatment of drug addiction." If a person is a faithful Black Muslim he cannot be an addict, just as if he is an Orthodox Jew he cannot be a pork eater. It is as simple as that. The Muslim perspective on drug use and drug avoidance is—like mine—moral and ceremonial, not medical and therapeutic. Of course, this does not mean that we come to all the same conclusions.

Malcolm X: Triumph through Resisting Temptation

Malcolm X's passion for honesty and truth led him to some remarkable drug demythologizings, that is, assertions that seemingly fly in the face of current medical dogmas about hard drugs and their addictive powers. "Some prospective Muslims," wrote Malcolm, "found it more difficult to quit tobacco than others found quitting the dope habit."[34] As I noted, for Muslims it makes no difference whether a man smokes tobacco or marijuana; what counts is the habit of self-indulgence, not the pharmacomythology of highs or kicks. Evidently, one good mythology per capita is enough: If a person truly believes in the mythology of Black Muslimism—or Judaism, or Christianity—then he does not need the ersatz mythology of medicalism and therapeutism.

The Muslims emphasize not only that addiction is evil, but also that it is deliberately imposed on the black man by the white man. "The Muslim program began with recognizing that color and addiction have a distinct connection. It is no accident that in the entire Western Hemisphere, the greatest localized concentration of addicts is in Harlem."[35] The monkey on the addict's back is not the abstraction of drug addiction as a disease, but the concrete reality of Whitey. "Most black junkies," explains Malcolm, "really are trying to narcotize themselves against being a black man in the white man's America."[36] By politicizing personal problems (defining self-medication with narcotics as political oppression), the Muslims neatly reverse the psychiatric tactic of personalizing political problems (defining psychiatric incarceration as hospitalization).

Because for Muslims drug use—legal or illegal—is not a disease, they have no use for pretentious drug treatment programs, especially if they consist of substituting one narcotic drug for another (methadone for heroin). Instead, they rely on breaking the drug habit by expecting the drug user to quit "cold turkey." The ordeal this entails helps to dramatize and ritualize the addict's liberation from Whitey. "When the addict's withdrawal sets in," explains Malcolm, "and he is screaming, cursing and begging, 'Just one shot, man!' the Muslims are right there talking junkie jargon to him, 'Baby, knock that monkey off your back! . . . Kick Whitey off your back!' "[37] Ironically, what Black Muslims tell their adherents is not very different from what white doctors told each other at the beginning of this century. In 1921, writing in the *Journal of the American Medical Association*, Alfred C. Prentice, M.D.—a member of the Committee on Narcotic Drugs of the American Medical Association—rejected "the shallow pretense that drug addiction is a 'disease' . . . [a falsehood that] has been asserted and urged in volumes of 'literature' by self-styled 'specialists.' "[38]

Malcolm X wore his hair crew-cut, dressed with the severe simplicity and elegance of a successful Wall Street lawyer, and was polite and punctual. Alex Haley describes the Muslims as having "manners and miens [that] reflected the Spartan personal discipline the organization demanded."[39] While Malcolm hated the white man—whom he regarded as the "devil"—he despised the black man who refused the effort to better himself: "The black man in the ghettoes . . . has to start self-correcting his own material, moral, and spiritual defects and evils. The black man needs to start his own program to get rid of drunkenness, drug addiction, prostitution."[40]

This is dangerous talk. Liberals and psychiatrists need the weak-willed and the mentally sick to have someone to disdain, care for, and control. If Malcolm had his way, such existential cannibals masquerading as do-gooders would be unemployed, or worse. Here, then, is the basic conflict and contradiction between the Muslim and methadone: By making the Negro self-responsible and self-reliant, Muslimism eliminates the problem and with it the need for the white man and the medicine man; whereas by making the white man and the doctor indispensable for the Negro as permanent social cripple and lifelong patient, medicalism aggravates and perpetuates the problem.

Malcolm understood and asserted—as few black or white men could understand or dared to assert—that white men want blacks to be on drugs, and that most black men who are on drugs want to be on them rather than off them. Freedom and self-determination are not only precious, but arduous. If people are not taught and nurtured to appreciate these values, they are likely to want to have nothing to do with them. Malcolm X and Edmund Burke shared a profound discernment of the painful truth that the state wants men to be weak and timid, not strong and proud. Indeed, perhaps the only thing Malcolm failed to see was that, by articulating his views as he did, he was in fact launching a religious war against greatly superior forces. I do not mean a religious war against Christianity. The religious war Malcolm launched was a war against the religion of Medicine—a faith other black leaders blindly worship. After all, blacks and whites alike now believe, as an article of faith, that drug abuse is an illness. That is why they demand and demonstrate for "free" detoxification programs and embrace methadone addiction as a cure for the heroin habit. Malcolm saw this, but I am not sure he grasped the enormity of it all. Or perhaps he did and that is why in the end, not long before he was killed, he rejected the Black Muslims as well—to whom, only a short while before, he gave all the credit for his resurrection from the gutter. He converted, one more time, to Orthodox Islam. Then he was murdered.

Do Drug Prohibitionists Protect Blacks?

Not surprisingly, drug prohibitionists systematically ignore the Black Muslim position on drugs. Neither bureaucratic drug criminalizers nor academic drug legalizers ever mention Malcolm X's name, much less cite his writings on drugs. The fact that Louis Farrakhan, the present leader of the Nation of Islam, continues to support Malcolm X's position on drugs does not help to make that position more acceptable to the white establishment.[41] In characteristically statist fashion, instead of seeing drug laws as racist, the drug prohibitionists see the absence of drug laws as racist. If "the legalizers prevail"—James Q. Wilson, a professor of management and public policy at UCLA, ominously predicts—

> then we will have consigned hundreds of thousands of infants and hundreds of neighborhoods to a life of oblivion and disease. To the lives and families destroyed by alcohol we will have added countless more destroyed by cocaine, heroin, PCP, and whatever else a basement scientist can invent. Human character is formed by society. . . . [G]ood character is less likely in a bad society.[42]

Virtually everything Wilson asserts here is false. Liberty is the choice to do right or wrong, to act prudently or imprudently, to protect oneself or injure oneself. Wilson is disingenuous in selecting alcohol and drugs as the "destroyers" of people. And as for his implying that our present prohibitionist mode of managing drugs has promoted the formation of "good character"—the less said, the better.

Wilson's argument brings us back full circle to the genocidal image of drugs, suggested here by a prominent white academic rather than a black priest-politician. As I observed before, this view casts the individual in a passive role, as victim. But if there are injured victims, there must be injuring victimizers. Wilson knows who they are: us. But he is wrong. Opportunity, choice, temptation do not constitute victimization. Wilson affronts the supporters of liberty by so categorizing them.

Finally, Wilson's explanation leaves no room for why some blacks succeed in not being consigned to what he revealingly calls "a life of oblivion and disease." Nor does Wilson consider the dark possibility that there might, especially for white Americans, be a fate worse than a few thousand blacks selling and using drugs. Suppose every black man, woman, and child in America rejected drugs, chose to emulate Malcolm X, and became a militant black separationist. Would that be better for American whites, or for the United States as a nation?

7

Doctors and Drugs: The Perils of Prohibition

Among the remedies which it has pleased the Almighty God to give to man to relieve his sufferings, none is so universal and so efficacious as opium.
—Thomas Sydenham, M.D. (1680)[1]

The undertreatment of pain in hospitals is absolutely medieval.
—Russell Portnoy, M.D., Pain Service, Sloan Kettering Memorial Hospital (1987)[2]

In the days before prescription laws, when lay people had the same access to drugs as doctors, there was no need for a person in pain to assume the patient role, find a physician, and obtain a prescription for an analgesic. He could simply go to a store and buy tincture of opium exactly as he now buys aspirin. Correspondingly, there was no need for the physician to assume the role of a medical expert whose duty is to ascertain whether the patient is telling the truth or lying, and decide whether he truly needs an analgesic drug, or merely wants one.

Why must lay persons and physicians now play these roles? Because the sale, possession, and use of potent analgesics without a prescription are illegal; and because the code of conduct of the medical profession and the laws of the United States mandate that physicians prescribe such drugs only to bona fide patients suffering from bona fide pain. These requirements make the issues of who counts as a bona fide patient, and what counts as bona fide pain, crucially important. For example, can the doctor be his own patient? Can the doctor's spouse or children be his patients? For the purpose of making a diagnosis, yes; for the purpose of prescribing a controlled substance, no.

Individuals who assume the patient role fraudulently and obtain prescription drugs under false pretenses—for example, by exaggerating or faking symptoms or signs of illness—are said to be guilty of prescription drug abuse; and doctors who dispense such drugs to persons who are not really their patients or who do not truly need the drugs are said to be guilty of abusing the prescription laws. The result is that regulations governing prescription writing have come to play a huge, and hugely distorting, role in determining what drugs physicians prescribe, what drugs patients obtain from their doctors, what drugs are sold over the counter, what drugs are advertised and to whom, and what drugs are traded on the black (drug) market.

Some personal recollections may be of interest in this connection. In the 1940s when I was a medical student, intern, and medical resident, cough syrup containing codeine was available over the counter, opiates were widely prescribed for pain, and barbiturates, bromides, and chloral hydrate were freely dispensed for insomnia. The terms *drug abuse*, *prescription drug abuse*, and *improper prescribing habits* had not yet entered our vocabulary. More than a decade later, in the late 1950s and early 1960s—as my daughters and I well remember—we would attend medical meetings in Atlantic City where, along with free Coca Cola and Campbell soups, tobacco companies handed out free samples of cigarettes by the carton, and pharmaceutical companies dispensed free samples of Darvon, Nembutal, and Seconal in bottles of one hundred—no prescription, no name, no questions asked. And the physician or his wife could come back again and again, stocking up to his or her heart's content.

THE PERILS OF DRUG PROHIBITION

One of the most tragic and publicly least understood side effects of the War on Drugs is that so many sick Americans suffering from painful illnesses are systematically deprived of adequate doses of painkilling drugs because of physicians' well-founded fears of prescribing so-called controlled substances. The reasons are obvious. The most effective analgesic drugs are opiates (morphine, heroin, dilaudid, and codeine) and methadone. The authors of the textbook of pharmacology used when I was a medical student stated, in italics: *"The opium alkaloids have no rival for the relief of pain"*; and to support this opinion, they added: "Sydenham . . . remarked that without opium few physicians would be sufficiently callous to practice therapeutics. [Sir William] Osler frequently referred to morphine as 'God's own medicine.' These statements serve to emphasize the *indispensable* nature of opium alkaloids, especially for the relief of pain."[3]

Practicing therapeutics without opiates, which Sydenham regarded as an unthinkable calamity for mankind, we now regard as the political and legal desideratum for good medical practice. Opiates are the most strictly controlled of our controlled substances. The Drug Enforcement Administration (DEA) watches doctors prescribing opiates like customs agents watch dark-complected travelers at Kennedy Airport.

Opiophobia or Fear of the Therapeutic State?

Physicians know they cannot prescribe for pain as they used to, as they would like to, or as their patients' welfare requires. But they have become so accustomed to state control of drugs that they never lay the blame for their loss of freedom to prescribe effective painkillers, or the patients' loss of access to such drugs, where it belongs: at the door of drug controls. On the contrary, they endorse drug controls (which, inter alia, make them the beneficiaries of a state-controlled drug monopoly), and then naively cast about for absurd explanations of the controls' inexorable consequences.

For example, C. Stratton Hill, Jr., director of the Pain Service in the Department of Neuro-oncology at the University of Texas in Houston, recognizes the problem but is reluctant to reach the conclusion to which his own experiences point. "As the tumor grows and spreads," he writes, "the pain becomes diffuse . . . and will require narcotic analgesics to control it. [Nevertheless, physicians] fail to use them properly in such cases." Why? Because "physicians have developed an 'opiophobia' that prevents prescribing opiates in adequate doses."[4]

It is sad enough that most physicians have never heard of Ludwig von Mises. It is sadder still that, having heard of Sigmund Freud, they mistake manufacturing psychiatric slang for making medical progress. "This phobia [of prescribing opiates]," declares Hill, "is like all others, not subject to rational correction." But Hill is wrong and he must know it. Physicians avoid prescribing opiates because of their perfectly rational fear of being apprehended by agents of the American drug-police state and punished by the courts for violating the drug laws.

What does Hill propose to remedy the situation? "Educational efforts . . . since it is unlikely that adequate doses of narcotics will be prescribed for patients until the phobia is dealt with." Like the patient's pain, the physician's license constricts his view of the world. Both are so preoccupied by their actual experiences that they have no energy or imagination left to look around and see themselves and their situation in a broader context and clearer light. In the end, Hill tranquilizes himself and his readers with pious platitudes and a patriotic denunciation of the medical miscreants: "Educational efforts must be directed to all segments of society. . . . Those who divert drugs from legitimate to illegitimate use—'script doctors'—are criminals and should be sought out and prosecuted."

But the vexing question remains, despite Hill's avoidance of it: Where is the line between legitimate and illegitimate pain, and hence between legitimate and illegitimate drug prescribing and drug use for pain? No one knows, and no one says. However, while the line between legitimate and illegitimate drug prescribing and drug use may be unclear, there is nothing unclear about what happens to people—doctors and patients alike—who cross it. They are shot down by the border guards—the physicians, as "script doctors"; the patients, as "drug abusers." Examples abound, especially among ambitious and conceited doctors who cater to VIP patients and who often become little more than pharmaceutical pimps procuring controlled substances for their prominent patrons. The physicians who prescribed for President Kennedy and for Elvis Presley played such a role and, after their patrons died, were prosecuted for it. More recently (in September 1990), three California physicians made the news when they were charged with "unprofessional conduct" for prescribing drugs to Elizabeth Taylor "in amounts that exceed a legitimate medical purpose."[5] Let *that* be a lesson to doctors prescribing painkillers.

Monitoring Prescription Writing

Today, the physician who prescribes a controlled analgesic or hypnotic drug (painkiller or sleeping pill) must carefully conform his prescribing behavior to the requirements of the law. It is not enough that he issue a controlled substance "in good faith." He must also "examine" his patient, and the patient must have an illness that justifies prescribing the controlled substance. Ironically, in the past, when the habitual use of barbiturates was not considered to be a disease, the physician who prescribed these drugs for regular use was not persecuted and punished; whereas today, when the habit is defined as a disease ("substance abuse"), the physician who prescribes controlled substances for such a person is persecuted and punished. This scenario has become so familiar that the fate of such medical miscreants now merits no more than a brief report as a "medicolegal decision," such as the following.

A physician in California treated a "back surgery patient for pain." The patient had twice been in a drug program and his mother had told the doctor that her son was abusing codeine and Doriden (gluthetimide, a controlled hypnotic). The physician prescribed one hundred tablets of Tylenol with codeine and fifty tablets of Doriden for the patient; the pharmacist reported the doctor to the State Bureau of Narcotic Enforcement; the bureau dispatched two undercover agents to entrap the doctor; the doctor treated both spies as if they were his patients and, without examining them, gave each a "single prescription for 30 Tylenol with codeine." The physician was arrested, tried, and "convicted on five counts of unlawful prescription of controlled substances."[6]

Some years ago, when doctors first began to be persecuted and punished for prescribing too many painkillers, there were occasional articles in medical journals about the plight of such hapless practitioners. A report in *Medical Economics* in 1984, entitled "Patients in Pain Can Put You in Jail"—about a California physician whom "a state panel found ... guilty of prescribing too many painkillers for his patients"—was a typical story.[7] Although the authorities concluded that "none of the violations were motivated by personal profit or gain," the doctor was "placed on probation for seven years, with severe restrictions on his prescribing privileges." His legal fees at the time the article was written stood at $130,000 and were still rising, since he was trying to appeal the verdict.

What did this doctor do wrong? According to *Medical Economics*, nothing. He was simply "caught in a head-on collision between two irreconcilable priorities—the nation's need to control drug abuse and the physician's humanitarian need to treat chronic-pain patients with compassion."[8] Pathetically, this physician tried to defend himself by accusing the state medical authorities of not having promulgated guidelines spelling out "precisely how much prescribing is too much, and under what circumstances." It did him no good. The rule of law—as scholars of liberty have long emphasized—is precious not because it guarantees good laws, but because it ensures that their application yields predictable results, permitting persons to plan their actions accordingly. It is precisely this feature that is absent in our drug laws, transforming doctors and patients alike into drug law violators.

The vile beauty of contemporary American anti-drug politics is that the authorities need no guidelines to recognize a drug malefactor. They know one when they see one. William W. Tucker, an internist and past president of the Sacramento–El Dorado Medical Society, said it well in this comment to *Medical Economics*: "As the situation now stands, there are no clear lines. It's like being stopped for speeding. When the driver asks the patrolman just what the speed limit is, he answers, 'I don't know, but you were over it.' "[9]

Although the analogy between the limit for drug prescribing and the speed limit is attractive, it fails in an important respect. The maximum speed for driving an automobile on a particular stretch of road can be precisely stated, and the speed with which a car travels can be objectively measured. But neither the severity of the patient's pain (which ostensibly legitimizes the prescribing) nor the nature and quantity of drugs he medically requires (which ostensibly legitimizes what the physician may prescribe for him) can be specified in the abstract.

These considerations lead us back to one of medicine's classic conundrums, namely, the distinction between legitimate and illegitimate pain, real and imaginary pain, physical and mental pain, organic and psychogenic pain, pain in medical patients and pain in psychiatric patients. Much can be, and has been, said on this interesting subject.[10] For our present purposes it is enough to emphasize that the distinction between these two kinds of pain may be entirely strategic; in other words, the distinction may not relate to anything *in* the patient at all, but may relate instead to what the physician treating the patient *says* and *does*. The latter phenomenon is exemplified by the fact that insurance companies pay for prescribed analgesics, but not for over-the-counter painkillers. If the physician prescribes ibuprofen for arthritis in 400-milligram or 600-milligram doses, the insurance company pays for it; but if he simply tells the patient to take it for pain, then the patient must get it in 200-milligram doses over the counter and pay for it himself.[11] Indeed, the notion that the reality of the patient's pain may be "validly" inferred not from examining the patient but rather from his doctor's response to him is officially affirmed by the Social Security system, whose agents ascertain whether a patient's pain is real and severe enough to qualify him for Social Security Disability Insurance payments by determining how his physician treats the pain: "Prescribed medication for pain is an indicator of the credibility of the client's complaints."[12]

Drug Controls vs. *Primum Non Nocere*

Nothing of what I have said so far is intended to imply that distinguishing between painful sensations that have their source in a bodily lesion from those that do not is unimportant. On the contrary. Making or failing to make that distinction correctly may mean the difference between the patient's life and death, between his receiving or not receiving the appropriate treatment for what ails him. My point is that we must scrutinize, in each particular instance, why a doctor or patient wants to know what kind of pain the patient experiences.

Typically, both doctor and patient try to make this distinction if the patient complains about his body and if both want to discover whether there is or is not something demonstrably wrong with the patient's body—which the physician may or may not be able to diagnose and remedy. Often, however, this is not what the patient wants his physician to do for him, nor is it what the physician would like to do for his patient. For example, a person may have pain whose nature is no longer in doubt because a correct diagnosis (say, of cancer of the prostate with metastases to the spinal column) has already been made on previous examinations. Or the person may feel pain, the doctor may be unable to determine its cause, and the patient may simply want relief from pain. In these and similar situations, the patient does not ask his physician to determine the anatomical source of the patient's pain. All he wants is relief from pain.

Faced with such a request, the doctor—like any moral agent—is free to accept it or reject it. Either choice is perfectly legitimate. What is morally illegitimate is the physician's allowing himself to be seduced by economic and political enticements into abandoning his role as healer and betraying his ethical obligation to the patient (*Primum non nocere!* First of all, do no harm!), and assuming instead the role of referee— arbitrating the conflict between the patient who wants a powerful analgesic and the state that wants to withhold it from him. (In psychiatry, the relationship is frequently reversed, inverting the conflict between healer and denominated sufferer: The state and its psychiatrist-agent want the patient to take the anti-psychotic drug, and the [involuntary] mental patient wants to reject it. It is a fundamental characteristic of the therapeutic state that, as a matter of medical principle and social policy, *it prevents sane adults from taking the drugs they want, and insane adults from rejecting the drugs they do not want.*)

The doctor who assumes this Solomonic role—and most practicing physicians do, the practical circumstances of their lives leaving them little other choice—victimizes his client qua patient, and compromises his own integrity as a healer. When I first addressed this dilemma almost forty years ago, the situation was not nearly so bad as it is today. The medical profession had not yet collectively thrown in the towel.[13] In a laudatory comment on my essay, the editor of the *Journal of the Iowa State Medical Society* wrote,

> As long as he [the physician] remains in his man's corner, he can be a true physician, able and willing to help him; but in the center of the ring, as the personification of the Rules of the Marquis of Queensberry, of the Selective Service System, or of whatever other authority is assumed to have jurisdiction, he is very nearly incapable of helping him at all.[14]

Even back then, the physician was pulled and pushed, with blandishments and threats, to abandon his traditional allegiance to his patient, stop his hopeless struggle to stem the onrushing tide of the alliance between medicine and the state, and become a double (or triple) agent—allegedly serving the patient, actually taking orders from the state, and still looking out mainly for himself. As more and more third parties entered into the previously (largely) private relationship between patient and doctor—ostensibly to protect the patient from economic and professional exploitation by the physician, but actually to enlist the physician as an agent of the state—the patient lost the most important means he possessed for controlling the medical situation: his clout over the physician's pocketbook.

Nevertheless, the illusion that the physician is primarily a doctor rather than a detective—an agent of the patient rather than of the state—lingers on. Indeed, how could it be shattered when we all depend on doctors to care for us when we are ill? Thus, even when reports in the popular press criticize the widespread practice of physicians undertreating pain, the doctors are never blamed for it. Either no one in particular is blamed for the suffering of the inadequately treated pain patient, or it is blamed on the scapegoat: drug abuse. I have never seen the physicians' fear to properly treat pain attributed directly to our drug laws. A report in *Newsweek* on cancer pain, misleadingly subtitled "Doctors Can Ease Suffering with Drugs," is illustrative.[15] Ironically, the story was not about how doctors *can* ease suffering with drugs, but about how they *fail to do so*. "The way we treat pain borders on a national disgrace," declared Dr. Charles Schuster, head of the National Institute of Drug Abuse. But the fact is that a hundred years ago doctors had no trouble controlling pain. Now they do. How does *Newsweek* explain this? By quoting the opinion of Dr. Mitchell Max, cancer-pain specialist at the National Institutes of Health, who offers this gem: "We treat infections, cut out tumors, set breaks in bones, but when it comes to pain, there's always the question of whether it's real or not.... All medicine is organized around what you can see."[16] There you have it. Doctors now undertreat pain because they cannot see it. Apparently they could see it better a hundred years ago. We are not told how or why doctors went pain-blind.

MEDICAL PRACTICE IN THE ANTI-NARCOTIC STATE

As I described in Chapter 2, we began to lose control of the pharmacopoeia in the early years of this century when certain drugs classified as prescription drugs were removed from the market, and dispensing them became a state monopoly controlled by physicians and pharmacists.

The penultimate transformation of medical practice from a privately entrepreneurial activity to a publicly bureaucratic one was brought about by the convergence of three critical economic and technological changes: (1) third-party payments for hospital and physicians' services and drugs; (2) new synthetic psychoactive drugs, such as Valium, replacing traditional "natural" drugs, such as opiates; and (3) computerized monitoring of doctors' prescription-writing habits and patients' prescription drug use. (I call this the "penultimate transformation" because we have not yet taken the ultimate step in this process: the formal nationalization of the country's health services.) In 1965, Medicare, Medicaid, and private third-party payers became prepotent participants in the doctor-patient relationship and assumed an appropriately decisive role in determining what drugs and other treatments were or were not necessary for the patient's proper medical care.

New anti-anxiety drugs and sleeping pills (such as Valium and Dalmane) offered ways of sedating patients without the use of the bad old "habit-forming" drugs (such as bromides and barbiturates). But before long, their use reopened the old medical-moral wound of "drug addiction," which was now regarded as more festering than ever. The abuse of recreational drugs thus became a medical as well as popular concern and led to the invention of the new disease "drug abuse," a term that subtly transformed self-medication into a genuine illness. Finally, the use of computers enabled bureaucrats to keep tabs on doctors and patients alike. This intrusion destroyed the last vestige of privacy in the medical arena and provided the evidence necessary to punish doctors and patients if they dispensed or consumed too many pleasure-producing drugs. Of course, before this glorious revolution could succeed, and before the guillotine decapitating our right to drugs could fall, the country had to be deluded into believing that the government was about to grant people lifelong protection from the threat of costly medical expenses, and that *it will cost them nothing*. It took people a while to realize—and most people still do not realize—that the "freedom" they gained is the freedom to be medical dependents whose therapeutic decisions are made for them by their parentified physicians acting as agents of the therapeutic state.

The Degradation of the Doctor-Patient Relationship

It should surprise no one that prescription laws have failed to fulfill their original purpose and promise of curing or curbing drug (ab)use. Instead, they have encouraged both patients and doctors to resort to indirect behaviors that help them achieve their goals. People who want prescription drugs have learned how to play the patient role and present the kinds of symptoms that will secure the needed medical document. When this (mis)behavior is detected, it is labeled "prescription drug abuse." Similarly, physicians who want to please and profit from serving important or indigent persons have learned how to write prescriptions that generate grateful VIPs or a large volume of medical visits billable to Medicaid. When this practice is detected, the physician is stigmatized as an "overprescriber" and punished as a "script doctor" running a "pill mill." Instead of remedying drug abuse, prescription drug laws have succeeded only in encouraging deception by patients and dishonesty by doctors, thus adding new dimensions to the drug problem.

The fact that our drug laws require people to secure a prescription for many of the drugs they want (but cannot get on the free market) fosters a mutually degrading dishonesty between physicians and patients, epitomized by the prescribing of sleeping pills. The law prohibits doctors from prescribing controlled substances to patients whom they have not examined. The result is a colossal charade—patients, doctors, insurance companies, and the government all pretending to believe that a person's telling his doctor that he cannot sleep and would like some sleeping pills may be a bona fide disease called "insomnia"; that doctors can diagnose this disease by distinguishing between patients who "medically" need, and patients who "merely" want, sleeping pills; and that prescribing sleeping pills is a bona fide medical treatment. The existential and economic importance of this charade—just one among many generated by drug prohibition combined with drug permission via prescriptions—cannot be overestimated. It is well established that "symptoms of insomnia are among the most common complaints in the doctors' office," and that hypnotic drugs are high on the list of best-selling drugs.[17] Accordingly, the cost saving from a free market in sleeping pills and painkillers alone would be immense.

Why is it is necessary that we all pretend that insomnia is a disease that only doctors can diagnose and treat? Because *wanting* a sleeping pill is not, but *needing* it is, a "proper medical indication" for prescribing it. How does a physician determine whether the patient suffers from the disease of insomnia and whether it is serious enough to require treatment? By examining him. But how can a doctor examine a person for insomnia in the middle of the day, in the doctor's office, when the patient is wide awake and is waiting impatiently to get out of the office and go about his business?

Mutatis mutandis, how can a physician prevent or treat drug abuse? By withholding controlled substances from patients he suspects of abusing drugs; and if the patient is already abusing drugs, by switching him to a different, supposedly non-habit-forming, drug. It does not matter that we have been through all this before—for example, when methadone was substituted for heroin, Dalmane for Seconal, and Valium for the older tranquilizers.[18] So now people abuse methadone and the benzodiazepines, which addicts and patients obtain legally from clinics and doctors, and nonpatients obtain illegally on the black market (supplied by resold or stolen prescription drugs).

All the while, a steady stream of new psychoactive drugs—like new Broadway plays—appear, get good reviews, then fall into disfavor and disappear. Who still remembers Miltown? The current stars on the hit parade of prescribed mind-altering drugs are lithium and Prozac, the latter already coming under attack for allegedly driving people to suicide. The catchy advertising slogan "Better living through chemistry" had clearly captured something basic in the modern American zeitgeist, namely, our seemingly limitless fear of *and* faith in drugs. The fear explains our timidity toward opiates; the faith, our belief that the habitual use of one narcotic (heroin) is a disease, which can be successfully treated with another narcotic (methadone). Grounded in pharmacomythology, not pharmacology, these fears and faiths cannot be dispelled by common sense or medical experience. Instead, we live according to the old adage *Credo quia absurdum est* (I believe it because it is absurd), which we find comforting because the credo lifts the burden of responsibility for our bad habits from our shoulders. Using one narcotic to cure the addict's taking another narcotic authenticates the doctors' expertise about habit-forming and habit-curing drugs, legitimizes them as pharmacological miracle workers, and makes them steadily more indispensable as the suppliers of *new* controlled substances. Rufus King was right—but no one listened to him—when he denounced the original Dole-Nyswander methadone program as having been "undertaken in tacit defiance of the federal Narcotics Bureau and local enforcement agencies in New York, but because of its eminent auspices [i.e., the Rockefeller University, and especially would-be U.S. president Nelson Rockefeller] it was not molested,"[19] and when he ridiculed and dismissed methadone treatment as "the final example of the cynicism and folly in the American drug saga."[20]

Prescribing old psychoactive drugs such as the barbiturates has thus become tantamount to medical malpractice, whereas prescribing new psychoactive drugs such as Prozac is viewed as the hallmark of practicing scientific medicine. The newer the drug the better, as the story of Prozac illustrates. Launched in 1988 by Eli Lilly and Company, Prozac was hailed for helping "to revolutionize the treatment of depression by stressing the biochemical nature of the disorder."[21] Sales for 1989 were approximately $600 million, up 65 percent from 1988. In 1992, sales of Prozac are expected to exceed $1 billion. I believe Prozac is so popular with patients and doctors alike not because it is therapeutically effective (what is the disease being treated?), but rather because most people like the way the drug makes them feel and because—it not being a controlled substance—doctors feel secure prescribing it. Moreover, the manufacturer is so eager to encourage the use of Prozac that it has done something unprecedented in the history of promoting so-called ethical (prescription) drugs: It has sent letters to physicians, promising to "defend, indemnify, and hold you harmless against claims, liabilities or expenses arising from personal injury alleged to have been caused by Prozac."[22]

Behind the mystifying pharmacomythology of contemporary mood-altering drugs lies a relatively simple situation. One class of these drugs consists of chemicals that people like to take because they make them feel better—for example, amphetamines and benzodiazapines. Another class consists of chemicals that people do not like to take because they make them feel worse—for example, Haldol and Thorazine (but which others, caring for troublesome persons, like to give them). Both classes of chemicals typically begin their medical careers as miracle drugs; those in the first class then become gradually transformed into drugs *abused by those who use them* (for example, Valium), whereas those in the second class become gradually transformed into drugs *abused by those who dispense them* (for example, Haldol).[23]

Intensifying the Drug Controls: The Triplicate Prescription Form

On January 1, 1989, a new law went into effect in New York State, requiring physicians prescribing benzodiazepines to use a triplicate prescription form, theretofore reserved for prescribing narcotics. Triplicate prescriptions can be written for no more than a month's supply of the drug and cannot be refilled. One copy of the form is for the physician's own records, another is for the pharmacist, and the third goes to the state bureaucracy monitoring the doctor's drug-prescribing and the patient's drug-using profiles. It would be difficult to imagine a more fitting emblem of the therapeutic criminalization of America. While in Eastern Europe and the Soviet Union people are revolting against the police monitoring their behavior, having at last recognized that state security is simply a pretext for the government's meddling in their lives, we supinely accept agents of the therapeutic state monitoring our drug-using behavior, refusing to recognize that it is simply a pretext for the government's meddling in our lives.

Why was this additional tightening of the prescription laws necessary? "Health officials say the controls are needed to identify physicians who prescribe the addictive drugs too liberally and to shut down 'pill mills' that sell prescriptions to addicts and teenagers."[24] As one might expect, the number of prescriptions physicians wrote for benzodiazepines fell precipitously, which the media idiotically interpreted as "success . . . in the effort to curb the misuse of tranquilizers."[25] Inasmuch as there are no criteria for what counts as drug misuse, the new law has succeeded only in withholding another class of drugs from the public.

Some of the specific consequences of New York State's new triplicate prescription law are worth detailing. The first and most fundamental consequence was that physicians became afraid to prescribe benzodiazepines. Two years after the law went into effect, only 27,000 of New York's 67,000 registered physicians obtained the necessary pads.[26] According to a report issued by the Medical Society of the State of New York, "Some physicians no longer prescribe benzodiazepines. . . . [Others] are referring patients . . . to an emergency room to obtain benzodiazepine prescriptions."[27]

Not surprisingly, in the first half of 1989, the number of benzodiazepine prescriptions written for the state's 1.2 million Medicaid recipients fell 55 percent compared to a year earlier. " 'We believe the regulation has been extremely effective in reducing [illegal street sales] and protecting patients from unnecessary drug dependence and injuries,' said John Eadie, director of public health protection for the State Health Department."[28] Note that Mr. Eadie's title is "director of public health protection." Who needs him, and why? Evidently, we in the State of New York need him, to protect us from physicians licensed by the State of New York to practice medicine. The ancient admonition *Quis custodiet ipsos custodes?* (Who shall guard the guardians?) has thus been given a new lease on life, creating jobs for the untold numbers of bureaucrats who are monitoring the prescribing habits of doctors, who monitor the drug habits of patients. In the meantime, old people in nursing homes are abused by the drug laws. According to the report by the Medical Society of the State of New York cited above, "In one study [of the consequences of the triplicate prescription law], 25 percent of nursing home residents taking benzodiazepines were switched to antipsychotic medications, which have more severe long-term adverse effects."[29]

The New York State Legislature's mania for drug monitoring is creating a steadily more lucrative black market in certain prescription drugs. For example, the street price of one Xanax pill rose from $1.50 in December 1988 (before the new triplicate prescription law went into effect) to $8 by mid–1989, while the price of a single Valium tablet rose from $2 to more than $6. "That's a measure of how we've been able to dry up the supply of these drugs on the street," Director of Public Health Protection Eadie explained. Other benefits of the triplicate prescription law have been the divestiture of one doctor's privilege to prescribe controlled substances, and the launching of more than three hundred criminal and civil investigations. Arthur Levin, director of the Center for Medical Consumers in New York City, concludes, "It shows that when doctors are being looked at, they behave somewhat differently."[30] So do the farmers "looked at" by Soviet bureaucrats. Thus is depriving people of what they want elevated by the communist state to a political virtue, and by the therapeutic state to a medical virtue.

Today the drug-scapegoating craze touches the lives of nearly every man, woman, and child in the United States. The initial targets of persecution were the foreign profiteers and domestic deviants—South American drug lords and intravenous drug abusers. Then, in quick succession, followed doctors, drug manufacturers, prescription drug abusers, smokers, and advertisers. "Drug companies and doctors," writes Congressman Pete Stark, Democrat of California, "present the biggest obstacle to prescription drug reform."[31] What does Stark mean by prescription drug reform? Saving hundreds of millions of dollars spent annually on Medicaid payments for controlled substances such as Valium and Xanax. Noting that, in the nine states that require multiple-copy prescription forms, prescriptions for controlled drugs fell 35–50 percent after such extra monitoring was instituted, Stark concludes that his "plan could save hundreds of millions a year." If Congressman Stark really wanted to save the taxpayer's money, he could do so more easily and effectively by restoring the free market in drugs. But, clearly, this is not his aim. Like every politician, Stark knows that you render people servile by making them dependent on the state. And you make them dependent on the state by depriving them of what they want and could—were it not for state interference—provide for themselves.

The Problem of the "Drug Abuse Problem"

The attention we give to the War on Drugs makes it appear as if we Americans were especially disposed to "abusing" drugs. Thus, protesting the FDA's plan to reclassify some prescription drugs as over-the-counter drugs, Dr. James Todd, executive vice-president of the American Medical Association, complains that "Americans are already the most over-self-medicated population."[32] Todd's assertion exemplifies the confused equation of self-medication with drug abuse, and the mindless assumption that self-medication is, a priori, undesirable. (As I noted in Chapter 2, some courageous and far-seeing persons predicted, back in the 1930s when Roosevelt undertook to destroy the free market in drugs, that self-medication would become a crime.) The same idea is voiced by Herbert D. Kleber, professor of psychiatry at Yale and one of the country's leading substance abuse experts, who states approvingly, "Medically, abuse is often defined as nonmedical use."[33] Todd's and Kleber's ideas are reminiscent of the now passé notion that self-abuse (that is, masturbation) is a disease. I submit that we ought to count knowledge-able and responsible self-medication as a moral and social good, not as a medical disease or moral evil. As for the claim that Americans are more over-self-medicated than other people, there is (as I observed ear-lier) not a shred of solid evidence for it, and much impressionistic evi-dence against it. Suffice it to add that alcohol has long been a popular drink in many parts of the world. Irishmen, Frenchmen, and Russians—to mention but a few nationalities—have been as fond of drink as Amer-icans, but only the American people saw fit to deputize their elected representatives to prohibit their favorite beverage. With the War on Drugs, we are witnessing a similar phenomenon, mistaking our ten-dency toward law intoxication with a tendency toward drug intoxication.

As anyone who travels abroad can observe, the use of nicotine—still called "smoking" by medically uncivilized people—is much more com-mon in Europe and Asia than in the United States. And so is the use of a variety of quack medicines in which we have no interest. In fact, we are less disposed to the nonmedical use of drugs than people in many other countries, but, as I noted, we *call* virtually all such drug use "drug abuse" and hence remain blissfully unaware of the fact that the maniacal pursuit of "good drugs" (which we expect to cure every disease on earth) and the maniacal persecution of "bad drugs" (to which we attribute a galaxy of human miseries) are not the manifestations of med-ical-scientific enlightenment, but are rather peculiarly American social phenomena.

WHEN NARCOTICS ARE OUTLAWED . . .

Like physicians, pharmacists too have good reasons to fear the drug laws. If they sell too many controlled substances —"too many" being undefined for them also—they are likely to be persecuted and punished by the government, especially if their clients are poor and the govern-ment pays for the drugs. In a typical raid on a pharmacy in Harlem, New York Congressman Charles B. Rangel led a group of reporters to two clinics to confront the pharmacists: " 'All you're involved in is le-galized drug pushing,' Mr. Rangel said to a pharmacist at Nino Drugs at 77–99 East 115th Street. 'This place makes more money off Medicaid than any other pharmacy its size in the city.' "[34]

Besides giving a good deal of space to Rangel's views on the profit motive, the gist of the report was that twenty-five physicians and twenty drugstores were "ousted from Medicaid" for what was considered to be an abuse of the system. The system is, of course, an invitation to abuse, and to being caught for it as well. One physician in Harlem—admiringly dubbed "the Dwight Gooden of Medicaid billers"—ordered nearly $4 million in prescriptions and services in a single twelve-month period, most of the drugs being "immediately sold back to black-market suppliers."[35] The pharmacists at least had an excuse, but it probably did them no good: "I am not doing anything illegal," said Saleem Rashid, a part-owner of RQS Pharmacy. "I am just filling their [the patients'] prescriptions."[36]

As if the threat of drug agents were not enough to instill fear into pharmacists, they also face the threat of addicts and criminals looking for narcotics to steal. These problems have led to a little-recognized medical advance: pharmacies without narcotics. "Even when doctors do prescribe narcotics," reports *Newsweek*, "their patients may find it amazingly hard to get the prescription filled."[37] A survey of twelve hundred drugstores around the country revealed that only half could supply morphine tablets. In New York City, the main reason pharmacists gave for not stocking the drug was fear of robbery; elsewhere, it was the lack of demand, "because physicians weren't prescribing narcotics."

A New Medical Specialty: Withholding Narcotics

How has the medical profession responded to the escalating restrictiveness of drug controls, especially with respect to narcotics? By creating special "pain clinics" and "pain services," staffed with physicians who specialize in the (non)treatment of pain. Perversely, these drug-denying doctors love to talk about the mistreatment they impose on their own patients, for which they invariably blame others. For example, Michael H. Levy, M.D., director of the Palliative Care Service at the Fox Chase Cancer Center in Philadelphia, complains, "There is still a good deal of resistance among physicians when it comes to pain control. That resistance comes out of lack of education."[38] Just the contrary. Physicians do not lack education about pain control. Instead, they have learned to withhold opioid analgesics even from dying patients because they are being taught that giving such painkillers in ample doses turns patients into "drug addicts" and exposes doctors to the risk of criticism or worse for abusing their prescription-writing privileges. When doctors run no risk for underprescribing painkillers but run a considerable and yet unpredictable risk for overprescribing them, what else can we expect but that patients will be systematically deprived of adequate pain relief?

The anti-narcotic zeal of the therapeutic state, which demands that even terminal patients suffering agonizing pain be denied adequate relief, pervades the entire medical scene. "Nurses," reports the *New York Times*, "are surprisingly stingy about dispensing pain killing drugs."[39] A study of nurses' drug-dispensing behavior revealed that "the doses of analgesics given the patients were one-fourth the amount permitted [prescribed] by the physician."

At the same time, doctors specializing in "cancer pain relief" reveal that physicians do not prescribe adequate doses of analgesics, driving some patients to suicide. In a group of two hundred patients treated in the pain clinic at the Memorial Sloan-Kettering Cancer Center in New York, "16 percent reported suicidal thoughts and impulses."[40] Mirabile dictu, the pain researchers have discovered "that ineffective treatment of pain is a major reason that cancer patients become depressed and suicidal." But what is a pain clinic for if not for the *in*effective treatment of pain? More often than not, the effective treatment of pain requires neither clinics nor doctors, but only a free market in drugs. However, such pharmaceutical freedom would make our highly paid pain researchers and pain clinicians unnecessary and unemployed. Clinging to their privileges, the experts pretentiously conclude, "Often, treating the underlying pain . . . may eliminate a person's wish to die."[41] What medical madness! First, doctors plead for the prohibition of opiates, to prevent people from using the drugs to kill themselves; then, doctors discover that people kill themselves because they have been deprived of opiates, and plead for letting the patients have more opiates.

The mind-numbingly banal conclusion of Charles S. Cleeland, chairman of the U.S. Cancer Pain Relief Committee, illustrates the intellectual bankruptcy of the pain specialists: "Millions of cancer patients [who] have pain . . . could be treated effectively if more narcotics were available and administered."[42] But narcotics are available, ad libitum, in the streets. Only in medical settings—in hospitals and doctors' offices—is the availability of narcotics so restricted that patients are harmed as a result. The gun lobby has long warned, "When guns are outlawed, only outlaws will have guns." We have outlawed narcotics, and now only outlaws have narcotics.

Physicians must, of course, bear a good deal of the blame for not having done more to stem the tide of the anti-narcotic restrictions imposed on them by the therapeutic state. Instead, they have endorsed drug controls and exploited them for their own selfish benefit—for example, by chairing and participating in various national and international drug commissions which, by the way, have conferences in elegant hotels in interesting cities. The experts did not really care what anti-libertarian policies these bureaucratic-medical commissions endorsed, so long as the patients remained dependent on the medical profession. Thus, for decades, international narcotic commissions composed of physicians labored to restrict both the medical and nonmedical uses of opiates. Now (in May 1990), acting as if this had never happened, *American Medical News* approvingly reports that "the International Narcotics Control Board has joined the World Health Organization in endorsing expanded use of narcotic drugs for treating cancer pain."[43]

The mind boggles. We spend more money on medical care than any other people in the world. And what is the result? That we live in a society in which people who, according to doctors, should have no access to narcotics seemingly have unlimited (illegal) access to them, while people who, according to doctors, have the most urgent need for narcotics have little or no access to them. Who is at fault? No one. Everyone is a victim, including the physicians, who are concerned that they will lose their licenses or be prosecuted if they prescribe narcotics "in the amounts necessary to treat chronic severe cancer pain."[44]

Sydenham, as I noted at the beginning of this chapter, attributed the miraculous powers of opium to relieve pain and suffering to the Almighty God. What God has given, the therapeutic state has taken away.

8

Between Dread and Desire: The Burden of Choice

In wise hands, poison is medicine; in foolish hands, medicine is poison.

—Casanova[1]

Better remembered for his erotic than for his medical expertise, Casanova offered this sagacious observation more than two hundred years ago. It could serve equally well as an epitaph for the free market in drugs, or as a promotional slogan for it.

THE TWIN TEMPTATIONS: DRUGS AND DRUG LAWS

The War on Drugs has had many undesirable consequences, not least among them the mass production of experts on drug abuse. As befits their role, these savants have written millions of words about "drugs," but the word *temptation* is not among them. Joining the current drug debate on the terms chosen by those in control of its accredited vocabulary thus requires that one be ignorant of history—especially religious history. I say this because so much of what we think of as the formation of personal character and human destiny—from the Old Testament Fall to the present moment—may be seen as the chronicle of temptation and the struggle against yielding to it. Aphoristic examples abound. "Was not Abraham found faithful in temptation?" the writers of the Apocrypha ask rhetorically, only to answer further on that "it was imputed unto him for righteousness."[2] The New Testament teaches this once familiar anti-temptation slogan: "Blessed is the man that endureth temptation";[3] and in the Lord's Prayer, the supplicant pleads, "And lead us not into temptation, but deliver us from evil."[4] (A bumper-sticker humorist has changed this to read: "Lead me not into temptation. I can find it myself.") Ralph Waldo Emerson sounds a modern, psychological note: "We gain the strength of the temptation we resist."[5]

The temptations that people always found, and probably always will find, hardest to resist are sex, money, and power. Drugs and food belong on this list, of course, but rank nowhere near the top. Nevertheless, our "drug problem" could profitably be viewed in terms of a struggle against temptation, which is precisely the way most Americans in the nineteenth century viewed it.[6] Mark Twain was much amused by this spectacle and offered many wise and witty recommendations on the subject. "There are," he characteristically remarked, "several good protections against temptations, but the surest is cowardice."[7] In a more serious mood, he mockingly pondered, "There are people who strictly deprive themselves of each and every eatable, drinkable and smokable which has in any way acquired a shady reputation. They pay this price for health. And health is all they get. How strange it is!"[8] Mark Twain did not live long enough to see something even stranger, namely, the American government's resorting to the use of naked force to impose this idea on people, at home and abroad. Thus, he never saw his fellow Americans electing and deputizing their representatives in Congress to deprive them of satisfying desires from which they could perfectly well have deprived themselves, if that is what they had really wanted to do. But note that the Volstead Act, which prohibited nearly everything connected with alcohol, *did not prohibit drinking it*. I interpret this paradox as one of the earliest symptoms of America's loss of faith in free will.

Unfree Will, Unfree Market

In contemporary political discourse, the issue of free will is raised only to assert its absence and, hence, the unsuitability of market relations in economic life in general, but especially where emotionally charged goods and services such as drugs and health care are at stake. Indeed, what is the point of giving people choices if we are convinced that they are unable to make the "right" choices because they are too young, too old, mentally ill, or otherwise incompetent?

In the War on Drugs in particular, whence do we draw our image of (un)free will? Sad to say, we draw it from and base it on the image of the enfeebled will of the stereotypical inner-city "kid" who is deprived of parenting, of education, and of hope, and is faced with the lure of using and trading in a powerful pleasure-producing drug—typically, "crack." The fact that drug warriors are so fond of resting their arguments on this image of abused children succumbing to temptation shows that they play with loaded dice: This caricature is offered to justify prohibiting the sale of drugs to *competent adults!* Needless to say, the fact that a drug is for sale (legally or illegally) does not mean that anyone has to buy it or use it. I reemphasize this truism because overlooking or denying it lays the foundations for the fallacious concept of drug (ab)use as an illness amenable to treatment. When even so staunch a defender of the free market as Milton Friedman regards treatment as the proper response to the drug problem, how can we expect ordinary people to resist this deadly delusion?

Friedman begins his "Open Letter to [Former Drug Czar] Bill Bennett" with a fatal concession. "The drug war," Friedman pleads, "cannot be won by those [Bennett's] tactics without undermining the human liberty and individual freedom that you and I cherish."[9] Because Bennett is nothing if not intelligent, we ought to assume that he realizes just as clearly as Friedman that his drug policies are destructive of dignity, liberty, and responsibility. Accordingly, we ought to assume that Bennett knowingly accepts this cost because, unlike Friedman, he believes that it is more important that America be drug free than that it be politically free. It is disingenuous to appeal to "treatment" as offering us, friend and foe of freedom alike, a common ground on which to meet. Thus, it is no use to say, as does Friedman in concluding his plea, "Moreover, if even a small fraction of the money we now spend on trying to enforce drug prohibition were devoted to treatment and rehabilitation, in an atmosphere of compassion not punishment, the reduction in drug usage and in the harm done to the users could be dramatic."[10] This is tantamount to giving away the game. Endorsing the expenditure of government funds for fictitious treatments of nonexistent diseases is prescribing more of the same poison: statism and therapeutism. (Friedman's endorsement of government-funded drug treatment programs is inconsistent with his support of the libertarian critique of medical licensure. Without state-sanctioned doctors, there could be no state-sanctioned "diagnoses" of "substance abuse" and no state-funded "treatments" for it. See Chapter 1.)

The therapeutic state is a totalitarian state—all the more so for masking its tyranny as therapy. Ironically, at the beginning of the twentieth century, educated people everywhere thought that ours was going to be a new golden age of scientific progress and personal freedom. Who would then have thought that ours was going to be the age that affirms the reality and near-universality of mental illness, denies free will and responsibility, and celebrates the abrogation of contract? Who would then have anticipated that half of the world's population would end up living in totalitarian states dedicated to protecting people from their anti-social desire for *private economic profit*? And that the other half would end up living in therapeutic states dedicated to protecting people from their anti-medical desire for *private pharmacological pleasure*? The Soviet Union—the model socialist state—became the incarnation of the principle that private property is evil and thus the desire for economic self-determination is inimical to the health of the body politic. The United States—the model therapeutic state—became the incarnation of the principle that self-medication is evil and thus the desire for pharmacological self-determination is inimical to the health of the body. Both the Soviet Union and the United States thus became persecutory states—one determined to find and punish people dealing in real money, epitomized by traffickers in hard currencies; the other determined to find and punish people dealing in pleasure-producing chemicals, epitomized by traffickers in hard drugs. And so, step by step, generation after generation, habits of law engendered habits of mind, and vice versa, until in the Soviet Union the idea of a free market in land and houses became unthinkable, and in the United States the idea of a free market in drugs became unthinkable.

Teaching America the Wrong Drug Lesson

Using any drug for any purpose entails risks. The same goes for drug laws. However, this is not the way we now perceive the drug problem. Instead, we see drugs as the problem, and drug controls as the solution. To maintain this distorted image, we exaggerate and even falsify the dangerousness of prohibited drugs, while we minimize and even deny the dangerousness of drug prohibitions. It is not surprising, then, that most people consider proposals even for limited drug "legalization"—much less for a genuine free market in drugs—to be unwise and impractical. Their "conservatism" with respect to drugs rests on having stopped questioning the following propositions and policies:

1. The use of illicit drugs is not only a crime, but also a disease.
2. Illicit drugs cause both crime and illness.
3. It is morally praiseworthy to attribute drug use to mental illness, peer pressure, parental neglect, poverty, social injustice, drug pushers, the addictive properties of drugs—to anything but the drug user's free will.
4. It is legally just to punish persons who trade in (prohibited) drugs, because they sell a harmful product; and to forcibly treat drug (ab)users, because they are sick (but deny it and refuse to be treated).

Although these explanations are plainly false, their scientific validity is authenticated by the medical profession; and although these explanations are patent evasions of personal choice and responsibility, their moral legitimacy is authenticated by the courts. For example, a brewery worker becomes fond of beer, is dismissed as a drunkard, develops cirrhosis of the liver, and dies when his hospital bed catches fire as a result of his smoking. Whose fault is his drinking and dying? His employer's. In a suit brought by the worker's widow against the brewery, the Michigan Court of Appeals ruled that "alcoholism is like any disease" and that the "circumstances of the job shaped the course of [this man's] disease . . . thus constituting a personal injury."[11] Such habits of mind and law preclude (at least for the time being) a serious examination of our so-called drug problem, much less a radical reorientation of our social policies vis-à-vis prohibited drugs.

As I have tried to show, of all the dangers that drugs pose, only one requires state intervention, namely, mislabeling. All the others can be effectively controlled by individuals assuming responsibility for their own behavior. Admittedly, in our contemporary American society, it is chimerical to expect people to assume responsibility for informing themselves about drugs and for adhering to the principle of caveat emptor. But this is because, with respect to drugs, the American government has consistently encouraged the public to conduct itself according to the maxim *Caveat emptor non necesse* (The buyer need not beware). Why not? Because the government will protect him. Can such paternalism on the part of the rulers lead to anything but infantilism on the part of the ruled?

Although the prohibitionist stubbornly denies it, drug controls foster precisely those moral values and personal behaviors that we mistakenly attribute to drugs. It is not drugs but drug prohibitions that lead to drug use that is uninformed, irresponsible, self-indulgent, and personally and socially self-destructive. If we were true to our political heritage, our aim would be not a "drug-free America," but an "America free of drug laws."

Why Do We Reject Responsibility for Drug Use?

The War on Drugs is a moral crusade and hence must be squarely met on moral grounds. The only morally coherent (and, in the United States, probably the only practical) alternative to drug prohibition is its repeal. The dearth of supporters for this option raises an obvious question: Why are we so afraid of a free market in drugs? For many reasons, the two most obvious ones being that people believe and fear that, if drugs were freely available, more people would choose an easy life of parasitism over a hard life of productivity, and more people would become "drug crazed" and thus commit criminal acts. Suffice it to say here that the problem of economic productivity—crucial for the prosperity and very survival of every society—has nothing to do with drugs but has everything to do with family stability, cultural values, education, and social policies. The second fear is equally misplaced. The "drug-crazed" criminal is a figure of psychiatric fiction. The idea this image engenders is not just incorrect; it is inverted: Drugs are not an inducement to crime; prohibiting drugs is. Instead of these displaced concerns, I want to examine a reason for our fear of the free market in drugs that we systematically ignore, but that I believe inclines us powerfully toward drug prohibition. Unlike the two fears just mentioned, this fear entails a very real connection between certain drugs and a form of behavior long prohibited by religious, legal, and psychiatric codes of conduct, namely, suicide. Although free-market access to drugs would not necessarily make it easier for people to become parasites or criminals, it would make it easier for them to commit suicide.

THE ULTIMATE CHOICE: SUICIDE

We have launched ourselves on a self-contradictory quest for a veritable medical dystopia, that is, for an America free of drug abuse because doctors effectively control drug use, and where everyone dies a painless and pleasant death because benevolent doctors kill "dying" people who want to be killed. My point is that—having combined a dread of dying a protracted, pointless, and perhaps painful death with a fear of living with a free market in drugs—we have negated our chances for attaining pharmacological autonomy, that is, freedom vis-à-vis drugs similar to the freedom we enjoy vis-à-vis food or religion.

Deprived of drugs useful for committing suicide, we nevertheless continue to cling to the hope of receiving the drugs we need to die a painless death when we are terminally ill. The result is that we now seriously entertain the preposterous idea of giving doctors and judges the right to kill us. In view of our faulty premises, the appalling conclusion that "medical euthanasia" is preferable to a free market in drugs is quite logical: We abhor and reject the idea of granting adults legally unrestricted access to drugs suitable for suicide; we view the desire to die as a symptom of mental illness; we interpret virtually all suicide as a tragedy that ought to have been prevented; and we forget that euthanasia, mercifully administered by "ethical" doctors, is a particularly sinister gift totalitarian governments have bestowed on modern man. In short, I believe that one of the main reasons we reject a free market in drugs is because we fear having an unfettered opportunity to kill ourselves (which a free market in drugs necessarily entails) and expect a grand alliance between medicine and the state to solve our existential tasks of living and dying for us.[12]

Drugs, Suicide, and the Right to Die

Because we enjoy a free market in food, we can buy all the bacon, eggs, and ice cream we want and can afford. If we had a free market in drugs, we could similarly buy all the chloral hydrate, heroin, and Seconal we wanted and could afford. We would then be free to die easily, comfortably, and surely—without any need for recourse to violent means of suicide or fear of being involuntarily kept alive "dying" in a hospital. We would then no longer have to complain about doctors, nurses, relatives, hospitals, nursing homes, lawyers, and insurance companies mistreating us, overtreating us, undertreating us, withholding pain medications from us, keeping us alive, and depriving us of our right to die.[13]

How did the idea of a "right to die" arise? What does the phrase mean? How can the inevitable biological destiny of all living beings be a right? Actually, the phrase refers primarily to our confused rejection of the spectacle of doctors keeping moribund persons alive with the aid of modern biotechnological machinery. Why do physicians do this? Because medical ethics ostensibly demands it; because they enjoy the powers science and the state have put in their hands; because they often have both professional and economic incentives for it; because they assume this is what the patient would want, could he express his wishes; because courts or kin command them to do "everything possible" to keep the patient alive; and lastly, because withholding life-sustaining measures could be regarded as deliberately killing the patient.

For many of us today, the term *sanctity of life* has lost virtually all meaning. No longer truly religious but not yet free of superstition masquerading as God-given rules for living, we cannot cope with the prospect of what seems a pointless prolongation of living or, rather, dying. At the same time, we cling to life—up to a point. After that, we want to be "allowed" to die—an imagery that falsely implies we are inescapably bound to persons determined to prevent us from dying. To deny them that role, we have complemented the proposition that we have a "right to life" (which has become the code phrase of the anti-abortion movement), with the seemingly contrary proposition that we have a "right to die."

However, the similarity between these two semantically reciprocal rights is illusory. Each addresses a completely different set of existential choices and ethical perplexities: The phrase *right to life* refers to our options regarding the ("natural" or spontaneous) beginning of life; the phrase *right to die* refers to our options regarding the ("unnatural" or artificially induced) ending of it. The right in the "right to life" thus belongs to the fetus, at risk of being aborted; whereas the right in the "right to die" (usually) belongs to persons other than the dying human being.

If a person executes a "living will" in which he requests the withholding of certain life-sustaining measures, then he is exercising his right to die or, more precisely, his right to reject certain medical interventions. A living will gives a person a chance or right to make certain decisions about his health or terminal care when he can no longer do so, just as a last will gives him such a right about his property. A living will may be a request for or against extraordinary measures of life preservation. Similarly, a terminal patient may or may not want to die. Attributing a right to die to him implies that those who keep him alive are injuring him by depriving him of a right.

However, if he does not execute a living will, then it seems to me that the phrase *right to die* identifies a "right" that does not belong to the dying person himself. Even the most ardent supporters of this fictitious right acknowledge that its designated beneficiary is usually past suffering and hence cannot, in good conscience, be said to have an urgent need of any right (except perhaps of the right not to be killed). The phrase thus refers, in a hypocritically distorted language, to the survivors' interest in bringing the moribund person's life to an end. I am not implying that this interest is, a priori, morally wrong. I am merely trying to clarify our use of the term *right to die*, and to suggest that, used approvingly (as it often is), it is a modern code term that expresses the speaker's endorsement of authorizing the state to grant doctors the "right to kill" (certain persons), of defining such an intervention as a "medical service," and of labeling it euphemistically as "aid in dying."[14]

It is not within the scope of the discussion here to analyze further this important issue. Let me add only that a great deal of the money we spend on what we call "health care" is in fact spent on extending life by a few months, weeks, or days, and that it is within the means of most people most of the time (accident victims forming the main exception) to take appropriate action to prevent their dying in a hospital, hooked to machines, deprived of their right to die.

The Right to Drugs vs. the Right to Euthanasia

In matters so heavily freighted with moral significance, the language we use is all-important. In 1990 a group calling itself Washington Citizens for Death with Dignity introduced an initiative in that state's legislature, phrased as follows: "Should adult patients who are in a medically terminal condition be permitted to request and receive from a physician aid-in-dying?" Recognizing the semantic trap thus laid, the Washington State Catholic Conference challenged the wording, but was unable to change "aid-in-dying" to "physician-caused death."[15]

The phrase *right to die* is thus emblematic not only of our skittishness about suicide and our longing for good doctors to kill us at just the right time and in just the right way, but—more fundamentally—of our repudiation of bodily self-ownership and the responsibilities that go with it. It remains to be seen how many Americans prefer legalizing doctors to kill them, over legalizing themselves to own drugs and shouldering the responsibilities that the ownership of such a valuable property entails.

So long as the phrase *right to die* does not include an unqualified *right to suicide*—a subject its supporters never mention—it is destined to be nothing more or less than just another step in the medicalization of life and in our headlong rush into the deadly embrace of the therapeutic state. On the other hand, if the phrase is intended to encompass the right to suicide, then—lest it be an empty slogan—the "right to die" must include the "right to drugs." We know, however, that most people (especially in the United States) consider the desire to commit suicide—much less the act itself—not a right, but a symptom of preventable and treatable mental illness. As against this view, I hold that the option to commit suicide is inherent in the human condition, that committing suicide ought to be considered a basic human right and may sometimes be a moral duty, and that the expectation or threat of suicide never justifies the coercive control of the (allegedly) suicidal person. At the same time, I consider it a basic moral wrong for a physician, *qua physician*, to kill a patient or anyone else and call it "euthanasia."[16] This does not mean that "pulling the plug" on a dying patient is (necessarily) an immoral act; it means only that doing so does not (necessarily) require medical expertise, should not be defined as a medical intervention, and should not be delegated (specifically) to physicians. I maintain that our longing for doctors to give us lethal drugs betokens our desire to evade responsibility for giving such drugs to ourselves, and that so long as we are more interested in investing doctors with the right to kill than in reclaiming our own right to drugs, our discourse about rights and drugs is destined to remain empty, meaningless chatter.

Of course, a people cannot expect to regain their right to acts and objects unless they are willing and prepared to assume responsibility for the conduct of the acts and the care of the objects in question. This principle applies now to the Soviet people with respect to the tools of free trade, and applies to us with respect to drugs. Specifically, since the most important practical consequence of our loss of the right to bodily self-ownership is the denial of legally unrestricted access to drugs, the most important symbol of the right to our bodies now resides in our reasserting our right to drugs—to all drugs, not just to one or another so-called recreational drug. At this point, we come face-to-face with our real drug problem, namely, that most Americans today do not want to have legally unrestricted access to drugs. On the contrary, they dread the idea and the prospect it portends. Indeed, the American people do not view access to drugs as a right, just as the Soviet people do not view "speculating" in currencies as a right. Illustrative of the persistence of this deeply ingrained anti-capitalist impulse was the Soviet government's decision, in February 1991 to confiscate all fifty- and hundred-ruble notes. The actual purpose of this scheme was to destroy the people's savings, for which there were no legally available goods to buy. However, then Prime Minister Valentin Pavlov justified the measure on the ground that it was a necessary "tool to combat illegal currency speculation and drug dealers."[17]

CORN LAWS AND DRUG LAWS

The first law of political dynamics is that the ruler's basic aim is always the same, namely, to deprive the ruled of liberty. The only thing that varies from time to time is the justification for the deprivation, namely, whether it is religious, political, economic, or medical. Thus, *protectionism* always plays a prepotent role in the government's regulating the affairs of men. This principle is illustrated by the similarities between the English Corn Laws and the American drug laws—two seemingly different systems of protection, each of which came into being, was motivated by, and achieved widespread popular support because each was regarded as indispensable for the safety, welfare, and preservation of the society that adopted it; and, over long periods of time, each of which was viewed as a necessary exception to the ideals and rules of the free market.

The English Corn Laws, c. 1100–1846

The Corn Laws provide us with an astonishingly relevant historical antecedent to the War on Drugs. Before the nineteenth century, England was still primarily an agricultural society, the people's survival depending mainly on grains (and, after the seveteenth century, also on potatoes). From the twelfth century onward, local governments and the king's council had the right to prohibit exports of grain during periods of failing harvests. After the sixteenth century, as methods of agriculture and transportation advanced, agricultural surpluses in one country became a threat to domestic producers of the same product in another country. Tariffs on imported grains were established to protect the interests of farmers and the land-owning classes. Since that time, the term *Corn Laws* became synonymous with regulations governing the import of grain into England, the term *corn* being used generically for grain.[18] Although the so-called Corn Laws were abolished in 1846—ushering in an era of unprecedented economic liberty and prosperity in Great Britain—and despite the popular Western rhetoric about "free trade" and "free markets," similar restrictions continue to govern international trade in many agricultural (and other) commodities.[19] Indeed, a free international market in food is an economic fiction similar to the physicist's ideal gas. Real markets and real gases do not behave like these models, which nevertheless are important—in physics, as scientific concepts; in commerce, as economic principles; and in politics, as libertarian ideals.

Of particular relevance to our understanding of our drug laws is the fact that, by the eighteenth century, the Corn Laws were so firmly established in England that even a free-market prophet such as Adam Smith believed it was altogether impossible to abolish them. He wrote,

> [The 1773 Corn Law,] though not the best in itself . . . is the best
> which the interests, prejudices and temper of the time would
> admit of. . . . The laws concerning corn may everywhere be com-
> pared to the laws concerning religion. The people feel them-
> selves so much interested in what relates either to their
> subsistence in this life, or their happiness in a life to come, that
> government must yield to their prejudices, and in order to pre-
> serve public tranquillity, establish that system of which they
> approve of. It is upon this account, perhaps, that we so seldom
> find a reasonable system established with regard to either of
> those two capital objects.[20]

Smith's seemingly casual comparison of the Corn Laws with religious laws was prescient, anticipating the Founding Fathers' insight into the necessity of separating church and state. Such a separation had never existed before, and still does not exist in so pure a form anywhere else. At the same time, Smith predicted that state support of religion (by any other name, such as health and drugs today) leads inexorably to an "unreasonable" system of regulations, such as the Corn Laws (or the War on Drugs).

As the nineteenth century dawned over England, that nation's position as the world's leading economic, intellectual, and military power was securely established. Conscientious observers of society began to recognize that, while the Corn Laws helped the superior classes (the farmers and landed aristocracy), they harmed the inferior classes—those most in need of protection from economic hardship. While the producers got a better price for their grain than they would have if they had been forced to compete with cheaper imports in a free market, the consumers (that is, everyone, with the poor hit the hardest) had to pay more for their daily bread than they would have had to, had they been free to buy foreign grain on the same terms as domestic. In effect, then, the Corn Laws were a form of price embargo whose burden was borne overwhelmingly by the poorest members of society.

The Case against the Corn Laws and the Drug Laws

During the 1830s, critics of the Corn Laws began to organize and quickly became influential. Their arguments apply perfectly to our drug laws. Note especially the critics' language and the fact that their aim was to abolish a restrictive legislation so as to ensure economic and personal freedom, not to reform or perfect methods of coercive state control of the economy and personal conduct. In 1838 John Benjamin Smith (no relation to Adam Smith) founded the Anti-Corn-Law Association and stated its purpose as follows.

> It [the association] had been established upon the same righteous principle as the Anti-Slavery Society. The object of that society was to obtain the free right for negroes to possess their own flesh and blood. The object of this was to obtain the free right of the people to exchange their labour for as much good as could be got for it; that we might no longer be obliged by law to buy our food at one shop, and that the dearest in the world, but be at liberty to go to that at which it can be obtained cheapest.[21]

When I wrote *Ceremonial Chemistry* and my earlier critiques of the drug laws, I did not realize the relevance of the Corn Laws to the drug laws. However, my reasoning in support of a free market in drugs was similar to the reasoning articulated above, as the following rephrasing of Smith illustrates:

> The Anti-Drug-Law Association ought to be established on the same righteous principle as the Anti-Slavery Society and the Anti-Corn-Law Association. . . . The object of this association shall be to obtain the free right of the people to exchange their labor for the drug of their choice; that we might no longer be obliged by law to obtain our drug in one way only, by securing permission from a physician for buying it, in an atmosphere in which doctors and drug agents are obsessed with the mission of ensuring that none of us receives a drug merely because he wants it.

It is obvious who the beneficiaries and victims of the Corn Laws were, and it is equally obvious who the beneficiaries and victims of the drug laws are. I shall not belabor the subject. Suffice it to say that doctors, lawyers, and politicians started the War on Drugs and continue to wage it, and that they are its real beneficiaries. In contrast, the drug war's ostensible beneficiaries—the poor, the uneducated, the young, the old, and the sick—are its actual victims.

What happened to England's leading Corn Law supporters after prohibitions on the trade in corn were lifted? They quickly discovered the truth and justice of the free market in grains. Lord John Russell's metamorphosis is illustrative. Born in 1792, Russell was prime minister from 1846 until 1852, and again from 1865 until 1866. (The Corn Laws were abolished in 1846 while Sir Robert Peel was prime minister, only a short time before Lord Russell succeeded him.) In 1845 Russell wrote,

> I confess that . . . my views have, in the course of twenty years, undergone a great alteration. I used to be of the opinion that corn was an exception to the general rules of political economy; but observation and experience have convinced me that we ought to abstain from all interference with the supply of food. . . . Let us then, unite to put an end to a system which has been proved to be the blight of commerce, the bane of agriculture, the source of bitter division among classes, the cause of penury, fever, mortality, and crime among the people.[22]

Every blight and bane Lord Russell attributed to the sacrosanct Corn Laws now applies, with even greater force, to our sacrosanct drug laws.[23]

ENVOI: TOWARD FREE-MARKET CONTROL OF DRUG USE

Although Jefferson had no trouble seeing the future darkly, I doubt he could have imagined a United States in which individuals who trade in drugs would be declared malefactors so dangerous as to deserve to be decapitated, and that at the behest of an American "czar."[24] However, Jefferson did foresee the day when the American people would be more interested in riches than in rights: "From the conclusion of this war," he warned, "we shall be going down hill. . . . They [the people] will be forgotten . . . and their rights disregarded. They will forget themselves, but in the sole faculty of making money, and will never think of uniting to effect a due respect for their rights."[25]

By the time Ludwig von Mises was born, Jefferson's prediction had come true and other political and social developments conspired to erode the ideals of Jeffersonian liberties. Mises's greatness lies in his lucid unmasking of, and courageous opposition to, the "protections" with which paternalistic statists are ever ready to injure us. (Mises overlooked one front, which in the long run may prove to be the Achilles heel of the free society, namely, psychiatry. Involuntary, institutional psychiatric interventions are the epitome of paternalist-statist protections that are, by definition, immune to effective opposition based on appeals to the subject-patient's rights).

In *Human Action*—his magnum opus—Mises wrote,

Opium and morphine are certainly dangerous, habit-forming drugs. But once the principle is admitted that it is the duty of government to protect the individual against his own foolishness, no serious objections can be advanced against further encroachments. . . . [W]hy limit the government's benevolent providence to the protection of the individual's body only? . . . The mischief done by bad ideologies, surely, is much more pernicious, both for the individual and for the whole society, than that done by narcotic drugs.[26]

Jefferson would have found it difficult to believe that the nation he helped found has embraced a political system based on the self-contradictory premise that people are competent enough to elect their own representatives to govern them, *but* so deeply distrust their own competence with respect to managing drugs that they deputize their elected representatives to permit them (the people) to use the drugs the state deems good for them, and prohibit them from using the drugs it deems bad for them. Mises rebelled against, and rejected, the legitimacy of the second half of this oxymoronic premise.

Jefferson and Mises were men of principle who sought to formulate political policies befitting a society of free and self-respecting people. No one can accuse our leading drug experts—in medicine, law, or politics—of being persons of principle. They have risen above that: They are persons of compassion. How can they be expected to worry about abstract principles when their attention is occupied by drug crises epitomized by mayors snorting coke and welfare mothers producing crack babies? It is easy enough to understand how the spectacle of a prominent person's pleasurable drug use might upset the envious, or how the prospect of a poor welfare mother's persistent production of muggers might disturb the racist wrapped in the liberal's mantle. But such ad hoc concerns cannot form the basis for a political order.

At this very moment in Eastern Europe, a complex political order based on fundamentally flawed principles seems to be coming apart at the seams. What, after all, is communism if not a political system based on (fake) compassion and (real) coercive paternalism? Rejecting the free market as uncaring toward the indigent and the infantile, the planned economies of Marxism-Leninism have substituted for it a system of political-economic directives aimed at supplying all with everything the omnicompetent state deems good, and denying to all everything it deems bad—precisely the features that drug controls share with other anti-capitalist political principles and practices.

If my critique of drug controls seems extreme or radical, let me observe that in fact it is neither. It is old-fashioned and, strictly speaking, conservative. I take my stand with the Old and New Testaments, where many sins are enumerated, but using drugs is not one of them; with the Constitution of the United States of America, which gives the government certain powers, but denying us the right to take drugs is not one of them; and with Ludwig von Mises, who fought—for a long time virtually alone—the threat posed by the paternalist-protectionist state.

Judging People: Meritorious Behavior vs. Abstinence from Drugs

We cannot intelligently examine the pros and cons of drug controls if we accept, as prima facie valid, the premise that it is in the best interest of individuals as well as of society to curtail or eliminate the use of (certain, so-called dangerous) drugs. This postulate, which virtually everyone now accepts, justifies punishing persons not only because they injure or kill others, but also because they produce, possess, sell, or use certain drugs.

Although the prospect is not imminent, it is possible that there will come a time when, once again, we shall prefer a drug peace to a War on Drugs. We shall then have to abandon our ideological opposition to drugs and reapproach the problem prudentially, as we approach most everyday problems. As a rule, we are rewarded and punished for the behaviors we display—not for the virtues or vices others attribute to our character, or for the drugs they detect in our urine. To illustrate this distinction, consider how we now treat professional athletes, and how we might treat them if they had the same right to use the drugs of their choice as they have to practice the religion of their choice. If our policy is that an athlete must be drug free, then we are justified in testing him and punishing him for being "on drugs." On the other hand, if our policy were that his taking a drug before a game is not any more of our business than is his praying before a game, then, if he used alcohol or sedatives, he would be "punished" by his opponents who would best him; whereas if he used anabolic steroids or stimulants, he would be "rewarded" by besting superior opponents.

Whether any particular drug would or would not have such an effect on a particular player's performance is irrelevant to this argument. What is relevant is that many drugs enhance performance, and many others impair it; and so, too, do many nonpharmacological factors, from the behavior of the weather to the disposition of one's spouse. The effect of a drug on behavior, like the effect of religion on it, may be for good or ill. Some of the greatest works of art in the world were created by men intoxicated with drugs, religion, or both. The point is that we have a choice about how to judge the other person's behavior: We can reward or penalize his performance because we are interested (only) in it, and eschew entering uninvited into his life; or we can reward or punish him for the drugs he avoids or seeks because we are obsessed with his drug-using habits, attribute deleterious consequences to the use of certain scapegoated drugs, and regard it as our duty to protect him (and others) from those consequences, whether he likes it or not.

This distinction between performance-oriented and prohibition-oriented rules rests on, and reprises, Lysander Spooner's distinction between vices and crimes. (See Chapter 2.) In the old days, if a factory worker showed up in the morning drunk, the foreman fired him. Today, a social worker from the company's employee assistance program refers him to a drug treatment program. In the end, the drunkard is still likely to lose his job. The only thing we can be sure of is that the drug treatment program will delay the worker's and his family's confronting the truth, and will make the company's product less competitive on the world market.

When a drug enhances rather than impairs the user's performance, the differing consequences of the performance-oriented and prohibition-oriented approaches are just as significant. Sigmund Freud might not have successfully endured the struggles of his early career had he been unable to augment his regular intake of nicotine with frequent doses of cocaine, and William Halstead might not have become America's most celebrated surgeon and one of the stars of the Johns Hopkins Medical School had he not been able to medicate himself with morphine whenever he felt the need for it.[27] In short, saying no to drugs may be neither to the individual drug user's nor to society's best interests—unless we postulate that a social parasite "off drugs" is a better person and a better citizen than a great athlete, entertainer, or surgeon "on drugs."

Limits on the Right to Drugs

Commitment to the belief that a person has a basic right to grow and smoke tobacco or marijuana does not imply that he has a right to do these things on someone else's property, without the owner's permission. The government can, therefore, rightfully prohibit smoking in a public building, just as it can rightfully prohibit growing tobacco on public land. Mutatis mutandis, driving a car places the driver in a position where his behavior may be a threat to the safety of the public. Hence, the state is justified in prohibiting people who do not know how to drive from driving, and in prohibiting those who know how to drive from driving if their ability is impaired by the use, or non use, of drugs. This principle justifies depriving persons guilty of driving while intoxicated (DWI) offenses of their drivers' licenses, and granting epileptics licenses only on condition that they maintain themselves on anti-convulsant drugs to control their seizures. Moreover, compulsory drug testing (periodically or randomly) is justified in occupations where a worker's impairment endangers the public—for example, in commercial aviation. However, here too the emphasis must be on a rational assessment of the worker's impairment (if any), not on the government's or public's pharmaceutical-ideological prejudices masked as medicine. Some diseases—for example, epilepsy or glaucoma—disqualify a person from being a pilot; others—for example, acne or athlete's foot—do not. Similarly, it makes sense to prohibit a pilot from taking LSD, but not from taking aspirin. Lastly, we must not forget that a commercial aircraft is not the pilot's private property. It belongs to the airline company, which, together with the government, has the right to set the rules for protecting its property and the safety of the service it renders the public.

I should like to say here that nothing in this book should be interpreted as my denying that we have a "drug problem." The drug problem exists. It is social reality. And it exhibits the two mutually reinforcing constituents of which it is comprised: drug producers/sellers and drug buyers/users. But let us be crystal clear what the problems are.

The drug user's "problem"—assuming *he* thinks he has a problem—is that he has a habit, say smoking, he wants to quit. To break his habit, he must want to stop smoking more than he wants to continue smoking. Easier said than done? Of course. But merely because a habit is difficult to break does not mean that indulging in it is a disease or a crime, or that the government has a right to punish or involuntarily treat the person who practices it.

Our problem—assuming *we* consider another person's trading in or using drugs to be a problem (the pusher has a business, the user a habit)—is that we too have a habit, namely, preferring a command economy in drugs to a free market in them. To break this habit, we must reinvert our moral preferences and reembrace the true basis of a liberal social order: Which means that we would have to value cooperation more highly than coercion, self-control and self-medication more highly than meddling and "therapy," a free market in drugs more highly than drug prohibition.

The so-called drug debate has become a bore. We are long past the point where declaring that the War on Drugs is not working or where offering proposals to reform our drug control policies makes any sense. Recall once more that, although the purpose of Prohibition was to stop people from drinking liquor (not from transporting it), the Eighteenth Amendment outlawed only "the manufacture, sale, or transportation" of alcohol. Why did the men who drafted that constitutional amendment not prohibit drinking alcohol, as Congress now prohibits drinking cough syrup with codeine? I submit that this question points in the direction we ought to go if we want to get past the deadlock on drugs. In the final analysis, the problem is not merely that the War on Drugs is a classic case of the cure being worse than the disease it purports to cure, but that we are unwilling to come to grips with what we, as a people, believe ought to form the moral foundations for the United States' interest in protecting our lives, liberties, and properties.

Today, the legitimacy of secular states—especially of the United States—rests primarily on the prudential interests of its citizens in maximizing the security of their lives, liberties, and properties. It does not lie in the state's commitment to saving us from falling into moral sin, political error, or medical illness. If this proposition is true, and if we desire to uphold it as a principle worth honoring, then we would have to conclude that our interests would be better served if our drug laws conformed with the principles of the free market. In practice, this would mean rejecting drug prohibitions and embracing, instead, a policy of consistently punishing people guilty of genuine crimes. But that would not be quite enough. In what may perhaps be an even more radical departure from our present practices, we would have to disallow drug use (intoxication) and mental illness (however defined) as excusing conditions from crimes, and would have to discontinue using state-sanctioned coercions to protect people from themselves.

In short, there is nothing particularly novel about our present drug problem. Nor is there anything particularly novel about envisioning a return to a free market in drugs. We need not reinvent the wheel to solve our drug problem. All we need to do is stop acting like timid children, grow up, and stand on our own two feet. "It is ordered in the eternal constitution of things," wrote Edmund Burke, "that men of intemperate minds cannot be free. Their passions forge their fetters."[28] Nor can men of infantile minds and childish habits be free. Their dependency—on the state, not on drugs—forges their fetters.

Notes

The epigraph at the front of this book is from Adams, J., "A Dissertation on the Canon and Feudal Law," 1765, reprinted in R. J. Taylor, ed., *The Papers of John Adams*, vol. 1 (Cambridge, MA: Harvard University Press, 1977), p. 112.

PREFACE

1. Hebra, F. von, quoted in L.-F. Celine, *The Life and Work of Semmelweis*, 1924, reprinted in *Mea Culpa & The Life and Work of Semmelweis*, trans. R. A. Parker (New York: Howard Fertig, 1979), p. 131. Hebra, a pupil of the famous Viennese pathologist Karl Rokitanksy, was the founder of the Vienna School of Dermatology.

2. For typical examples, see "Drug war a battle of law vs. treatment," *Syracuse Herald-Journal*, Syracuse, NY, April 17, 1991; and Kris, E., "State to force classes on adult sex offenders," *Syracuse Herald-Journal*, May 2, 1991.

INTRODUCTION

1. Butler, S., quoted in R. V. Sampson, *The Psychology of Power* (New York: Pantheon, 1966), p. 110.

2. Hopkins, J. F., *A History of the Hemp Industry in Kentucky* (Lexington: University of Lexington Press, 1951); Moore, B., *A Study of the Past, the Present and the Possibilities of the Hemp Industry in Kentucky* (Lexington, KY: James E. Hughes, 1905); and Washington, G., "Diary Notes," cited in L. Grinspoon, *Marihuana Reconsidered*, 2nd ed. (Cambridge, MA: Harvard University Press, 1977), pp. 10–12.

3. Constitution of the United States, Art. I, sec. 2.

4. Bastiat, F., *Economic Sophisms*, 1845/1848, reprint, trans. Arthur Goddard (Princeton,NJ: Van Nostrand, 1964), p. 4.

5. See, for example, Jacob, J. B., "Imagining drug legalization," *Public Interest* 101 (Fall 1990): 28–42.

6. Dicey, A. V., *Lectures on the Relations between Law and Public Opinion in England during the Nineteenth Century*, 1905, 1914, reprint, 2nd ed. (London: Macmillan, 1963), p. lxxix.

CHAPTER 1

1. Madison, J., "Property," *National Gazette*, March 29, 1792, reprinted in *The Writings of James Madison*, vol. 6, ed. Gaillard Hunt, (New York: G. P. Putnam's Sons), p. 101.

2. Locke, J., "The Second Treatise of Government," bk. 2, ch. 5, sec. 27, in *Two Treatises of Government*, 1690, reprint, ed. Peter Laslett (New York: Mentor Books, 1965), pp. 328–29.

3. Madison, "Property," p. 103; for a more sustained analysis of this theme, see Szasz, S. M., "Resurfacing the road to serfdom," *Freeman* 41 (February 1991): 46–49.

4. Friedman, M., "Private property," *National Review* (November 5, 1990): 55–56; quote at p. 56.

5. Erler, E. J., "The Great Fence to Liberty: The Right to Property in the American Founding," in E. F. Paul and H. Dickman, eds., *Liberty, Property, and the Foundations of the American Constitution* (Albany: State University of New York Press, 1989), pp. 43, 56.

6. See Barnett, R. E., ed., *The Rights Retained by the People* (Fairfax, VA: George Mason University Press, 1989).

7. Madison, "Property," p. 105; see also Nedelsky, J., *Private Property and the Limits of American Constitutionalism* (Chicago: University of Chicago Press, 1990), esp. pp. 16–66.

8. *Scott v. Sandford*, 60 U.S. (19 How.) 393 (1857), cited in V. G. Rosenblum and A. D. Castberg, eds., *Cases on Constitutional Law* (Homewood, IL: Dorsey Press, 1973), pp. 73–85; quote at pp. 74–79.

9. Burke, E., *Reflections on the Revolution in France*, 1790, reprint, ed. Conor Cruise O'Brien (London: Penguin, 1986), pp. 247–48.

10. Jefferson, T., "Notes on the State of Virginia," 1781, reprinted in A. Koch and W. Peden, eds., *The Life and Selected Writings of Thomas Jefferson* (New York: Modern Library, 1944), p. 275.

11. Twain, M., "Osteopathy," 1901, quoted in C. T. Harnsberger, ed., *Mark Twain at Your Fingertips* (New York: Beechhurst Press, 1948), pp. 341–42.

12. See Szasz, T. S., "The Ethics of birth control—Or: Who owns your body?" *Humanist* 20 (November/December 1960): 332–36.

13. Friedman, M. *Capitalism and Freedom* (Chicago: University of Chicago Press, 1962) p. 138.

14. See *Griswold v. Connecticut*, 381 U.S. 479 (1965), and *Roe v. Wade*, 410 U.S. 113 (1973).

15. See, for example, " 'Grass' could cost a rancher his land," *Syracuse Herald-Journal*, March 19, 1991.

16. *McDermott v. Wisconsin*, 228 U.S. 115 (1913); emphasis added.

17. Christopher, T. W., *Constitutional Questions in Food and Drug Laws* (Chicago: Commerce Clearinghouse, 1960), p. 3; emphasis added.

18. Ibid., pp. 3–4.

19. *Wickard v. Filburn*, 317 U.S. 111 (1942), p. 84.

20. Ibid., p. 86. I wish to thank Arthur Spitzer, legal director of the ACLU's Washington, D.C., office, for kindly calling my attention to this case. The interpretation I advance is solely my responsibility.

21. Mackay, C., *Extraordinary Popular Delusions and the Madness of Crowds*, 1841, 1852, reprint (New York: Noonday Press, 1962).

22. *Webster's Third New International Dictionary*, unabridged (Springfield, MA: G&C Merriam, 1961), p. 2162.

23. Mises, L. von, *Socialism*, 1922, reprint, trans. from the 2nd German edition by J. Kahane (Indianapolis, IN: Liberty Classics, 1981), p. 469.

24. Freud, S., *Civilization and Its Discontents*, 1929, reprint in SE, vol. 21, p. 113.

25. Freud, S., *The Introductory Lectures on Psychoanalysis*, 1916–17, reprint in SE, vol. 16, p. 389.

26. Mises, *Socialism*, p. 107.

27. Mises, L. von, *Human Action* (New Haven, CT: Yale University Press, 1949), p. 874.

28. Even many libertarians do not support a free market in drugs—a market uncontaminated by the presumption that drug (ab)use is a disease. Among those who do, see, for example, Rothbard, M. N., *For a New Liberty* (New York: Collier, 1973), pp. 111–112; Mitchell, C. N., *The Drug Solution* (Ottawa, Canada: Carleton University Press, 1990); and Ebeling, R. M., "The economics of the drug war," *Freedom Daily* 1 (April 1990): 6–10.

29. *Lear's* (March 1990).

30. *TV Guide* (May 19–25, 1990).

31. *People* (May 21, 1990).

32. *Time* (December 17, 1990): 19.

33. Purvis, A., "Just what the patient ordered," *Time* (May 28, 1990): 42.

34. Ibid.

35. Anglin, M. D., and Hser, Y., "Legal Coercion and Drug Abuse Treatment: Research Findings and Social Policy Implications," in J. A. Inciardi and J. R. Biden, Jr., eds., *Handbook of Drug Control in the United States* (Westport, CT: Greenwood Press, 1990), pp. 151–76; quote at p. 152.

36. Bastiat, F., *Economic Sophisms*, 1845/1848, reprint, trans. Arthur Goddard (Princeton, NJ: Van Nostrand, 1964), pp. 125–26.

37. Jones, L., "Evaluation of drug treatment research urged," *American Medical News* (October 26, 1990): 4.

38. *Calero-Toledo v. Pearson Yacht Leasing Co.*, 416 U.S. 663 (1974).

39. Ibid., p. 665.

40. Ibid., p. 663.

41. Ibid., p. 695.

42. *United States v. One Assortment of 89 Firearms*, 465 U.S. 354 (1974), p. 356.

43. Ibid.

44. Ibid.

45. See, for example, Szasz, T. S., *Law, Liberty, and Psychiatry*, 1963, reprint (Syracuse, NY: Syracuse University Press, 1989) and *Psychiatric Justice*, 1965, reprint (Syracuse, NY: Syracuse University Press, 1988).

46. See Herpel, S. B., *"United States v. One Assortment of 89 Firearms,"* *Reason* (May 1990): 3–36.

47. Dillin, J., "Nation's liberties at risk," *Christian Science Monitor*, February 2, 1990.

48. For example, see Treaster, J. B., "Agents arrest car dealers in sales to drug traffickers," *New York Times*, October 4, 1990.

49. "Marshalls faulted on drug property: Report says mismanagement of seized real estate has cost the U.S. millions," *New York Times*, April 21, 1991.

50. McDonald, F., quoted in L. M. Werner, "If Jefferson et al. could see us now," *New York Times*, February 12, 1987.

51. Lewis, D., "Prohibition and persuasion," *North American Review* 139 (August 1884): 188–99, quote at p. 194, reprinted in C. Watner, "Foreword," in L. Spooner, *Vices Are Not Crimes: A Vindication of Moral Liberty* 1875, reprint (Cupertino, CA: Tanstaafl, 1977), pp. viii–ix.

52. Hobbes, T., *Leviathan*, 1651, reprint, ed. Michael Oakeshott (New York: Collier Macmillan, 1962), p. 105.

53. Mandeville, B., *The Fable of the Bees*, 1732, reprint, F. B. Kaye edition, 2 vols. (Indianapolis, IN: Liberty Press, 1988); see also Hunter, R. and Macalpine, I., eds, *Three Hundred Years of Psychiatry, 1535–1860* (London: Oxford University Press, 1963), p. 296.

It may be of interest to note that Bernard de Mandeville was also a pioneer in psychiatry (psychotherapy)—an enterprise closely related to economics, albeit this connection is no longer officially recognized. Mandeville's medical practice was limited to patients suffering from what the alienists called "nerve and stomach disorders" or, as he called them, the "hypochondriack and hysterick passions." In 1711 he published *A Treatise of the Hypochondriack and Hysterick Passions*, written explicitly "by way of Information to Patients [rather] than to teach other Practitioners." Although Mandeville's books went through numerous printings and he was one of the most famous and influential figures of his age, his name is now rarely mentioned except by libertarian writers.

54. Johnson, P., *Modern Times* (New York: Harper & Row, 1983), p. 728.

CHAPTER 2

1. Rogers, W., quoted in P. Yapp, ed., *The Traveller's Dictionary of Quotations* (London and New York: Routledge & Kegan Paul, 1983), p. 919.

2. McDonald, F., *Novus Ordo Seclorum* (Lawrence: University Press of Kansas, 1985), pp. 10 and 16.

3. See Burke, K., "Interaction: III. Dramatism," in D. L. Sils, ed., *International Encyclopedia of the Social Sciences*, vol. 7 (New York: Macmillan and Free Press, 1968), p. 450.

4. Although the similarity between these two problems is based on nothing more than a strategic analogy, it is now commonly misunderstood as a literal equivalence; see, for example, Schrage, M., "Vaccine to fight drug addiction is needed," *Los Angeles Times*, March 1, 1990.

5. "It is better to know nothing than to know what ain't so." Shaw, H. W. ("Josh Billings"), quoted in J. Bartlett, *Familiar Quotations*, 12th ed. (Boston: Little, Brown, 1951), p. 518.

6. Reagan, N., quoted in S. V. Roberts, "Mrs. Reagan assails drug users," *New York Times*, March 1, 1988.

7. Bennett, W., quoted in "In the news," *Syracuse Herald-Journal*, June 13, 1990.

8. Nelis, K., "Cuomo applauds students for taking on 'the devil,' " *Post Standard*, Syracuse, NY, January 28, 1988.

9. See Mackay, C., *Extraordinary Popular Delusions and the Madness of Crowds*, 1841, 1852, reprint (New York: Noonday Press, 1962); and Moore, R. I., *The Formation of a Persecuting Society* (Oxford, England: Basil Blackwell, 1987).

10. See Tuveson, E. L., *Redeemer Nation* (Chicago: University of Chicago Press, 1968).

11. Bush, G., "Transcript of Bush's Inaugural Address," *New York Times*, January 21, 1989.

12. Tuveson, *Redeemer Nation*, p. 132.

13. "Censorship," in the *Encyclopaedia Britannica* vol. 5 (Chicago: Encyclopaedia Britannica, 1973), p. 161.

14. *Webster's Third New International Dictionary*, unabridged (Springfield, MA: G&C Merriam, 1961), p. 468.

15. Lader, L., "Margaret Sanger: Militant, pragmatist, visionary," *On the Issues* 14 (1990): 10–12, 14, 30–35; quote at p. 30.

16. Ibid.

17. Broun, H., and Leech, M., *Anthony Comstock* (New York: Literary Guild of America, 1927), pp. 15–16.

18. "Plea, *U.S. v. D. M. Bennett*," quoted in ibid., epigraph, p. i, and p. 89.

19. Broun and Leech, *Anthony Comstock*, p. 88.

20. "Censorship," *Encyclopaedia Britannica*, vol. 6, p. 249.

21. See Shryock, R. H., *Medical Licensing in America, 1650–1965* (Baltimore: Johns Hopkins University Press, 1967).

22. Food and Drugs Act, 34 Stat. 768, ch. 3915 (June 30, 1906). This act is often erroneously called the Pure Food and Drug Act.

23. Temin, P., *Taking Your Medicine* (Cambridge, MA: Harvard University Press, 1980), p. 33.

24. I wish to thank Sheldon Richman for calling my attention to this antilibertarian aspect of the 1906 Food and Drugs Act.

25. Food and Drugs Act, 34 Stat. 768, p. 770.

26. See *United States v. Johnson*, 221 U.S. 488 (1911).

27. Ibid., p. 505; emphasis added.

28. Harrison Narcotic Act, 38 Stat. 785 (1914).

29. *United States v. Jin Fuey Moy*, 241 U.S. 394 (1915), p. 394; emphasis added.

30. *Whipple v. Martinson*, 256 U.S. 41 (1921), p. 45; emphasis added.

31. Musto, D. F., *The American Disease* (New Haven, CT: Yale University Press, 1973), p. 64.

32. Sontheimer, M., "Ein Hustenmittel aus Elberfeld" [A cough medicine from Elberfeld], *Die Zeit*, April 6, 1990, p. 64.

33. Carpenter, T. G., and Rouse, R. C., "Perilous Panacea: The Military in the Drug War," CATO Institute Policy Analysis, Washington, DC, February 15, 1990, p. 24.

34. See Szasz, T. S., *Law, Liberty, and Psychiatry*, 1963, reprint (Syracuse, NY: Syracuse University Press, 1989), pp. 212–22, and *The Therapeutic State* (Buffalo, NY: Prometheus Books, 1984).

35. Spooner, L., *Vices Are Not Crimes*, 1875, reprint (Cupertino, CA: Tanstaafl, 1977), p. 1.

36. Ibid.

37. Kolata, G., "Temperance: An old cycle repeats itself," *New York Times*, January 1, 1991.

38. Spooner, *Vices Are Not Crimes*, p. 4.

39. Ibid., pp. 29–30.

40. Spargo, J., *Social Democracy Explained* (1918), pp. 306–7, quoted in J. H. Timberlake, *Prohibition and the Progressive Movement, 1900–1920* (New York: Atheneum, 1970), p. 98.

41. Strong, J., *The Gospel of the Kingdom* 8 (July, 1914): 97–98, quoted in Timberlake, *Prohibition and the Progressive Movement*, p. 27.

42. Tennant, F. S., quoted in D. L. Breo, "NFL medical adviser fights relentlessly against drugs," *American Medical News* (October 24/31, 1986): 18–19.

43. Quoted in Timberlake, *Prohibition and the Progressive Movement*, p. 180.

44. Ibid., p. 38.

45. For an excellent, though uncritical, account of drug legislation during Roosevelt's first two terms, see Jackson, C. O., *Food and Drug Legislation in the New Deal* (Princeton, NJ: Princeton University Press, 1970).

46. Hornberger, J. G., "Democracy vs. constitutionally limited government," *Freedom Daily* 1 (June, 1990): 1–5; quote at p. 4.

47. See, for example, Kallett, A., and Schlink, F. J., *100,000,000 Guinea Pigs* (New York: Vanguard Press, 1932).

48. Jackson, *Food and Drug Legislation*, p. 19.

49. Ibid., pp. 151–60.

50. Young, J. H., *The Medical Messiahs* (Princeton, NJ: Princeton University Press, 1967), p. 159; see also Young, J. H., *The Toadstool Millionaires* (Princeton, NJ: Princeton University Press, 1961).

51. Young, *The Medical Messiahs*, p. 160.

52. Ibid., p. 165; emphasis added.

53. Federal Food, Drug, and Cosmetic Act, 52 Stat. 1040 (1938).

54. Jackson, *Food and Drug Legislation*, p. 37.

55. Ibid., p. 38.

56. Ibid., p. 46.

57. King, R., *The Drug Hang-up* (New York: Norton, 1972), pp. 348–49; in this connection, see also Mark, J. F., "The drug laws and the Ninth and Tenth Amendments," *Drug Law Report* 1 (May/June 1986): 241–50.

58. Temin, P., "The origin of compulsory drug prescription," *Journal of Law and Economics*, 22 (1979): 91–106. For a comprehensive history of prescription laws, see Mitchell, C. N., *The Drug Solution* (Ottawa, Canada: Carleton University Press, 1990).

59. Temin, *Taking Your Medicine*, p. 48.

60. U.S. Congress, *Quackery: A $9 Billion Scandal*, 1984, quoted in P. Skrabanek, "Health quackery—holding back the tide," *International Journal of Risk and Safety in Medicine* 1 (1990): 65–69; quote at p. 65.

61. Beck, M., et al., "Peddling youth over the counter: Wanna buy some eternal life?" *Newsweek* (March 5, 1990): 50–52.

62. Ibid.; see also Sullum, J., "Cold comfort," *Reason* 22 (April 1991): 22–29.

63. See Skrabanek, P., and McCormick, J., *Follies and Fallacies in Medicine* (Glasgow, Scotland: Tarragon Press, 1989).

64. Berkmoes, R. V., "A flamboyant crusader against overmedication of elderly," *American Medical News* (November 23–30, 1990): 26; and Garrard, J., et al., "Evaluation of neuroleptic drug use by nursing home elderly under proposed Medicare and Medicaid regulations," *Journal of the American Medical Association* 265 (January 23–30, 1991): 463–67.

65. Szasz, T. S., "AIDS and drugs: Balancing risk and benefits," *Lancet* (London), 2 (August 22, 1987): 450; and LeBrun, M., "AIDS stalks women," *Syracuse Herald-Journal*, November 30, 1990.

66. Quoted in Kinsky, L., "The FDA and Drug Research," in T. R. Machan, ed., *The Libertarian Alternative* (Chicago: Nelson-Hall, 1974), p. 183.

67. "Safety questions on nonprescription drugs," *U.S. News & World Report* (November 12, 1990): 93.

68. Young, *The Medical Messiahs*, p. 167.

69. Ibid., p. 168.

70. Ibid., p. 169; emphasis added.

71. Ibid., p. 215.

72. Peterson, M. B., *The Regulated Consumer* (Ottawa, IL: Green Hill Publisher, 1971), p. 38.

73. See, for example, Nader, R., "Endorsement," for Torrey E. F., *Nowhere to Go* (New York: Harper & Row, 1988), back jacket; and Torrey, E. F., et al., "Washington's grate society: Schizophrenics in the shelters and on the streets," *Public Citizen*, Washington, D.C., Health Research Group, (April 23, 1985).

74. Jackson, *Food and Drug Legislation*, pp. 52–53.

75. Tuveson, *Redeemer Nation*, pp. 73–74; emphasis added.

76. Spooner, *Vices Are Not Crimes*, pp. 12–13.

CHAPTER 3

1. *Hamlet*, act I, scene iii, line 43.

2. Vienne, M., quoted in J. Delumeau, *Sin and Fear*, 1983, reprint, trans. Eric Nicholson (New York: St. Martin's Press, 1990), p. 555.

3. Roosevelt, F. D., "First Inaugural Address," March 4, 1933, quoted in J. Bartlett, ed. *Familiar Quotations*, 12th ed. (Boston: Little, Brown, 1951) p. 915.

4. Seneca (c. A.D. 54), quoted in B. Stevenson, *The Macmillan Book of Proverbs, Maxims, and Famous Phrases* (New York: Macmillan, 1948), p. 786.

5. Delumeau, *Sin and Fear*, pp. 556–57.

6. Douglas, M., and Wildavsky, A., *Risk and Culture* (Berkeley: University of California Press, 1983), p. 7.

7. Anslinger, H. J., quoted in J. Kaplan, *Marijuana* (New York: Pocket Books, 1972), p. 92.

8. See, for example, Rorabaugh, W. J., *The Alcoholic Republic* (New York: Oxford University Press, 1979), pp. 5–21.

9. Musto, D. F., *The American Disease* (New Haven, CT: Yale University Press, 1973), p. 248.

10. See, for example, Mintz, M., "Tobacco decimating world, says WHO epidemiologist," *Washington Post*, April 5, 1990; also, Cook, G., "Africa: Ashtray of the world," *Sunday Times*, London, May 13, 1990.

11. For an example of such nonreforms, see Trebach, A. S., "The Need for Reform of International Narcotics Laws," in R. Hamowy, ed., *Dealing with Drugs* (Lexington, MA: Lexington Books, 1987), p. 103.

12. Burke, E., *Reflections on the Revolution in France*, 1790, reprint, ed. Conor Cruise O'Brien (London: Penguin, 1986), p. 248; emphasis added.

13. Girard, R., *The Scapegoat*, 1982, reprint, trans. Yvonne Freccero (Baltimore: Johns Hopkins University Press, 1986), p. 16.

14. Szasz, T. S., *Ceremonial Chemistry*, 1974, reprint, rev. ed. (Holmes Beach, FL: Learning Publications, 1985).

15. John 11:48–50.

16. Girard, *Scapegoat*, p. 113; emphasis added.

17. Ibid., p. 114. *The Compact Edition of the Oxford English Dictionary* (Oxford, England: Clarendon Press, 1971) gives "to cut" and "cutting a knot" as the etymological roots of the term.

18. Marcus, R., "Court: States can ban peyote rites," *Washington Post*, April 18, 1990; see *Employment Division, Department of Human Resources of Oregon v. Smith*, 110 S. Ct. 1595 (1990).

19. Greenhouse, L., "Court is urged to rehear case on ritual drug use: Religious groups team with legal scholars, " *New York Times*, May 11, 1990; also Neuhaus, R. J., "Church, state and peyote," *National Review* (June 11, 1990): 40–44.

20. Starchild, A., "U.S. imports criminals to fill domestic shortage," *Liberty* 3 (November 1989): 25.

21. Ibid.

22. Douglas and Wildavsky, *Risk and Culture*, p. 184.

23. Bourne, R., *The Radical Will* (New York: Urizen Books, 1977), p. 360.

24. See, for example, Anderson, G. M., "Parasites, profits, and politicians: Public health and public choice," *Cato Journal* 9 (Winter 1990): 557–78.

25. Ibid., p. 573.

26. See, for example, Andrew E., *Shylock's Rights* (Toronto: University of Toronto Press, 1988).

27. Tofani, L., "Unapproved drugs given limited use," *Syracuse Herald-Journal*, May 22, 1990.

28. Winerip, M., "Drug works, but insurer won't pay," *New York Times*, November 27, 1990.

29. "Mom's addiction results in conviction," *Syracuse Herald-Journal*, May 23, 1990.

30. Lewin, T., "Appeals court in Florida backs guilt for drug delivery by umbilical cord," *New York Times*, April 20, 1991.

31. U.S. House of Representatives, Select Committee on Children, Youth, and Families, "Women, Addiction, and Perinatal Substance Abuse: Fact Sheet," mimeographed, April 19, 1990.

32. Hey, R. P., "US targets maternal drug abuse as cost problems escalate," *Christian Science Monitor*, May 22, 1990.

33. See "National Foundation," in *The World Book Encyclopedia*, vol. 14 (Chicago: Field Enterprises, 1966), p. 37; and Gunn, S. M., and Platt, P. S., *Voluntary Health Agencies* (New York: Ronald Press, 1945), p. 34.

34. Macklis, R. M., "Radithor and the era of mild radium therapy," *Journal of the American Medical Association* 264 (August 1, 1990): 614–18; quote at pp. 614–15.

35. Ibid.

36. Douglas and Wildavsky, *Risk and Culture*, p. 10.

37. For a delightful satire on this subject, see Romains, J., *Knock*, 1923, reprint, trans. James B. Gidney (Great Neck, NY: Barron Educational Series, 1962).

38. See Lewis, H. W., *Technological Risk* (New York: Norton, 1990); also Paulos, J. A., "What we fear least kills most," *New York Times Book Review*, November 25, 1990, pp. 11–12.

39. Douglas and Wildavsky, *Risk and Culture*, p. 53.

40. See Shenon, P., "Bennett defends plan to fight drugs in Peru," *New York Times*, June 22, 1990.

41. Steele, K. D., "Hanford: America's nuclear graveyard," *Bulletin of the Atomic Scientists* 45 (October 1989): 15–23; quote at p. 15.

42. Ibid., p. 17; see also Wald, M. L., "Wider peril seen in nuclear waste bomb making: Washington soil tainted," *New York Times*, March 28, 1991.

43. Wald, M. L., "Disposal of mild radioactive waste to be less restricted in new policy," *New York Times*, June 26, 1990.

44. Satchell, M., "A vicious 'circle of poison': New questions about American exports of powerful pesticides," *U.S. News & World Report* (June 10, 1991): 31–32; quote at p. 31.

45. Coolidge, C., quoted in Stevenson, *Macmillan Book of Proverbs*, p. 2117.

46. Mill, J. S., *On Liberty*, 1859, reprinted in J. S. Mill, *The Six Great Humanistic Essays*, with an introduction by Albert William Levi (New York: Washington Square Press, 1969), p. 220.

47. Kleber, H. D., "The nosology of abuse and dependence," *Journal of Psychiatric Research* 24, suppl. 2 (1990): 57–64; quote at p. 59.

48. I wish to thank Charles S. Howard for suggesting these scenarios. Some months after he proposed them, truth overtook fiction (see below in the text), proving that insightful speculation about a crowd madness can approximate the predictive power of a hard science.

49. "Jailing of pregnant captain questioned," *Arkansas Democrat*, May 25, 1991.

50. See Szasz, T. S., *Insanity* (New York: Wiley, 1987).

CHAPTER 4

1. Rogers, W., "Slogans, Slogans Everywhere," 1925, reprinted in W. Rog-

ers, *A Will Rogers Treasury*, ed. Bryan B. Sterling and Frances N. Sterling (New York: Bonanza Books, 1982), p. 71.

2. "Drug lecture prompts girl to turn parents in to police," *Post-Standard*, Syracuse, NY, August 15, 1986.

3. "Hollywood seeks girl who turned in parents," *New York Times*, August 20, 1986; emphasis added.

4. Bennett, W. J., quoted in R. L. Berke, "Drug chief urges youth: Just say who," *New York Times*, May 19, 1989.

5. Ibid.

6. Cummings, J., "Agents call but in vain for girl who got police," *New York Times*, August 22, 1986.

7. "More children informing on parents for drug abuse," *Syracuse Herald-Journal*, November 13, 1986.

8. "Bush inspires boy to turn in his mom for using cocaine," *Syracuse Herald-Journal*, September 15, 1989.

9. "Teen who sold drug shown by Bush jailed," *Syracuse Herald-Journal*, November 1, 1990.

10. "For show and tell, beer," *New York Times*, February 6, 1990.

11. Naylor, S. W., "Teen suspended for dispensing over-the counter medication," *Syracuse Herald-Journal*, June 2, 1990.

12. Ibid.

13. Reagan, R., *An American Life* (New York: Simon and Schuster, 1990), cited from M. Dowd, "Where's the rest of him?" *New York Times Book Review*, November 18, 1990, pp. 1 and 43.

14. See Szasz, T. S., "Reagan should let jurors judge Hinckley," *Washington Post*, May 6, 1981, reprinted in T. S. Szasz, *The Therapeutic State* (Buffalo, NY: Prometheus Books, 1984), pp. 147–48.

15. Lewin, T., "Drug-testing kit for parents spurs stormy debate," *New York Times*, September 12, 1990.

16. Ibid.

17. Hite, R., "The double danger of AIDS," *Free Market* 6 (November 1988): 3–4; quote at p. 4; see also Judson, F. N., "What do we really know about AIDS control?" *American Journal of Public Health* 79 (July 1989): 878–82.

18. "Public polled on attitudes about cocaine users, sellers," *American Medical News* (February 16, 1990): 26.

19. See Oliver, C. "Brickbats," *Reason* (April 1990): 20.

20. "Billboards in War on Drugs bring criticism and lawsuits in Carolina," *New York Times*, April 1, 1990.

21. Quindlen, A., "Raising a generation of judgmental zealots," *Syracuse Herald-Journal*, October 16, 1990.

22. "Candidates' survival guide," *Newsweek* (March 18, 1988): 13.

23. Ibid.

24. Jefferson, T., quoted in S. Platt, ed., *Respectfully Quoted* (Washington, D.C.: Library of Congress, 1989), pp. 8–9; attributed to Jefferson, and possibly spurious.

25. Lincoln, A., quoted in ibid., p. 9.

26. Burke, E., *Reflections on the Revolution in France*, 1790, reprint, ed. Conor Cruise O'Brien (London: Penguin, 1986), p. 136.

27. Reagan, R., quoted in "Teens at Covenant House give Reagan mixed reviews," *Syracuse Herald-Journal*, November 15, 1989.

28. Ritter, B., *Covenant House* (New York: Doubleday, 1987), p. 5.

29. Ibid., p. 8.

30. Farber, M. A., "O'Connor is moving to clear up 'mess' at Covenant House," *New York Times*, March 10, 1990.

31. McLaughlin, J., "Let Covenant House survive Ritter's woes," *Syracuse Herald-Journal*, February 14, 1990.

32. See Collier, P., and Horowitz, D., *The Kennedys* (New York: Summit Books, 1984).

33. See Szasz, T. S., *Ceremonial Chemistry*, 1974, reprint, rev. ed. (Holmes Beach, FL: Learning Publications, 1985), p. 13; also Rensenberger, B., "Amphetamine used by a physician to lift moods of famous patients," *New York Times*, December 4, 1962.

34. Heymann, C. D., *A Woman Named Jackie* (New York: Lyle Stuart, 1989), p. 301.

35. Ibid., p. 303.

36. Lindsey, R., "Mrs. Ford, in hospital statement, says: 'I'm addicted to alcohol,' " *New York Times*, April 22, 1978; see further Szasz, T. S., "A dialogue about drug education," in Szasz, *Therapeutic State*, pp. 254–60.

37. Ford, B., quoted in "Review, *Betty: A Glad Awakening*," *Time* (March 16, 1987): 81.

38. Blumenthal, D., "A day in the life of the Betty Ford Center," *New York Times*, February 27, 1987.

39. Shapiro, W., "A mild dose of candor: Kitty Dukakis reveals a former drug dependency," *Time* (July 20, 1987): 34.

40. Kunen, J. S., et al., "From Kitty Dukakis, a cry of despair," *People* (November 27, 1989): 115–19.

41. Shapiro, "Mild dose of candor."

42. "Kitty Dukakis on the soapbox," *U.S. News & World Report* (August 1, 1988): 30 and 46–51.

43. Kunen et al., "From Kitty Dukakis."

44. Ibid.

45. Ibid.

46. Quoted in Gelman, D., "Roots of Addiction," *Newsweek* (February 20, 1989): 52.

47. Dukakis, K., *Now You Know* (New York: Simon and Schuster, 1990).

48. Dowd, M., "Kitty Dukakis's life of sad uncertainties and self-made mists," *New York Times*, September 6, 1990.

49. Clift, E., "More than you ever imagined: The startling confessions of Kitty Dukakis," *Newsweek* (September 3, 1990): 64.

50. Sheppard, R. Z., "Public life, private trouble," *Time* (September 10, 1990): 85.

51. Szasz, T. S., "Bad habits are not diseases: A refutation of the claim that alcoholism is a disease," *Lancet* (London) 2 (July 8, 1972): 83–84.

52. Rado, S., "The psychoanalysis of pharmacothymia (drug addiction)," *Psychoanalytic Quarterly* 2 (1933): 1–23; quote at p. 23; emphasis added.

53. Kleber, H., quoted in H. Fishman, "Whatever happened to the War on Drugs?" *Psychiatric Times* 8 (May 1991): 44–46; quote at p. 44.

54. Ibid., pp. 44–45.

55. Ibid., p. 45.

56. Simons, M., "Gluttons for tranquilizers, the French ask, 'Why?' " *New York Times*, January 21, 1991.

57. Ibid.

58. Mill, J. S., *On Liberty*, 1859, reprinted in J. S. Mill, *The Six Great Humanistic Essays*, with an introduction by Albert William Levi (New York: Washington Square Press, 1969), pp. 224–25.

59. *Encyclopaedia Britannica* vol. 11 (Chicago: Encyclopaedia Britannica, 1973), pp. 351–53.

60. Ibid., vol. 4, pp. 783–84.

61. See Szasz, T. S., "The uses of naming and the origin of the myth of mental illness," *American Psychologist* 16 (February 1961): 59–65, reprinted as "The Rhetoric of Rejection," in *Ideology and Insanity*, 1970, reprint (Syracuse, NY: Syracuse University Press, 1991), pp. 49–68.

62. See Moore, B., *A Study of the Past, the Present and the Possibilities of the Hemp Industry in Kentucky* (Lexington, KY: James E. Hughes, 1905); Hopkins, J. F., *A History of the Hemp Industry in Kentucky* (Lexington: University of Lexington Press, 1951); and Herer, J., *The Emperor Wears No Clothes*, 1985, reprint (Van Nuys, CA: HEMP Publishing, 1980).

63. See Schoeck, H., *Envy*, 1966, reprint, trans. Michael Glenny and Betty Ross (New York: Harcourt, Brace, 1969).

CHAPTER 5

1. Bastiat, F., *Economic Sophisms*, 1845/1848, reprint, trans. Arthur Goddard (Princeton, NJ: Van Nostrand, 1964), p. 142.

2. See Szasz, T. S. "The myth of the rights of mental patients," *Liberty* 2 (July 1989): 19–26.

3. See, for example, Inciardi, J. A., and Biden, J. R., Jr., eds., *Handbook of Drug Control in the United States* (Westport, CT: Greenwood Press, 1990).

4. Schmoke, K. L., "We're making progress in the movement to end the War on Drugs," *Drug Policy Letter* 1 (November/December, 1989): 2–3; quote at p. 3.

5. Drug Policy Foundation, "Biennial Report, 1988 & 1989," p. 7 (Drug Policy Foundation, 4801 Massachusetts Ave., N.W., Suite 400, Washington, D.C. 20016–2087).

6. Campbell, F. B., "To control drugs, legalize," *New York Times*, January 23, 1990.

7. See, for example, Hankins, J., "Casualties of the drug war," *New York Times*, January 31, 1990.

8. Glasser, I., "Now for a drug policy that doesn't do harm," *New York Times*, December 18, 1990.

9. See Weaver, R. M., *The Ethics of Rhetoric* (Chicago: Regnery, 1953).

10. "The federal drugstore," *National Review* (February 5, 1990): 34–41.

11. Ibid., p. 41.

12. Hagerty, B.,"Drug-legalization debate gets louder," *Wall Street Journal/ Europe*, January 9, 1990.

13. Quoted in Roberts, S., "On the question of legal drugs, a vote for maybe," *New York Times*, January 25, 1990.

14. Rosenthal, A. M., "A chat with Jesse," *New York Times*, January 25, 1990.

15. Rangel, C. B., "Legalize drugs? Not on your life," *New York Times*, May 17, 1989; emphasis added.

16. Ibid.

17. Twain, M., *Following the Equator*, vol. 1 (Hartford, CT: American Publishing, 1903), p. 98.

18. Buckley, W. F., "Who cares if leaders make things up?" *Post-Standard*, Syracuse, NY, March 31, 1990.

19. Ibid.

20. "United Nations Convention against Illicit Traffic in Narcotic Drugs and Psychotropic Substances," concluded at Vienna on December 20, 1988, in United Nations, *Multilateral Treaties Deposited with the Secretary-General* (New York: United Nations, 1989), pp. 269–71.

21. See Inglis, B., *The Forbidden Game* (London: Hodder and Staughton, 1975), pp. 154–77.

22. "Should we legalize the illegal?" *Parade* (February 4, 1990): 4; emphasis added.

23. Labaton, S., "Federal judge urges legalization of crack, heroin, and other drugs," *New York Times*, December 13, 1989.

24. Baer, D., "A judge who took the stand: It's time to legalize drugs," *U.S. News & World Report* (April 9, 1990): 27.

25. Douglas, W. O., concurring opinion in *Robinson v. California*, 370 U.S. 660 (1961), p. 676.

26. Sweet, R., "Admit that the drug war is not successful; abolish prohibition," *Drug Policy Letter* 1 (November/December 1989): 5–6; quote at p. 5.

27. Sweet, R., remarks made on "Firing Line Special Debate: 'Resolved: Drugs Should Be legalized,' " *Firing Line* TV show, March 26, 1990.

28. Guest, T., "The growing movement to legalize drugs," *U.S. News & World Report* (January 22, 1990): 22–23.

29. Sweet "Admit that drug war is not successful," p. 5.

30. Treaster, J. B., "Bush proposes more anti-drug spending," *New York Times*, February 1, 1991.

31. Keillor, G., "Where there's smoke, there's is ire," *American Health* (December 1989): 50–53; quote at p. 53.

32. Morley, J., "De-escalating the war," *Family Therapy Networker* 14 (November/December 1990): 25–27 and 30–35; quote at p. 27.

33. Nadelmann, E., quoted in E. Yoffe, "How to legalize," *Mother Jones* (February/March 1990): 18–19.

34. Ibid.

35. So too does Richard Miller in *The Case for Legalizing Drugs* (New York: Praeger, 1991).

36. Haggerty, J., "Decriminalizing narcotics use advocated," *Morning Times*, Scranton, PA, March 29, 1990.

37. Grinspoon, L., quoted in L. Jones, "Legalize or prohibit?" *American Medical News* (January 26, 1990): 2 and 32.

38. Grinspoon, L., Ewalt, J. R., and Shader, R. I., *Schizophrenia* (Baltimore: Williams & Wilkins,1972), p. 230.

39. Grinspoon, L., *Marihuana Reconsidered*, 2nd ed. (Cambridge, MA: Harvard University Press, 1977), p. 399.

40. See, for example, "Marijuana for ill is curbed by U.S." *New York Times*, June 23, 1991.

41. "American Bar Association rescinds policy on decriminalization of marijuana," *National Drug Policy Network's Newsbriefs* (February 15, 1990): 1–2.

42. Grinspoon, L., and Bakalar, J. B., *Cocaine*, rev. ed. (New York: Basic Books, 1985), p. 260.

43. Jacobs, J. B., "Imagining drug legalization," *Public Interest* 101 (February 1990): 28–42; quote at p. 31.

44. Anderson, D. C., "Legal crack? No sale: The idea fails on practical grounds," *New York Times*, November 26, 1990.

45. Ibid.

46. "Bush's drug control strategy is more of the same," National Drug Policy Network, news release, January 25, 1990, pp. 1–2. The National Drug Policy Network should not be confused with the Drug Policy Foundation, a Washington-based organization devoted to education, research, and the legal defense of individuals persecuted under the drug laws. See note 5 above.

CHAPTER 6

1. Williams, C., "Crack is genocide, 1990's style," *New York Times*, February 15, 1990.

2. Rosenthal, A. M., quoted in L. H. Lapham, "A political opiate," *Harper's Magazine* (December 1989): 43–48; quote at p. 46.

3. Williams, "Crack is genocide."

4. Murray, C. L., " 'We cannot make poison the norm,' " *Los Angeles Times*, March 21, 1990; emphasis added.

5. Ibid.

6. Warner, K. E., "Health and economic implications of a tobacco-free society," *Journal of the American Medical Association* 258 (October 16, 1987): 2080–86; quote at p. 2080.

7. Jackson, J., quoted in D. Lazare, "How the drug war created crack," *Village Voice*, January 23, 1990, pp. 20–24; quote at p. 22.

8. Ibid.

9. See, for example, Anderson, H., et al., "The global poison trade," *Newsweek* (November 7, 1988): 66–68.

10. Jackson, J., "Barry's ordeal offers a lesson for all of us," *Syracuse Herald-American*, January 29, 1990.

11. Rowan, C., "Wake up white America: Stereotypes fogging war on drugs," *Syracuse Herald-Journal*, December 28, 1989.

12. Meddis, S., "Drug arrest rate is higher for blacks," *USA Today*, December 20, 1989.

13. "Just the facts," *FCNL Washington Newsletter* of the Friends Committee on National Legislation (February 1990): 2.

14. McAllister, B., "23% of U.S. black men in their 20s under penal authority, study finds," *International Herald Tribune*, February 28, 1990.

15. Page, C., "Our fear of young black males," *Chicago Tribune*, March 4, 1990.

16. Ibid.

17. Harris, R., "Blacks feel brunt of drug war," *Los Angeles Times*, April 22, 1990.

18. Quoted in ibid.

19. Quoted in ibid.

20. DeParle, J., "Talk grows of government being out to get blacks," *New York Times*, October 29, 1990.

21. Wright, L., and Glick, D., "Farrakhan mission: Fighting the drug war—his way," *Newsweek* (March 19, 1990): 25.

22. Belkin, L., "Airport anti-drug nets snare many people fitting 'profiles,' " *New York Times*, March 20, 1990.

23. Ibid.

24. Ibid.

25. Sullivan, R., "Police say drug-program profiles are not biased," *New York Times*, April 26, 1990.

26. Ibid.

27. London, R., "Judge's overruling of crack law brings turmoil," *New York Times*, January 11, 1991.

28. Ibid.

29. Kolata, G., "Racial bias seen on pregnant addicts," *New York Times*, July 20, 1990.

30. Smith, V. E., "A frontal assault on drugs: Reuben Greenberg's methods actually get results," *Time* (April 30, 1990): 26.

31. Ibid.

32. Boyce, J. N., "Tailoring treatment for black addicts," *Wall Street Journal*, April 10, 1990.

33. Szasz, T. S., *Ceremonial Chemistry*, 1974, reprint, rev. ed. (Holmes Beach, FL: Learning Publications, 1985), pp. 89–103.

34. Malcolm X, *The Autobiography of Malcolm X*, with the assistance of Alex Haley (New York: Grove Press, 1966), p. 259.

35. Ibid.

36. Ibid., p. 260.

37. Ibid., p. 261.

38. Prentice, A. C., "The problem of the narcotic drug addict," *Journal of the American Medical Association* 76 (June 4, 1921): 1551–56; quote at p. 1553.

39. Malcolm X, *Autobiography*, p. 384.

40. Ibid., p. 276.

41. See, for example, Kurtz, H., "Drug scourge is conspiracy by whites, some blacks say," *Washington Post*, December 29, 1989.

42. Wilson, J. Q., "Against the legalization of drugs," *Commentary* (February 1990): 21–28; quote at p. 28.

CHAPTER 7

1. Sydenham, T., quoted in L. Goodman and A. Gilman, *The Pharmacological Basis of Therapeutics* (New York: Macmillan, 1941), p. 186.

2. Portnoy, R., quoted in D. Goleman, "Physicians said to persist in undertreating pain and ignoring evidence," *New York Times*, December 31, 1987.

3. Goodman and Gilman, *Pharmacological Basis of Therapeutics*, pp. 218, 217.

4. Hill, C. S., Jr., "Narcotics and cancer pain control," *Ca: A Cancer Journal for Clinicians* 38 (December 1988): 322–25.

5. "Chronicle: 3 doctors charged with overprescribing for Elizabeth Taylor," *New York Times*, September 8, 1990.

6. "Medicolegal decisions: Physician prescribes, court convicts," *American Medical News* (October 19, 1990): 24; a summary of *People of the State of California v. Lonergan*, 267 Cal. Rptr. 887, Cal. Ct. of App. (March 26, 1990).

7. Carlova, J., "Patients in pain can put you in jail," *Medical Economics* (November 12, 1984): 195–203.

8. Ibid.

9. Ibid.

10. For a review and discussion, see Szasz, T. S., *Pain and Pleasure*, 1957, reprint (Syracuse, NY: Syracuse University Press, 1989).

11. Meier, B., "Widening drug availability: Two views," *New York Times*, February 23, 1991.

12. Quoted in Lupus Foundation of America, *A Legal Manual for Lupus Patients* (St. Louis, MO: Lupus Foundation of America, 1982), p. 28. I owe this reference to my daughter Suzy.

13. Szasz, T. S., "Malingering: Diagnosis or social condemnation?" *American Medical Association Archives of Neurology and Psychiatry* 76 (October 1956): 432–43.

14. Editorial, "Judge not!" *Journal of the Iowa State Medical Society* 47 (January 1957): 35–36.

15. Clark, M., et al., "Cancer hurts before it kills: Doctors can ease suffering with drugs," *Newsweek* (December 19, 1988): 58–59.

16. Ibid.

17. Editorial, "Whatever happened to insomnia (and insomnia research)?" *American Journal of Psychiatry* 148 (April 1991): 419.

18. See, for example, Szalavitz, M., "Methadone addicts are as far from recovery as heroin addicts," letters to the editor, *New York Times*, April 26, 1990.

19. King, R., *The Drug Hang-up* (New York: Norton, 1972), p. 257.

20. Ibid, p. 260.

21. Value Line, Inc., "The Value Line Investment Survey," New York, February 9, 1990, p. 1268.

22. Marcus, A. D., and Lambert, W., "Eli Lilly to pay doctors' Prozac-suit costs," *Wall Street Journal*, June 6, 1991.

23. Garrard, J., et al., "Evaluation of neuroleptic drug use by nursing home elderly under proposed Medicare and Medicaid regulations," *Journal of the American Medical Association* 265 (January 23–30, 1991): 463–67; and Winslow, R., "New rules to cut use of medication by nursing homes," *Wall Street Journal*, January

23, 1991. Also see, for example, Cowley, G., et al., "The promise of Prozac," *Newsweek* (March 26, 1990): 36–41; and Clark, D. B., et al. "Surreptitious drug use by patients in a panic disorder study," *American Journal of Psychiatry* 147 (April 1990): 507–10.

24. Hinds, M. deC., "Anxiety rises as New York limits tranquilizer prescriptions," *New York Times*, January 21, 1989.

25. Winslow, R., "Tranquilizer prescription law studied," *Wall Street Journal*, January 30, 1990.

26. Medical Society of the State of New York, "Triplicate prescription: Issues and answers," *News of New York* (February 28, 1991): 5.

27. Ibid., pp. 2 and 5.

28. Ibid.

29. Ibid, p. 1.

30. Ibid.

31. Stark, P., "Not all drug lords are outlaws," *New York Times*, August 12, 1990.

32. Todd, J., quoted in Meier, "Widening drug availability."

33. Kleber, H. D., "The nosology of abuse and dependence," *Journal of Psychiatric Research* 24 suppl. 2 (1990): 57–64; quote at p. 58.

34. "20 drugstores, 25 doctors off Medicaid," *New York Times*, January 28, 1989.

35. Verhovek, S. H., "Doctor charged with Medicaid fraud," *New York Times*, May 31, 1991.

36. "20 drugstores."

37. Clark et al., "Cancer hurts."

38. Jones, L., "Hospice's next step: Into medical mainstream," *American Medical News* (January 7, 1991): 17.

39. Goleman, "Physicians said to persist."

40. Shuchman, M., "Depression hidden in deadly disease," *New York Times*, November 15, 1990.

41. Ibid.

42. Cleeland, C. S., quoted in "Group backs more narcotics use for cancer," *American Medical News* (May 11, 1990): 28.

43. Ibid.

44. Ibid.

CHAPTER 8

1. Casanova (Giovanni Jacobo Casanova de Seingalt, 1725–1798), quoted in M. Schnyder, "Gedanken zur Drogen—und Suchtprophylaxe" [Reflections on drug abuse—and drug addiction prevention], *Neue Zurcher Zeitung* (October 20–21, 1984): 37; the translation is mine.

2. The Apocrypha 1 Maccabees 2:52.

3. James 1:12.

4. Matthew 6:12.

5. Emerson, R. W., *Essays*, quoted in B. Stevenson, ed., *The Macmillan Book of Proverbs, Maxims, and Famous Phrases* (New York: Macmillan, 1948), p. 2291.

6. See Szasz, T. S., *Ceremonial Chemistry*, 1974, reprint, rev. ed. (Holmes Beach, FL: Learning Publications, 1985), ch. 11.

7. Twain, M., *Following the Equator*, vol. 1 (Hartford, CT: American Publishing, 1903), p. 339.

8. Twain, M., *Wits and Wisecracks*, selected by Doris Benardete (Mount Vernon, NY: Peter Pauper Press, 1961), p. 28.

9. Friedman, M., "An open letter to Bill Bennett," *Wall Street Journal*, September 7, 1989.

10. Ibid.

11. "Widow of alcoholic at brewery wins suit," *New York Times*, October 31, 1990.

12. See, for example, Rothman, D. J., "M.D. doesn't mean 'more deaths,' " *New York Times*, April 20, 1991. For my general critique, see Szasz, T. S., *The Therapeutic State* (Buffalo, NY: Prometheus Books, 1984) and *The Untamed Tongue* (LaSalle, IL: Open Court, 1990).

13. See, for example, Somerville, J., "Illinois task force issues model right-to-die bill," *American Medical News* (April 20, 1990): 20.

14. See, for example, Gianelli, D. M., "Compassion or murder? Washington state considers legalizing euthanasia," *American Medical News* (November 2, 1990): 3 and 6.

15. See Gianelli, D. M., "Wash. voters asked if MDs may offer active euthanasia," *American Medical News* (May 18, 1990): 1 and 35; quote at p. 35.

16. See Szasz, T. S., "The ethics of suicide," 1971, reprinted in *The Theology of Medicine*, 1977, reprint (Syracuse, NY: Syracuse University Press, 1988), pp. 68–85; "The case against suicide prevention," *American Psychologist* 41 (July 1986): 806–12; and *The Untamed Tongue*, pp. 245–52.

17. Editorial, "Mr. Pavlov's ruinous reflexes," *New York Times*, February 15, 1991.

18. Barnes, D. G., *A History of the English Corn Laws from 1660–1846*, 1930, reprint (New York: Augustus M. Kelley/Reprints of Economic Classics, 1965); and McCord, N., *The Anti–Corn Law League, 1838–1846* (London: George Allen & Unwin, 1958).

19. See Dam, K. W., *The GATT: Law and International Economic Organization* (Chicago: University of Chicago Press, 1970). The acronym *GATT* stands for General Agreement on Tariffs and Trade.

20. Smith, A., quoted in N. Longmate, *The Breadstealers* (New York: St. Martin's Press, 1984), p. 4.

21. Smith, J. B., quoted in ibid., p. 19.

22. Russell, J., quoted in ibid., p. 211.

23. For a libertarian critique of the Corn Laws, see Spall, R. F., "Landlordism and liberty: Aristocratic misrule and the Anti-Corn-Law League," *Journal of Libertarian Studies* 8: (Summer 1987): 213–36.

24. Bennett, W. J., quoted in *Newsweek* (June 26, 1989): 15; also Editorial, "Off with their heads: A strange recipe for morality from our leader in drug war," *Syracuse Herald-Journal*, June 17, 1989.

25. Jefferson, T., "Notes on the State of Virginia," 1781, reprinted in A. Koch and W. Peden, eds., *The Life and Selected Writings of Thomas Jefferson* (New York: Modern Library, 1944), pp. 276–77.

26. Mises, L. von, *Human Action* (New Haven, CT: Yale University Press, 1949), pp. 728–29.

27. Szasz, *Ceremonial Chemistry*, pp. 75–79.

28. Burke, E., "A Letter from Mr. Burke to a Member of the National Assembly in Answer to Some Objections to His Book on French Affairs," in *The Works of the Right Honorable Edmund Burke*, vol. 3 (Boston: Wells & Lilly, 1826), p. 315.

Bibliography

Andrew, E. *Shylock's Rights: A Grammar of Lockian Claims*. Toronto: University of Toronto Press, 1988.

Baker, G. P., and Hacker, P.M.S. *Language, Sense and Nonsense*. Oxford, England: Basil Blackwell, 1984.

Barnes, D. G. *A History of the English Corn Laws from 1660–1846*. 1930. Reprint. New York: Augustus M. Kelley/Reprints of Economic Classics, 1965.

Barnett, R. E., ed. *The Rights Retained by the People: The History and Meaning of the Ninth Amendment*. Fairfax, VA: George Mason University Press, 1989.

Bartlett, J., ed. *Familiar Quotations*, 12th ed. Boston: Little, Brown, 1951.

Bastiat, F. *Economic Sophisms*. 1845/1848. Reprint. Trans. Arthur Goddard. Princeton, NJ: Van Nostrand, 1964.

Bork, R. H. *The Tempting of America: The Political Seduction of the Law*. New York: Free Press, 1990.

Bourne, R. *The Radical Will: Selected Writings, 1911–1918*. New York: Urizen Books, 1977.

Broun, H., and Leech, M. *Anthony Comstock: Roundsman of the Lord*. New York: Literary Guild of America, 1927.

Burke, E. *The Philosophy of Edmund Burke: A Selection from His Speeches and Writings*. Ed. Louis I. Bredvold and Ralph G. Ross. Ann Arbor: University of Michigan Press, 1961.

———. *Reflections on the Revolution in France*. 1790. Reprint. Ed. Conor Cruise O'Brien. London: Penguin, 1986.

———. *The Works of the Right Honorable Edmund Burke*. 12 vols. Boston: Wells & Lilly, 1826.

Celine, L.-F. *Mea Culpa & The Life and Work of Semmelweis*. Trans. R. A. Parker. New York: Howard Fertig, 1979.

Christopher, T. W. *Constitutional Questions in Food and Drug Laws*. Chicago: Commerce Clearinghouse, 1960.

Collier, P., and Horowitz, D. *The Kennedys: An American Drama*. New York: Summit Books, 1984.

The Compact Edition of the Oxford English Dictionary. 2 vols. Oxford, England: Clarendon Press, 1976.

Dam, K. W. *The GATT: Law and International Economic Organization*. Chicago: University of Chicago Press, 1970.

Delumeau, J. *Sin and Fear: The Emergence of a Western Guilt Culture, 13th–18th Centuries*. 1983. Reprint. Trans. Eric Nicholson. New York: St. Martin's Press, 1990.

Dicey, A. V. *Lectures on the Relations between Law and Public Opinion in England during the Nineteenth Century*. 1905, 1914. Reprint. 2nd ed. London: Macmillan, 1963.

Douglas, M., and Wildavsky, A. *Risk and Culture: An Essay on the Selection of Technical and Environmental Dangers*. Berkeley: University of California Press, 1983.

Dukakis, K. *Now You Know*. New York: Simon and Schuster, 1990.

Encyclopaedia Britannica. Chicago: Encyclopaedia Britannica, 1973.

Ford, B. *Betty: A Glad Awakening*. New York: Doubleday, 1987.

Freud, S. *The Standard Edition of the Complete Psychological Works of Sigmund Freud*. 24 vols. London: Hogarth Press, 1953–1974. (Cited in notes as SE.)

Friedman, M. *Capitalism and Freedom*. Chicago: University of Chicago Press, 1962.

Girard, R. *The Scapegoat*. 1982. Reprint. Trans. Yvonne Freccero. Baltimore: Johns Hopkins University Press, 1986.

Goodman, L., and Gilman, A. *The Pharmacological Basis of Therapeutics*. New York: Macmillan, 1941.

Grinspoon, L. *Marihuana Reconsidered*. 2nd ed. Cambridge, MA: Harvard University Press, 1977.

Grinspoon, L., and Bakalar, J. B. *Cocaine: A Drug and Its Social Evolution*. Rev. ed. New York: Basic Books, 1985.

Grinspoon, L., Ewalt, J. R., and Shader, R. I. *Schizophrenia: Pharmacotherapy and Psychotherapy*. Baltimore: Williams & Wilkins, 1972.

Gunn, S. M., and Platt, P. S. *Voluntary Health Agencies*. New York: Ronald Press, 1945.

Hamowy, R., ed. *Dealing with Drugs: Consequences of Government Control*. Lexington, MA: Lexington Books, 1987.

Harnsberger, C. T., ed. *Mark Twain at Your Fingertips*. New York: Beechhurst Press, 1948.

Hayek, F. A. *The Constitution of Liberty*. Chicago: University of Chicago Press, 1960.

———. *The Fatal Conceit: The Errors of Socialism*. Ed. W. W. Bartley III. Chicago: University of Chicago Press, 1989.

Herer, J. *The Emperor Wears No Clothes*. 1985. Reprint. Van Nuys, CA: HEMP Publishing, 1990.

Heymann, C. D. *A Woman Named Jackie*. New York: Lyle Stuart, 1989.

Hobbes, T. *Leviathan, Or the Matter, Forme and Power of a Commonwealth Eccle-*

siastical and Civil. 1651. Reprint. Ed. Michael Oakeshott. New York: Collier Macmillan, 1962.

Hopkins, J. F. *A History of the Hemp Industry in Kentucky*. Lexington: University of Lexington Press, 1951.

Hunter, R., and Macalpine, I., eds. *Three Hundred Years of Psychiatry, 1535–1860*. London: Oxford University Press, 1963.

Inciardi, J. A., and Biden, J. R., Jr., eds. *Handbook of Drug Control in the United States*. Westport, CT: Greenwood Press, 1990.

Inglis, B. *The Forbidden Game: A Social History of Drugs*. London: Hodder and Staughton, 1975.

Jackson, C. O. *Food and Drug Legislation in the New Deal*. Princeton, NJ: Princeton University Press, 1970.

Johnson, P. *Modern Times: The World from the Twenties to the Eighties*. New York: Harper & Row, 1983.

Kallett, A., and Schlink, F. J. *100,000,000 Guinea Pigs: Dangers in Everyday Foods, Drugs, and Cosmetics*. New York: Vanguard Press, 1932.

Kaplan, J. *Marijuana: The New Prohibition*. New York: Pocket Books, 1972.

King, R. *The Drug Hang-up: America's Fifty-year Folly*. New York: Norton, 1972.

Koch, A., and Peden, W. eds. *The Life and Selected Writings of Thomas Jefferson*. New York: Modern Library, 1944.

Lewis, H. W. *Technological Risk*. New York: Norton, 1990.

Locke, J. *Two Treatises of Government*. 1690. Reprint. Ed. Peter Laslett. New York: Mentor Books, 1965.

Longmate, N. *The Breadstealers: The Fight against the Corn Laws, 1838–1846*. New York: St. Martin's Press, 1984.

Lupus Foundation of America. *A Legal Manual for Lupus Patients*. St. Louis, MO: Lupus Foundation of America, 1982.

Machan, T. R., ed. *The Libertarian Alternative: Essays in Social and Political Philosophy*. Chicago: Nelson-Hall, 1974.

Mackay, C. *Extraordinary Popular Delusions and the Madness of Crowds*. 1841, 1852. Reprint. New York: Noonday Press, 1962.

Madison, J. *The Writings of James Madison*. 9 vols. Ed. Gaillard Hunt. New York: G. P. Putnam's Sons, 1900–1910.

Malcolm X. *The Autobiography of Malcolm X*. With the assistance of Alex Haley. New York: Grove Press, 1966.

Mandeville, B. *The Fable of the Bees: Or Private Vices, Publick Benefits*. 1732. Reprint. F. B. Kaye Edition. 2 vols. Indianapolis, IN: Liberty Press, 1988.

McCord, N. *The Anti-Corn Law League, 1838–1846*. London: George Allen & Unwin, 1958.

McDonald, F. *Novus Ordo Seclorum: The Intellectual Origins of the Constitution*. Lawrence: University Press of Kansas, 1985.

Menninger, K. *The Crime of Punishment*. New York: Viking, 1968.

Mill, J. S. *On Liberty*. 1859. Reprinted in J. S. Mill, *The Six Great Humanistic Essays*, with an Introduction by Albert William Levi. New York: Washington Square Press, 1969.

Miller, R. L. *The Case for Legalizing Drugs*. New York: Praeger, 1991.

Mises, L. von. *Human Action: A Treatise on Economics*. New Haven, CT: Yale University Press, 1949.

————. *Socialism: An Economic and Sociological Analysis.* 1922. Reprint. Trans. from the 2nd German ed. (1932) by J. Kahane. Indianapolis, IN: Liberty Classics, 1981.

Mitchell, C. N. *The Drug Solution.* Ottawa, Canada: Carleton University Press, 1990.

Moore, B. *A Study of the Past, the Present and the Possibilities of the Hemp Industry in Kentucky.* Lexington, KY: James E. Hughes, 1905.

Moore, R. I. *The Formation of a Persecuting Society: Power and Deviance in Western Europe, 950–1250.* Oxford, England: Basil Blackwell, 1987.

Musto, D. F. *The American Disease: Origins of Narcotic Control.* New Haven, CT: Yale University Press, 1973.

Nedelsky, J. *Private Property and the Limits of American Constitutionalism: The Madisonian Framework and Its Legacy.* Chicago: University of Chicago Press, 1990.

Paul, E. F., and Dickman, H., eds. *Liberty, Property, and the Foundations of the American Constitution.* Albany: State University of New York Press, 1989.

Peterson, M. B. *The Regulated Consumer.* Ottawa, IL: Green Hill Publisher, 1971.

Platt, S., ed. *Respectfully Quoted: A Dictionary of Quotations Requested from the Congressional Research Service.* Washington, D.C.: Library of Congress, 1989.

Reagan, R. *An American Life.* New York: Simon and Schuster, 1990.

Ritter, B. *Covenant House: Lifeline to the Street.* New York: Doubleday, 1987.

Robinson, V. *An Essay on Hasheesh.* New York: Medical Review of Reviews, 1912.

Rogers, W. *A Will Rogers Treasury.* Ed. Bryan B. Sterling and Frances N. Sterling. New York: Bonanza Books, 1982.

————. Quoted in *The Traveller's Dictionary of Quotations: Who Said What, about Where.* London and New York: Routledge & Kegan Paul, 1983.

Romains, J. *Knock (Knock, ou le triomphe de medecine).* 1923. Reprint. Trans. James B. Gidney. Great Neck, NY: Barron Educational Series, 1962.

Rorabaugh, W. J. *The Alcoholic Republic: An American Tradition.* New York: Oxford University Press, 1979.

Rosenblum, V. G., and Castberg, A. D., eds. *Cases on Constitutional Law: Political Roles of the Supreme Court.* Homewood, IL: Dorsey Press, 1973.

Rothbard, M. N. *For a New Liberty: The Libertarian Manifesto.* Rev. ed. New York: Collier, 1973.

Sampson, R. V. *The Psychology of Power.* New York: Pantheon, 1966.

Schoeck, H. *Envy: A Theory of Social Behavior.* 1966. Reprint. Trans. Michael Glenny and Betty Ross. New York: Harcourt, Brace, 1969.

Shryock, R. H. *Medical Licensing in America, 1650–1965.* Baltimore: Johns Hopkins University Press, 1967.

Sils, D. L., ed. *International Encyclopedia of the Social Sciences.* New York: Macmillan and Free Press, 1968.

Skrabanek, P., and McCormick, J. *Follies and Fallacies in Medicine.* Glasgow, Scotland: Tarragon Press, 1989.

Spooner, L. *Vices Are Not Crimes: A Vindication of Moral Liberty.* 1875. Reprint. Cupertino, CA: Tanstaafl, 1977.

Stevenson, B., ed. *The Macmillan Book of Proverbs, Maxims, and Famous Phrases.* New York: Macmillan, 1948.

Szasz, T. S. *Ceremonial Chemistry: The Ritual Persecution of Drugs, Addicts, and Pushers*. 1974. Reprint. Rev. ed. Holmes Beach, FL: Learning Publications, 1985.

————. *Ideology and Insanity*. 1970. Reprint. Syracuse, NY: Syracuse University Press, 1991.

————. *Insanity: The Idea and Its Consequences*. New York: Wiley, 1987.

————. *Law, Liberty, and Psychiatry: An Inquiry into the Social Uses of Mental Health Practices*. 1963. Reprint. Syracuse, NY: Syracuse University Press, 1989.

————. *The Manufacture of Madness: A Comparative Study of the Inquisition and the Mental Health Movement*. New York: Harper & Row, 1970.

————. *The Myth of Mental Illness: Foundations of a Theory of Personal Conduct*. New York: Hoeber-Harper, 1961. Rev. ed. New York: Harper & Row, 1974.

————. *Pain and Pleasure: A Study of Bodily Feelings*. 1957. Reprint. Syracuse, NY: Syracuse University Press, 1989.

————. *Psychiatric Justice*. 1965. Reprint. Syracuse, NY: Syracuse University Press, 1988.

————. *The Theology of Medicine: The Political-philosophical Foundations of Medical Ethics*. 1977. Reprint. Syracuse, NY: Syracuse University Press, 1988.

————. *The Therapeutic State: Psychiatry in the Mirror of Current Events*. Buffalo, NY: Prometheus Books, 1984.

————. *The Untamed Tongue: A Dissenting Dictionary*. LaSalle, IL: Open Court, 1990.

Taylor, R. J., ed. *The Papers of John Adams*. Cambridge, MA: Harvard University Press, 1977– .

Temin, P. *Taking Your Medicine: Drug Regulation in the United States*. Cambridge, MA: Harvard University Press, 1980.

Timberlake, J. H. *Prohibition and the Progressive Movement, 1900–1920*. New York: Atheneum, 1970.

Torrey, E. F. *Nowhere to Go: The Tragic Odyssey of the Homeless Mentally Ill*. New York: Harper & Row, 1988.

Tuveson, E. L. *Redeemer Nation: The Idea of America's Millennial Role*. Chicago: University of Chicago Press, 1968.

Twain, M. *Following the Equator: A Journey around the World*. 2 vols. Hartford, CT: American Publishing, 1903.

————. *Wits and Wisecracks*. Selected by Doris Benardete. Mount Vernon, NY: Peter Pauper Press, 1961.

United Nations. *Multilateral Treaties Deposited with the Secretary-General*. New York: United Nations, 1989.

Weaver, R. M. *The Ethics of Rhetoric*. Chicago: Regnery, 1953.

Webster's Third New International Dictionary. Unabridged. Springfield, MA: G & C Merriam, 1961.

World Book Encyclopedia. Chicago: Field Enterprises, 1966.

Yapp, P. ed. *The Traveller's Dictionary of Quotations: Who Said What, about Where?* London and New York: Routledge & Kegan Paul, 1983.

Young, J. H. *The Medical Messiahs: A Social History of Health Quackery in Twentieth Century America*. Princeton, NJ: Princeton University Press, 1967.

————. *The Toadstool Millionaires: A Social History of Patent Medicines before Federal Regulation*. Princeton, NJ: Princeton University Press, 1961.

Name Index

Subject Index